HOME PLANNERS
Gold

200 Of Our Finest Home Plans in Full Color!

HOME PLANNERS
TUCSON, ARIZONA

Produced and Designed By Home Planners, LLC
Wholly owned by Hanley-Wood, Inc.

Published By Home Planners, LLC
Wholly owned by Hanley-Wood, Inc.
Editorial and Corporate Offices:
3275 West Ina Road, Suite 110
Tucson, Arizona 85741

Distribution Center:
29333 Lorie Lane
Wixom, Michigan 48393

Rickard D. Bailey, CEO and Publisher
Cindy Coatsworth Lewis, Publications Manager
Paulette Mulvin, Senior Editor
Jan Prideaux, Associate Editor
Paul Fitzgerald, Book Design
Nancy Metcalf, Book Production

Photo Credits
Bob Greenspan: pages 62, 63, 175, 192
Nick Kelsh: page 80
Andrew D. Lautman: Front Cover, pages 3, 6, 11, 32, 37, 38, 45,
   58, 66, 95, 106, 118, 139, 171, 177, 199
Allen Maertz: pages 10, 147
Laszlo Regos: Back Cover, pages 15, 39, 187
Carl Socolow: pages 9, 61

10 9 8 7 6 5 4

Printed in the United States of America.

Library of Congress Catalog Card Number: 95-076603

ISBN Softbound: 1-881955-23-0
ISBN Hardbound: 1-881955-24-9
ISBN Bookware: 1-881955-25-7

On the front cover: A farmhouse with a nod to Victorian charm,
Design HH3309 is featured on page 62. (Home is shown in reverse
of original plan.) Photos by Andrew D. Lautman.

On the back cover: This lovely Cape Cod traditional is spacious as
well as appealing. For more information, see page 25. Photos by
Laszlo Regos.

Table of Contents

Additional Products and Services

DECK PLANS
To enhance the backyards of many of the plans, matching orcorresponding Deck Plans are available. The blueprint package includes a Deck Frontal Sheet, Deck Framing and Floor Plans, Deck Elevations and a Deck Materials List. A Standard Deck Details package, also available, provides all the how-to information necessary for building any deck. Buy the Complete Deck Building Package and receive 1 set of Custom Deck Plans of your choice, plus 1 set of Standard Deck Building Details all for one low price.

COST ESTIMATES
Available in two separate stages, the Quote One® system helps you estimate the cost of building a Home Planners design. The Summary Cost Report shows the total cost per square foot for a home in your zip-code area and then breaks that cost down into ten categories showing the costs for building materials, labor and installation. The report is furnished in three grades: Budget, Standard and Custom. The Detailed Cost Estimate furnishes an even more detailed report. The material and installation (labor + equipment) cost is shown for each of over 1,000 line items provided in the Standard Grade. Space is allowed for additional estimates from contractors and subcontractors. The Detailed Cost Estimate must be purchased with a set of blueprints (a Materials List is included in the price).

CUSTOMIZATION
For available homes, the Home Customizer® service allows you to make changes at prices much lower than those charged by other architectural or drafting services. Among the many changes that can be made:
- exterior elevation changes
- roof, wall and foundation changes
- room additions, and more!

To get started, you will order the Home Customizer® kit which includes an instruction book, architectural scale, clear acetate work film, removable correction tape, 1/4" scale furniture cutouts, erasable red marker, and 1 set of Customizable drawings with floor plans. Then you'll work with our Customization Specialist to cost out the changes you'd like and make them a reality. The price of the Customizer kit is refunded to you after you place your customization order.

LANDSCAPE PLANS
Many homes have matching or complementary Landscape Blueprint packages available. These comprehensive blueprint packages contain everything you'll need to install a superb front-yard landscape: Frontal Sheet, Plan View, Regionalized Plant & Materials List, a sheet on Planting and Maintaining Your Landscape, Zone Maps and a Plant Size and Description Guide. These plans help you achieve professional results, even if you install the landscape yourself. Each set is 18" x 24" in size with clear, complete instructions and easy-to-read type.

Regional Order Map

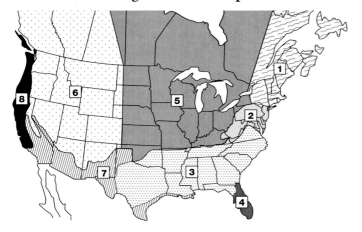

Region	**1**	Northeast
Region	**2**	Mid-Atlantic
Region	**3**	Deep South
Region	**4**	Florida & Gulf Coast
Region	**5**	Midwest
Region	**6**	Rocky Mountains
Region	**7**	Southern California & Desert Southwest
Region	**8**	Northern California & Pacific Northwest

Please specify Geographic Region when ordering your Landscape Plan. See page 218 for prices, ordering information and regional availability.

For prices on the above products and services, see pages 216-221.

HOME PLANNERS—
A Legacy Of Design

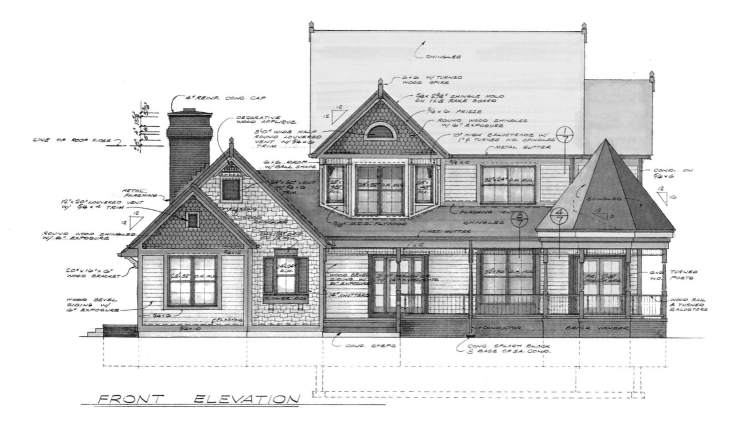

FRONT ELEVATION

As often happens after an idea becomes a reality, Home Planners beginnings took the company down a road less traveled. It came about in 1946 when well-known Detroit home designer, Richard B. Pollman, was commissioned by a leading heating equipment manufacturer to design homes for its national ad campaign. A graduate of the University of Michigan Architectural School, Mr. Pollman's talent as a designer manifested itself in houses whose exteriors were delightfully proportioned and whose floor plans offered practical and convenient livability. Because of this, the commissioned plans that he designed were so popular that there were hundreds of inquiries about the availability of construction blueprints for them. Soon afterwards, the company's first twenty-six stock plans were developed and Home Planners was founded. For many years, Mr. Pollman's design work appeared as a regular feature in the *Detroit News*. The popularity of this creative work led to the first of over 200 Home Planners plan books and magazines.

Joining Mr. Pollman was architect Irving E. Palmquist, a fellow graduate of the University of Michigan Architectural School. Together, during their career at Home Planners, they created over 2,500 home designs, a portfolio which formed the basis for the Home Planners line of fine stock plans and working drawings. In addition to Home Planners own publications, this portfolio of designs has been featured in many outstanding shelter magazines such as House Beautiful's *Houses and Plans*, *Colonial Homes*, Better Homes and Gardens' *Home Plan Ideas*, and other successful quarterlies and special publications.

The Fabulous Forties And Fifties

In addition to his exquisite sense of proportion and exterior appeal, Richard B. Pollman gave heavy consideration to practicality in design. The first of the Home Planners line—like those of today—were homes that people could afford to build and live in. The initial twenty-six, designed just after World War II, catered to a renewed interest in home, family and getting on with the business of a much-changed world. Many returning GIs had buying power and wanted a place to call their own—where they could raise a family and begin to put the war behind them.

Anticipating the exterior design and floor plan diversity that would eventually become a Home Planners trademark, Pollman's group of twenty-six plans ranged in size from 900 square feet to 1,460 square feet.

DESIGN 12

COLD RM. | HTR. RM.

ACTIVITIES
16⁶ x 22⁹

DRYER | WASHER | IRONER

LT.

MODEL OF DESIGN 12

57'0"

| B.R. 15 x 13⁴ | LIVING DINING 24 x 13 | TERRACE |

CL. CL. CL. | REF. RANGE | WORKBENCH

DN UP

KIT. 14 x 8 | NOOK | GARAGE 14 x 22

B.R. 11 x 12 | B 8 x 7⁴ | P.

32'6"

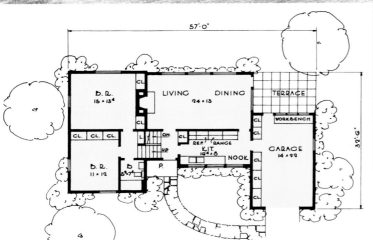

65'9"

ENTRANCE YARD

27'6"

GARAGE 13⁶ x 23

WORKBENCH

W.R. | DESK | KIT. 9 x 9⁴ | LAUND. 9 x 9⁴ | ENT. | B.R. 12⁶ x 11⁴

RANGE REF.

B 7 x 5

CL. CL.

HTR.

H.

DINING 10 x 8 | LIVING 18 x 11⁴ | B.R. 11 x 8 | B.R. 9 x 11⁴

CL. CL.

TERRACE

OUTDOOR LIVING

DESIGN 24

They were affordable and appealed to style trends of the day. Most were one-story, ranch-style homes with exceptions such as Design 8, a Cape Cod with a second floor that could be finished as needed, and Design 12, a tri-level with a lower-level activities room. The floor plans of these homes focused on family living and, for the most part, featured two or three bedrooms, a living room, a dining room, a one-car garage or car port, and in some cases a separate activities room (which would later be known as the family room). Many of the plans were innovative for their time with a full-service laundry room or an eating nook attached to the kitchen. Radiant floor heating and passive solar elements were used in several of the plans. Both were developmental projects in which Mr. Pollman was interested.

Two of the plans, Designs 24 and 25, were ahead of their time with characteristics based on the International Style that had its roots in the late 1930s and early 1940s. Blockish modular-looking framework with large areas of glass dominated the style.

Another early plan (circa 1950s), Design 133 became a true mainstay for Home Planners. Small in square footage, homeowners found it large in livability and it soon become an extremely popular seller. It offered both a slab and a basement option as part of the blueprint package.

The Growth Of The Sixties

By the mid-1950s and on through the 1960s, Home Planners had begun to establish itself as a stock plan provider for professional builders, as well as for individuals who wanted to build their own home. The plans portfolio reached the thousands in number and included a wide variety of homes that would appeal to a variety of tastes.

Of particular interest during this time were homes that broke away from the tradition of squares or rectangles and employed more original styles. French, Tudor, Spanish and Dutch Colonial details were cropping up in many of the designs—not supplanting the stalwart Cape Cods and Colonials, but adding a broader dimension to the portfolio. The contemporary line was also significantly expanded in both one- and two-story models.

Multi-level homes were added in significant numbers to satisfy an increasing demand. Tri-levels, split-levels, bi-levels, and other multi-level options gave homeowners a chance to add living space to their homes without using up more site space. It also allowed them to build on difficult sloping or hillside lots.

Homes designed at Home Planners during this period were also larger than ever before—some approaching the 3,000-square-foot range. They often sported four bedrooms and generally included a designated master bedroom with a private full or half bath. Garages were expanded to two-car versions and the family room became the spot for casual living—complementing the more formal living room.

At this time, Home Planners also began testing some creative floor planning ideas. Concepts such as split-bedroom options—which placed the master suite in one area of the home and secondary bedrooms in another—were well received and continue as popular floor-plan features today. Bathrooms built on interior walls freed up valuable outside wallspace for more innovative floor planning. Family rooms also became

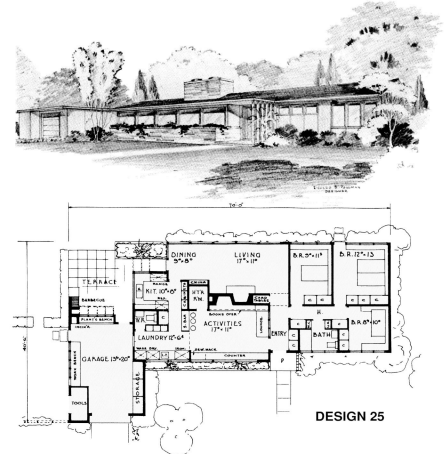

DESIGN 25

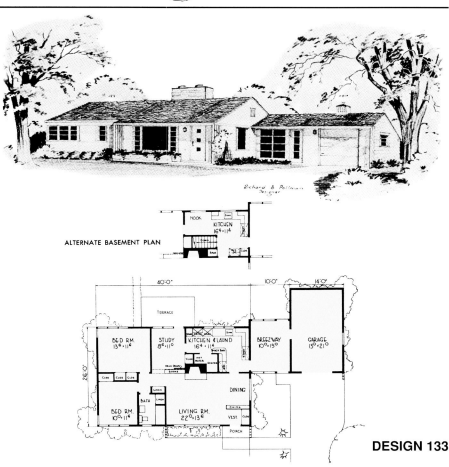

DESIGN 133

more popular as an adjunct to the formal living room. U-shaped and L-shaped kitchens were introduced and proved to be welcome work-center setups—maximizing the "work triangle" theory of efficiency. Aesthetic details such as sloped ceilings, beamed ceilings and raised-hearth and through (two-way) fireplaces gave plans an added appeal. Particular attention was given to indoor/outdoor relationships which included atriums, terraces, porches, balconies and decks.

One notable plan from this period, Design 271, shows a vast departure from all previous homes. A Y-shaped plan, 271 contained a sunken living room, a large activities/dining room and an abundance of storage. Its appeal was so great that it remained a popular seller well into the early 1970s.

During the 1960s, the History House series of famous houses and styles from our own country's architectural heritage became popular in House Beautiful's *Building Manual*. It continues today as a favorite feature in *Colonial Homes*.

The Leaders Of The Seventies And Eighties

Throughout the 1970s and 1980s, Home Planners, under the guidance of Charles W. Talcott, became recognized as the leader in the stock-plan industry, publishing its portfolio of unique homes in its own nationally distributed magazines and books as well as in a number of popular shelter magazines. The plans developed during this time period were reflective of a country-wide prosperity and included features that catered to the tastes and living requirements of families with varying budgets.

While the smaller, one-story ranch-style home held its own as a choice for many homeowners, other styles and livability options were also explored. The ubiquitous two-story house became the staple of the Home Planners design inventory. Blueprints for construction could be obtained for such styles as Early American, Georgian, Southern Colonial, Greek Revival, French Mansard and Tudor adaptations. Square footages grew—some well over 3,000 square feet and some as high as 4,000 square feet. The con-

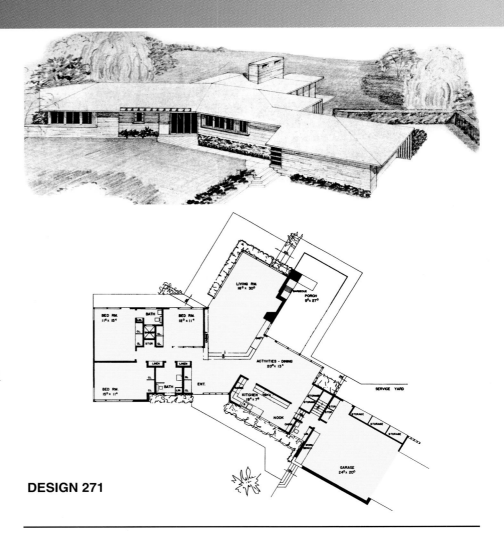

DESIGN 271

temporary line of homes was expanded and a line of vacation and second homes was developed. The Trend House series offered refreshing exteriors and singular floor plans. The Signature Series presented readers with a selection of designs for unlimited building budgets. Plans with optional elevations were tried and found to be a great success.

Floor plans during this time showed an increased emphasis on leisure living and separation of formal and informal living and dining areas. Plans became more open and airy, giving an appearance of space to homes with smaller square footages. Multi-purpose gathering rooms and great rooms began to be preferred over a formal living room with a separate family room for casual gatherings. Breakfast rooms came to complement the formal dining room. The appearance of studies (or study/bedroom options) indicated that homeowners were looking for quiet space where they could work at home.

Many of the newly designed master suites in Home Planners homes

from this era showed an increasing emphasis on luxury. Some had separate His and Hers dressing areas; some featured fireplaces and private terraces. Many had walk-in closets and elegant baths with dual vanity sinks, sunken tubs and compartmented toilet facilities.

Kitchen layouts took on vast changes by the 1980s. Many featured island work areas and/or snack-bar counters. Walk-in pantries were added in response to demand and planning desks were often incorporated to ease some of the burden of a family with two working adults. Space was allowed for time-saving conveniences such as dishwashers, double sinks, trash compactors, Lazy Susans and microwave ovens. Pass-through counters to the breakfast or family rooms were common.

It was during this time that the quintessential Home Planners farmhouse was developed—Design HH2774. A best seller by any standard, HH2774 took its place at the top of the charts and continues to sell well in both the United States

This home, as shown in the photograph, may differ from the actual blueprints.
For more detailed information, please check the floor plans carefully.

DESIGN HH2774

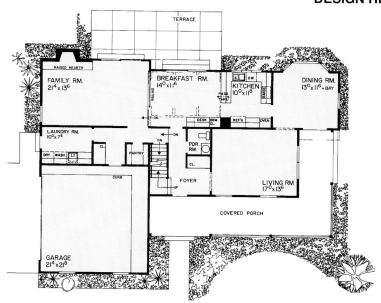

and Canada. Its simple, straightforward floor plan is eminently livable and its warm country exterior appeals to homeowners from coast to coast. With the perfect square footage for most families (2,335 square feet), four bedrooms and a comfortable look, HH2774 is a tried-and-true winner.

The New Nineties

Poised to meet perhaps its most significant challenges, Home Planners moved its corporate offices from Michigan to Tucson, Arizona in late 1989. Under the leadership of Rickard D. Bailey, the firm has embraced state-of-the-art CAD technology, computerized publishing procedures, telemarketing and new product development.

Perhaps one of the most interesting additions to the company's portfolio came with the development of Southwestern designs. Relocating Home Planners offices allowed a Western influence to pervade its design creation with a new line of Santa Fe, Mission and Pueblo-style

Width 59'-6"
Depth 46'

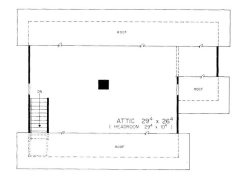

Photos by Allen Maertz

This home, as shown in the photograph, may differ from the actual blueprints.
For more detailed information, please check the floor plans carefully.

DESIGN HH3471

Width 154"
Depth 94'-8"

homes that, though seemingly regional in nature, appeal to homeowners throughout the country. The development of these plans led to a truly innovative idea in design—the Contemporary Farmhouse. Maintaining the properties of a true farmhouse—with porches and a country flavor—the Contemporary Farmhouse portfolio introduced some exciting new features to update the look and capture the attention of those seeking something different. This group of homes borrowed design elements from the sun-protected homes of the sun-belt areas: Southern Plantation houses of Florida and the Southwest, Plains Farmhouses of West Texas, California Farmhouses of the Sacramento Valley, and even Outback homes of Australia. Rustic in nature, they incorporate fine contemporary details such as vertical wood siding or stucco, numerous single-pane windows and spectacular entryways.

The flagship of the Contemporary Farmhouse series became a project house for Home Planners and was built just outside of Tucson in the shadows of the magnificent Santa Catalina mountains. The home is a showcase of '90s design: open floor planning, flexible space, separate guest quarters, abundant outdoor living space and a truly opulent master suite. Special features such as a large gathering room with a full wall of windows, fireplaces in five separate

This home, as shown in the photograph, may differ from the actual blueprints. For more detailed information, please check the floor plans carefully.

DESIGN HH2947

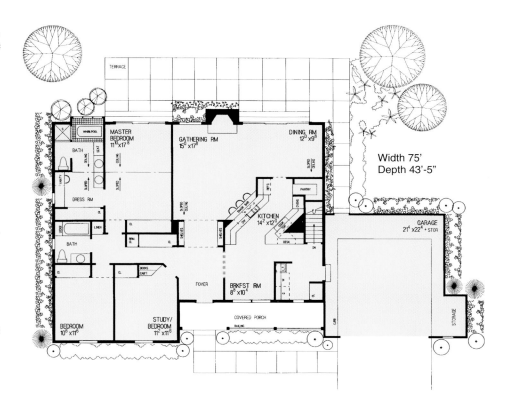

Width 75'
Depth 43'-5"

areas, and a breezeway game area make this home, Design HH3471, a real standout.

But Home Planners is not just Western in its approach to the 1990s. In fact, new plans show a remarkable sensitivity to changing lifestyles in all parts of the country. For example, Design HH2947, which has become Home Planners newest best seller, caters to empty-nesters and starter families. Decidedly country on the outside, this mid-size one-story features three bedrooms (or two plus a study), an open gathering room/dining room combination and a rather unique, angled kitchen. Its size and great livability have made it a hallmark plan for today's living patterns.

In addition to creating innovative home plans with stylish exteriors and exciting interiors, Home Planners has made the 1990s a time for developing a number of other products and services for home builders. Among them are Landscape and Deck plans to enhance a new home; Specification Outlines, Materials Lists, and Construction Detail sets to help plan and organize a building project; a Customization service to help homeowners make minor or major changes to blueprints; and a unique custom estimating service called Quote One® that gives localized cost information for building a Home Planners home in any zip-code area in the United States. To learn more about these unique products and services, see pages 4 and 216-221.

What is in store for Home Planners in the next fifty years? This remains to be seen. But what is certain is that the company will actively continue its long history of providing distinguished new design creations, appealing quality-laden publications, accurate and professional working drawings, a variety of new home planning products, and attentive service to you, our valued customer.

Home Planners
The Leader In Quality Stock Plans

oversee the creation and production of each home plan and check the finished product for accuracy.

The quality of our plans has been proven time and time again—millions of blueprints have been sold to satisfied home builders all across the United States. Here is what some of them have to say about Home Planners:

"The blueprints we received from Home Planners were of excellent quality and provided us with exactly what we needed to get our successful home-building project underway. We appreciate Home Planners invaluable role in our home-building effort."

T.A.
Concord, TN

"Home Planners blueprints saved us a great deal of money. I acted as the general contractor and we did a lot of the work ourselves. We probably built it for half the cost! We are thinking about more plans for another home. I purchased a competitor's book but my husband only wants your plans!"

K.M.
Grovetown, GA

"We instructed our builder to follow the plans including all of the many details which make this house so elegant... Our home is a fine example of the results one can achieve by purchasing and following the plans which you offer. "

S.P
Anderson, SC

"I have been involved in the building trades my entire life... Since building our home we have built two other homes for other families. Their plans from local architects were not nearly as good as yours. For that reason we are ordering additional plan books from you."

T.F.
Kingston, WA

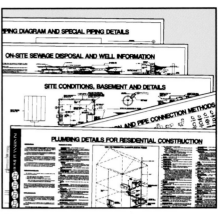

PLUMBING

Home Planners Service

Producing a quality product is just one way Home Planners can help you build a great home. The company provides unparalleled service to all their customers. Home Planners knows that, for most people, building a home is a once-in-a-lifetime experience and that it is a very personal, close-to-the-heart proposition. Home Planners wants that experience to be not only easy but enjoyable.

Believing that an informed builder is a happy builder, Home Planners gives you all the information you need to order the right blueprint product for your project. You won't be rushed through your order or forced into making snap decisions. If you have questions that even our knowledgeable operators can't answer, they'll make note of your questions, ask the experts and get back to you with a complete answer.

Once you've placed your order, you can count on Home Planners to process it with care. And even though blueprints are produced in response to your order, you'll be surprised at the quick turn-around time.

If you have questions or concerns once you've placed an order, or after you've received your sets of blueprints, Home Planners won't ignore you. We have on staff qualified Customer Service representatives who will review your questions or concerns and contact you with answers promptly. Your concerns

Home Planners Quality

Many stock plan companies can offer you plans for building your new home, so why should you choose Home Planners? Because Home Planners can provide the quality, the service and the additional products that will make your home-building experience positive and successful. Since 1946, Home Planners has been committed to the development of fine working drawings that are designed to meet or exceed all national building codes. The experienced design team at Home Planners is headed by licensed architects who

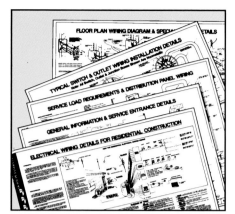

ELECTRICAL

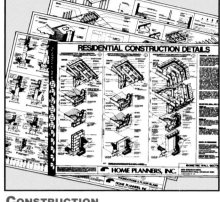

CONSTRUCTION

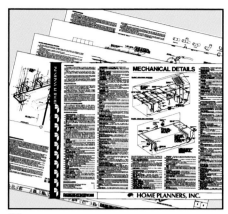

MECHANICAL

will be taken seriously—after all, Home Planners has a fifty-year-old reputation to maintain.

Additional Products And Services

Home Planners also looks beyond its main blueprint service to give you other advantages—products that will help with your building project and products that will enhance your finished home.

Building a home requires a working knowledge of technical subjects—knowledge that most homeowners just don't have. In order to give you the background you need, Home Planners offers **Information Sets** that cover the subjects of plumbing, electrical, general construction and mechanical. Though the sets are not specific to any one design, they do contain enough information to allow you to deal confidently with contractors and subcontractors through the building process. Included are:

- *Plumbing Details* that give general information on pipe schedules, fittings, sump-pump details, water softener hookups, septic system details and much more;
- *Electrical Details* that have helpful information on wire sizing, switch installation schematics, cable-routing details, appliance wattage, door-bell hookups, and typical panel circuitry among other things;
- *Construction Details* that depict the materials and methods used

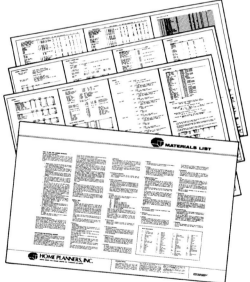

to build foundations, fireplaces, walls, floors and roofs and show acceptable alternatives;

- *Mechanical Details* that show various heating and air-conditioning systems and allow you to make load calculations and preliminary sizing and costing analysis.

For use as a workbook, Home Planners **Specification Outline** lists 166 items or stages crucial to the building process. When combined with the blueprints, a signed contract and a schedule, it becomes a legal document and record for the building of your home.

Customized **Materials Lists** are available for most of our homes—a truly invaluable tool for planning and estimating the cost of your new home. This comprehensive list outlines the quantity, type and size of materials (with the exception of mechanical system items) needed to build your house. It provides a ready reference to help you or your builder cost out materials and serves as a reference sheet when compiling bids.

To help you design a new home or arrange furniture in a new or existing home—or even to help you plan a remodeling project—

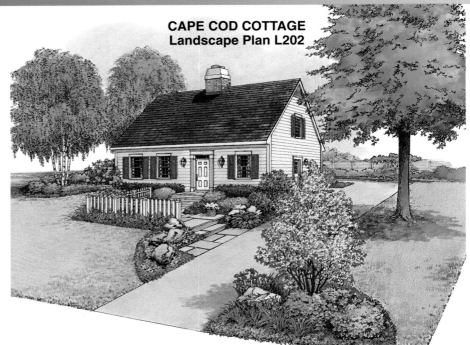

CAPE COD COTTAGE
Landscape Plan L202

Home Planners offers its handy **Plan-A-Home® kit.** Each package contains over 700 reusable peel-off planning symbols (walls, doors, windows, furniture, etc.) and a transparent planning grid that forms the layout for the house. Tracing paper and a felt-tip pen, also included, allow you to transfer your completed plans.

An exciting new service offered by Home Planners is the revolutionary **Quote One® System.** Available in two stages, the *Summary Cost Report* and the *Materials Cost Report*, this unique tool will give you customized cost estimates for building the home you want in your zip code area. The Summary Cost Report contains the total cost per square foot and then breaks that cost down into ten categories showing the costs for building materials, labor and installation. It is offered in three grades: Budget, Standard and Custom. The Materials Cost Report furnishes an even more detailed report in which the material and installation cost for each of over 1,000 line items are shown. This product must be purchased with a blueprint (a materials list is included as well!). Every one of the homes featured on pages 15-213 has the exclu-

sive Quote One® Service available to tell exactly what it will cost to build the home in your area.

Once your home is built, look to Home Planners for additional products to make it more beautiful and livable. For many of our designs, we have developed **Landscape Plans** that match or are complementary to the house plan. When you order any of these plans, you'll receive a plot plan for the landscape as well as a Regionalized Plant and Material List that works for your area. Also included are tips on planting and maintaining your landscape, Zone Maps and a Plant Size and Description Guide.

Many of the houses also have a complementary **Deck Plan** available to enhance outdoor livability. The Deck Plan set includes Deck

Framing and Floor Plans, Elevations and Materials List. A separate *Deck Details* set is also available to give you general guidance on deck building techniques and practices, as well as specific pointers on items such as railings, stairs, planter boxes, etc.

For more complete information about all of Home Planners products and services and for blueprint ordering information see pages 214-224. Each of the home plans on pages 15-213 has special services and products available. Check for the product/service symbols at the bottom of each page and then see the full descriptions on page 4. Remember—home plans are just the beginning. At Home Planners, the aim is to provide products and services that carry you all the way through planning, building and enhancing your new home!

WEEKEND ENTERTAINER DECK
Deck Plan D112

This home, as shown in the photograph, may differ from the actual blueprints.
For more detailed information, please check the floor plans carefully.

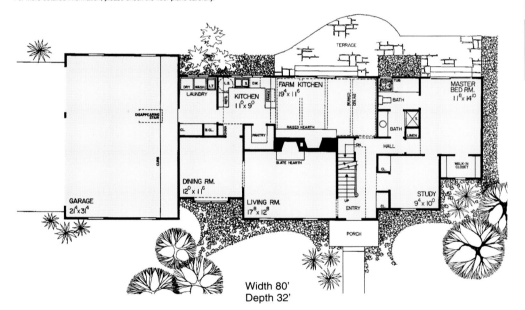

Width 80'
Depth 32'

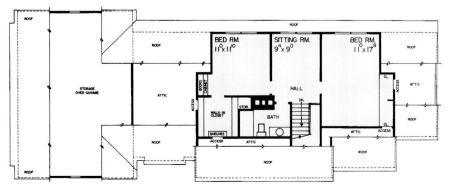

DESIGN HH2563

First Floor:	1,500 sq. ft.
Second Floor:	690 sq. ft.
Total:	2,190 sq. ft.

Half-House Provides Full Livability

In Colonial America's infancy, many great ideas were born, including the half-house. This updated design easily accommodates today's family.

A warm greeting emanates from the fireplace in the living room, combining well with the dining room for formal entertaining. An adjacent kitchen features windows above the sink, providing unobstructed views of the back yard, and a large walk-in pantry. Cold weather may find the family gathered in the farm kitchen sharing S'mores melted over a cozy fire. A first-floor master bedroom supplies a private retreat and a relaxing bath. The nearby study may also double as an office. Upstairs, two bedrooms share a full bath and a sitting room.

DESIGN HH2661

First Floor:	1,020 sq. ft.
Second Floor:	777 sq. ft.
Total:	1,797 sq. ft.

Cloaked In Comfort

This diminutive Cape Cod home cloaks a very comfortable interior. In the living room select a good book from the built-in bookcase, curl up in front of the blazing corner fireplace, and feel the contentment enfold you.

For the best of entertaining options, choose the dining room for formal occasions or the country kitchen for casual gatherings. The country kitchen contains an efficient layout for meal preparation, a sunlit window seat and a corner fireplace. A study completes the first floor.

The second floor is dedicated to the sleeping area. Here, a room-to-stretch master bedroom is complemented by a private bath. Two family bedrooms share a full hall bath. A linen closet provides convenient access for everyone.

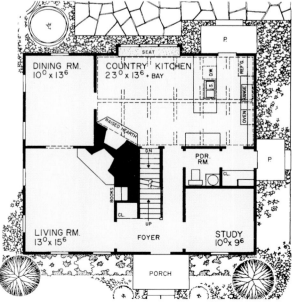

Width 34'
Depth 30'

Additional products and services available. See page 4.

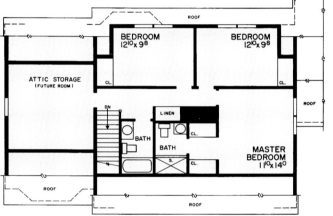

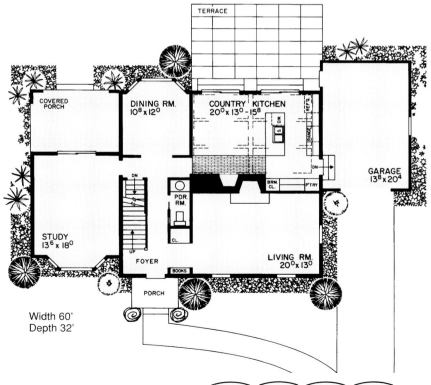

DESIGN HH2682

First Floor (Basic Plan):	976 sq. ft.
First Floor (Expanded Plan):	1,230 sq. ft.
Second Floor (Both Plans):	744 sq. ft.
Total (Basic Plan):	1,720 sq. ft.
Total (Expanded Plan):	1,974 sq. ft.

Expand Your Horizons

This home delivers an extra measure of Cape Cod charm—it offers a grow-as-you-go floor plan. If you prefer, begin with the basic plan. Only 32-feet wide, this plan includes a living room with a central fireplace, a dining room, a country kitchen with a fireplace and lots of room for large family gatherings, and a powder room. The second floor contains the master bedroom and bath, two family bedrooms and a full bath.

When needed, the first floor may be expanded to include a bay-windowed study for quiet pursuits, a covered porch for additional outdoor living space and a garage. The second floor is enlarged to accommodate a large room for attic storage or an additional bedroom.

Additional products and services available. See page 4.

17

DESIGN HH2657

First Floor:	1,217 sq. ft.
Second Floor:	868 sq. ft.
Total:	2,085 sq. ft.

Cape Cod Style Spans The Ages

This Cape Cod exterior is so authentic, it's easy to imagine a young woman standing at the picket fence, sea breezes tossing her hair while she waits for her sea captain's return. However, the interior brings you immediately to the present with an amenity-filled floor plan that complements today's lifestyle.

The foyer opens to the formal dining room on the right, and a living room enhanced by a bay window and a fireplace on the left. A country kitchen includes a corner fireplace with a raised hearth, a bay window and a meal preparation area designed for efficiency. The master bedroom features dual closets, a window seat with storage, a dressing room and a private bath. Two family bedrooms share a hall bath, completing the second floor.

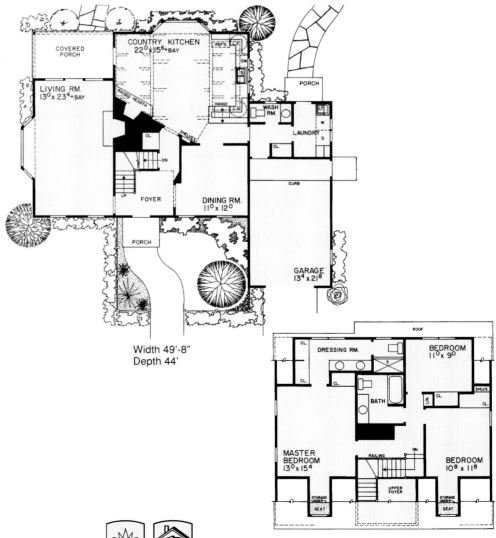

Width 49'-8"
Depth 44'

Additional products and services available. See page 4.

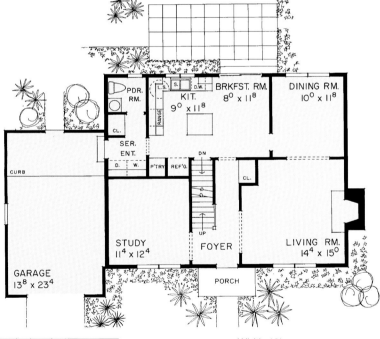

Width 48'
Depth 32'

DESIGN HH3571

First Floor:	964 sq. ft.
Second Floor:	783 sq. ft.
Total:	1,747 sq. ft.

Cape Cod Update

Capture the warmth and drama of traditional Cape Cod style while enjoying the up-to-date features desired in today's floor plans.

The study guarantees a quiet retreat for developing business plans or completing that unfinished novel. Nearby, the living room is cheered by a warming fireplace and combines with the dining room for formal entertaining. Adjacent to the dining room is the breakfast room and the kitchen. Sliding glass doors provide access to a rear terrace—an ideal spot to savor your morning coffee or evening dessert. A convenient powder room and laundry room complete the first floor.

Retire to the second-floor master bedroom and pamper yourself in the relaxing whirlpool tub. Two family bedrooms, one with a dormer, share a full bath on this floor.

DESIGN HH2145

First Floor:	1,182 sq. ft.
Second Floor:	708 sq. ft.
Total:	1,890 sq. ft.

Legendary Cape Cod

The Cape Cod half-house has roots deep in the heritage of New England. Historically, these homes were developed in stages—a concept that works as well today as it did in the 17th Century.

The living room contains built-in bookcases and a corner fireplace with room to spare for special galas. Old movies and a crackling fire will make the family room a favorite place for casual times. A snack-bar pass-through from the kitchen to the covered porch makes dining al fresco a delight. The right wing of the first floor contains two bedrooms that share a full bath.

As the family grows and the need for more space arises, the second floor may be developed, providing two additional bedrooms and another full bath.

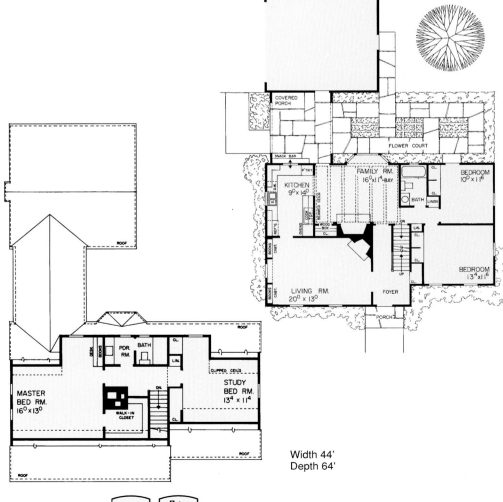

Width 44'
Depth 64'

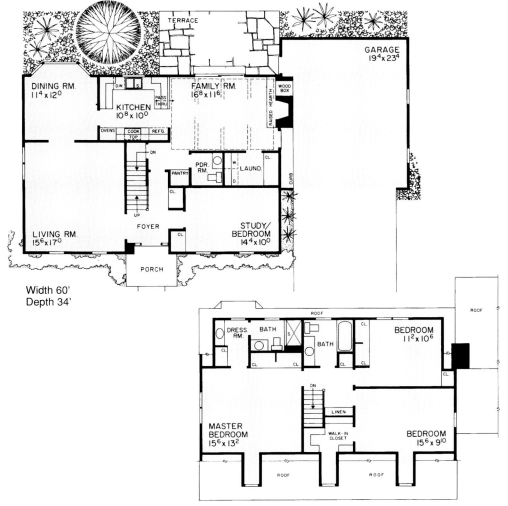

DINING RM.
11⁴ x 12⁰

TERRACE

GARAGE
19⁴ x 23⁴

KITCHEN
10⁸ x 10⁰

FAMILY RM.
16⁸ x 11⁶

OVENS | COOK TOP | REF'G.

PASS THRU

WOOD BOX

RAISED HEARTH

DN

PANTRY

PDR. RM.

LAUND.

UP

LIVING RM.
15⁶ x 17⁰

FOYER

STUDY/
BEDROOM
14⁴ x 10⁰

PORCH

Width 60'
Depth 34'

DRESS. RM.

BATH

BATH

ROOF

BEDROOM
11² x 10⁶

ROOF

DN

LINEN

MASTER
BEDROOM
15⁶ x 13²

WALK-IN
CLOSET

BEDROOM
15⁶ x 9¹⁰

ROOF

ROOF

DESIGN HH1791

First Floor:	1,157 sq. ft.
Second Floor:	875 sq. ft.
Total:	2,032 sq. ft.

Dressed-Up Cape Cod

Three dormers, two carriage lights and a dove cote dress up this full Cape Cod as easy as 1-2-3. Inside, the study/bedroom provides a quiet place to contemplate the day's events. For formal occasions, a living room and an adjacent dining room with bay-windowed views of the rear grounds are ready and waiting. The U-shaped kitchen is flooded with sunlight—compliments of a window located above the sink. A beam ceiling and a raised-hearth fireplace enhance the family room. Completing the first floor are the conveniently located powder and laundry rooms.

Upstairs, retreat to the serenity of the master bedroom with a dressing room and a private bath. Two family bedrooms and a full bath complete the second floor.

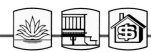

DESIGN HH2615

First Floor:	2,563 sq. ft.
Second Floor:	552 sq. ft.
Total:	3,115 sq. ft

New England, Rockwell-Style

It's easy to imagine this lovely New England home in a Norman Rockwell painting. Two arched entryways form covered porches, while the center front door conveys a special welcome.

A warming fireplace greets you in the formal living room, providing passage to a sun-drenched solarium. The kitchen is situated to serve both formal and informal areas well and the family room, featuring a corner bar, allows plenty of space for activities. The master bedroom rests to the rear of the first floor. His and Hers walk-in closets and a private bath complete this restful retreat.

The second floor holds two family bedrooms, a full bath, dual linen storage and a built-in desk/vanity.

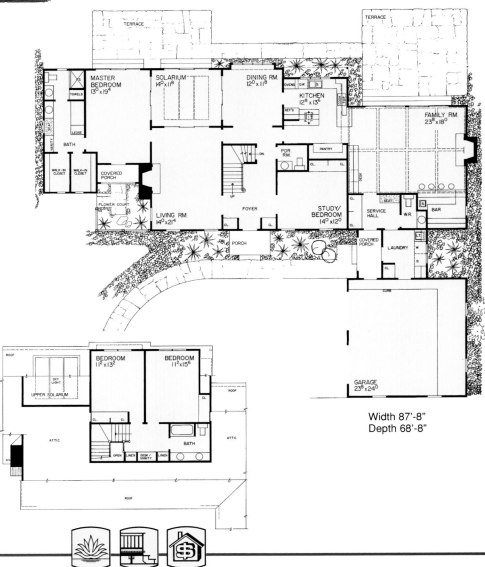

Width 87'-8"
Depth 68'-8"

Additional products and services available. See page 4.

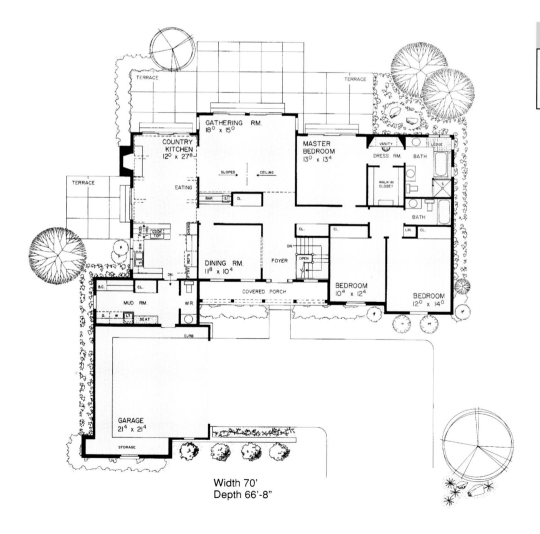

Width 70'
Depth 66'-8"

DESIGN HH2916

Square Footage:	2,129

Copious Colonial Style

The textures of Early New England are present on this inviting Colonial exterior. Inside, thoughtful planning furnishes space for the entire family on one floor.

A country kitchen sized to accommodate a casual family meal or, if necessary, a football team, shares eating space with a step-saving kitchen. For special occasions, a dining room is located nearby. The gathering room opens up with a sloped ceiling and two sets of sliding glass doors providing passage to the rear terrace.

A special haven, the master bedroom features a large walk-in closet and a room-to-relax bath. Two family bedrooms that provide space to sleep and study share a full bath. A mud room with washer/dryer space and a wash room are convenient to the garage.

DESIGN HH2880

| Square Footage: | 2,758 |

A Dash Of Colonial Charm

For generations, the Farmer's Almanac has been a source for weather predictions. This design sustains perfect weather for growers all year long—integrated with this comfortable Colonial home is a 149-foot greenhouse!

A crackling fire and a quiet game may be enjoyed in the country kitchen, while at the same time the media room hosts a frenzy of electronic games. Unobstructed views of the rear grounds enhance the combined living and dining rooms.

Stretch out in the master bedroom, or pass between the His and Hers walk-in closets to a luxurious bath. Here you may relax in a whirlpool tub and take a daydream vacation to Tahiti. Two family bedrooms and a full bath offer their own privacy.

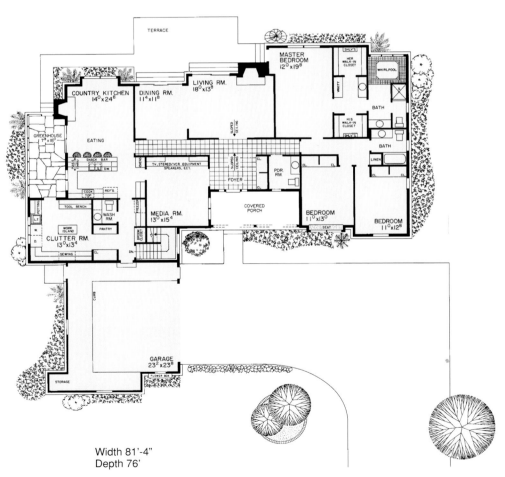

Width 81'-4"
Depth 76'

Additional products and services available. See page 4.

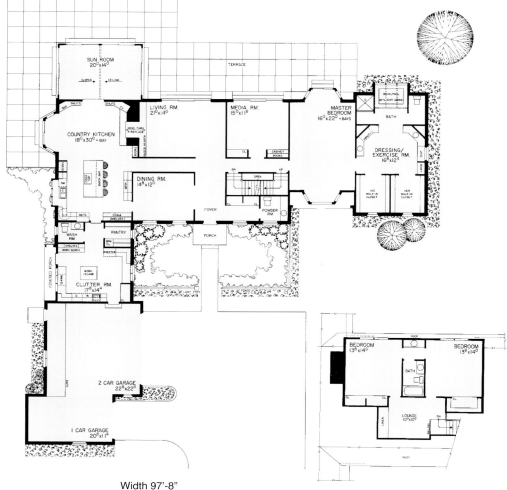

Width 97'-8"
Depth 101'-4"

DESIGN HH2921

First Floor:	3,215 sq. ft.
Second Floor:	711 sq. ft.
Total:	3,926 sq. ft.

Setting A Colonial Example

Bricks, shutters, a fanlight and a cupola on the highest peak—this is the embodiment of classic Colonial design.

The foyer opens to the dining room on the left and the living room straight ahead. An L-shaped kitchen, fit for a gourmet, shares space with a bay-windowed country kitchen and a through-fireplace. The sun room provides a front row view of all four seasons, while blanketing you in solar warmth. The spacious first-floor master bedroom is a dream-come-true with a bay window at each end. If you prefer to pick up the pace, tone up in the dressing/exercise room and then enjoy a relaxing soak in the skylit whirlpool tub. The second floor is reserved for two family bedrooms and a full bath.

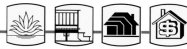

Additional products and services available. See page 4.

25

DESIGN HH2699

First Floor:	2,188 sq. ft.
Second Floor:	858 sq. ft.
Total:	3,046 sq. ft.

Uncommonly Luxurious Colonial

It's hard to improve upon the Colonial perfection founded by our forefathers, but perhaps it can be expanded a bit! Luxury is found throughout this plan, beginning with the elegantly proportioned dining room and living room.

The country kitchen is spacious, with a U-shaped kitchen and an island cooktop at one end, an eating area and built-ins at the other, and a fireplace that provides the central focus.

Far from the hustle and bustle is the secluded master bedroom. Curl up with a good book in the adjoining lounge or pamper yourself in the relaxing whirlpool tub. A handy laundry room, wash room and mud area are near the three-car garage. Two second-floor bedrooms each enjoy a private bath and share a lounge area.

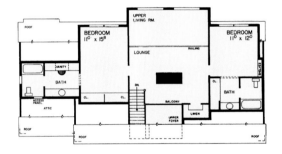

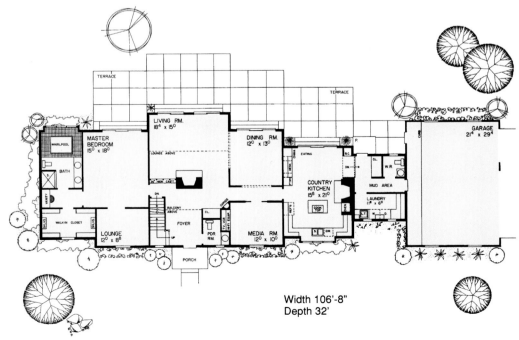

Width 106'-8"
Depth 32'

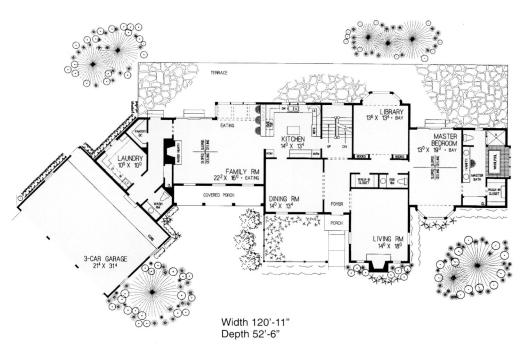

Width 120'-11"
Depth 52'-6"

DESIGN HH2995	
First Floor:	2,465 sq. ft.
Second Floor:	617 sq. ft.
Total:	3,082 sq. ft.

Combining Old And New

This New England Colonial combines the distinct character of the past with the amenities of the present.

Inside, the foyer opens to the dining room and the large living room warmed by a fireplace. The kitchen combines with the family room where an eating area and a raised-hearth fireplace encourage casual living. The library supplies an extra measure of quiet. Search the built-in bookcases for a favorite author and settle comfortably by the bay window.

Privacy is paramount in the first-floor master suite. Here, natural light filters through the bay window and the sliding glass doors. The master bath contains a whirlpool tub and a separate shower. The second floor is comprised of a full bath and two family bedrooms, each with a built-in desk.

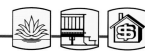

Additional products and services available. See page 4.

27

DESIGN HH1113

Square Footage: 1,008 sq. ft.

Less Is More

In these complicated times, wouldn't it be wonderful to possess an uncomplicated lifestyle? This just-right American classic is well-suited to meet the needs of a small family or empty-nesters.

A covered front porch extends a warm invitation to enter. Inside, the living room combines with the dining room to afford a spacious living area. Just steps away from the dining room is an efficient kitchen, supplying access to a rear terrace perfect for outdoor dining. The master bedroom possesses a private bath and a good deal of closet space. Linen storage is handy to a full bath shared by two family bedrooms.

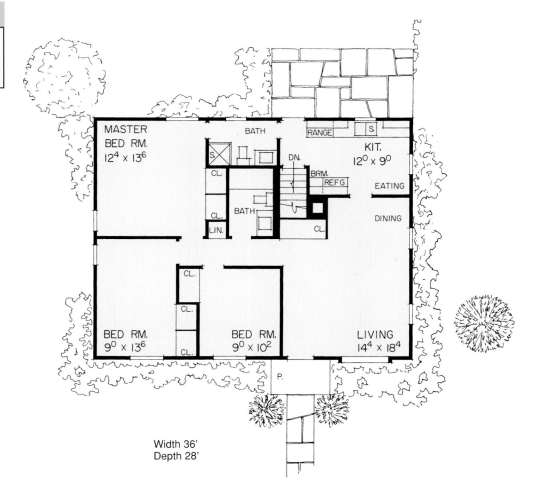

MASTER BED RM. 12⁴ x 13⁶

BATH

RANGE   S

KIT. 12⁰ x 9⁰

CL.

S

DN.

BRM.

REFG

EATING

CL.

BATH

DINING

LIN.

CL.

CL.

CL.

BED RM. 9⁰ x 13⁶

CL.

BED RM. 9⁰ x 10²

LIVING 14⁴ x 18⁴

P.

Width 36'
Depth 28'

Additional products and services available. See page 4.

DESIGN HH1323

Square Footage: 1,344 sq. ft.

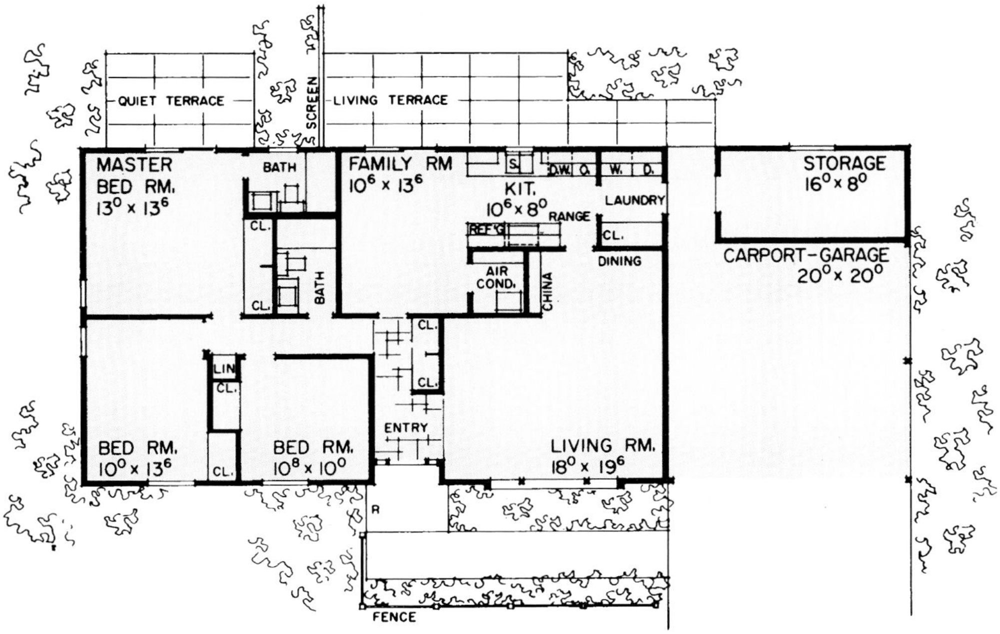

Exercise Your Options

When faced with a multitude of choices, it often becomes difficult to know which is right. Here, the choice is simple. These classic American designs incorporate three alternate exteriors with a excellent floor plan. It's a win-win situation!

The floor plan is thoughtfully designed with the living area located on the right and the sleeping area on the left. Sunlight streams through the large living room window, catching the sparkle of china in the built-in cabinet located in the adjoining dining room. Efficient planning places the kitchen near the family room, which accesses the living terrace for outdoor pursuits. The master bedroom possesses its own quiet terrace and a private bath. Two family bedrooms and a bath complete the plan.

Width 68'
Depth 28'

Floor plan labels:
QUIET TERRACE — LIVING TERRACE — SCREEN
MASTER BED RM. 13⁰ x 13⁶ — BATH — FAMILY RM. 10⁶ x 13⁶ — KIT. 10⁶ x 8⁰ — RANGE — S — DW — O — W. D. — LAUNDRY — STORAGE 16⁰ x 8⁰
CL. — BATH — CL. — REFG — CHINA — AIR COND. — CL. — DINING — CARPORT-GARAGE 20⁰ x 20⁰
BED RM. 10⁰ x 13⁶ — LIN CL. — BED RM. 10⁸ x 10⁰ — CL. — CL. — ENTRY — LIVING RM. 18⁰ x 19⁶
CL. — R — FENCE

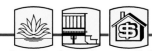

Additional products and services available. See page 4.

29

DESIGN HH2622

First Floor:	624 sq. ft.
Second Floor:	624 sq. ft.
Total:	1,248 sq. ft.
Bonus Room:	247 sq. ft.

Great Design, Small Package

A 5-carat diamond is small, yet massive. The same may be said for this charming Early American adaptation which is diminutive in size, but extends enormous livability.

A fireplace in the living room invites cozy evenings and lazy afternoons. Space in the dining room accommodates large gatherings for special occasions as well as romantic dinners for two. Casual meals may be taken at the nook in the adjacent L-shaped kitchen which enjoys a pantry and a window above the sink. A handy powder room completes the first floor.

The second floor contains three bedrooms, two baths and a room-to-grow area as future needs arise.

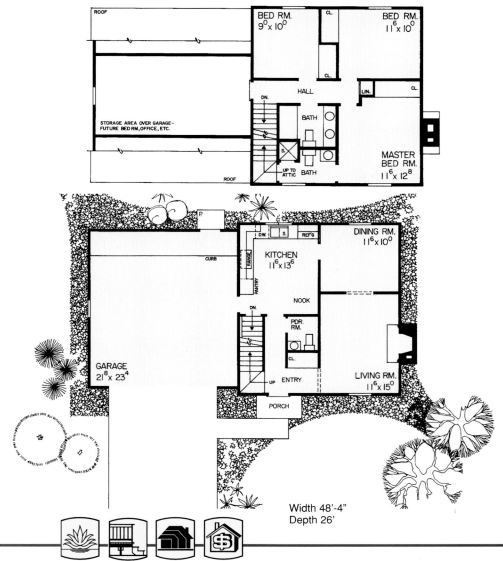

Width 48'-4"
Depth 26'

Additional products and services available. See page 4.

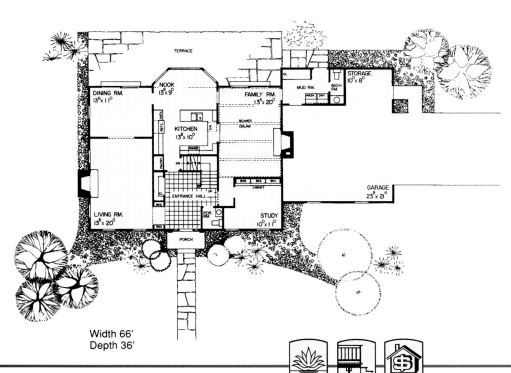

Width 66'
Depth 36'

DESIGN HH2610

First Floor:	1,505 sq. ft.
Second Floor:	1,344 sq. ft.
Total:	2,849 sq. ft.

New England Images

Narrow horizontal siding, corner boards and trademark window placement evoke strong memories of New England design. A large entrance hall makes a grand impression, leading into a study that dedicates a wall to built-in bookcases and a formal living room that possesses an entry flanked with bookcases.

The formal dining room, the bay-windowed nook and the family room offer unobstructed views of the rear yard. An efficient kitchen handily serves all areas.

The second floor is reserved for the sleeping zone. A spacious master bedroom features two walk-in closets, a dressing room and a private bath. Three family bedrooms, a large bath and an abundance of closet storage complete this floor.

Additional products and services available. See page 4.

31

This home, as shown in the photograph, may differ from the actual blueprints. For more detailed information, please check the floor plans carefully.

Photo by Andrew D. Lautman

DESIGN HH1956

First Floor:	990 sq. ft.
Second Floor:	728 sq. ft.
Total:	1,718 sq. ft.

Two Bedroom Options

This fine two-story home is graced with Colonial touches. Best of all, the plan includes two choices for completing the second floor: select the three-bedroom option, or if you prefer, the four-bedroom option. Whichever you choose, the tremendous livability remains unchanged.

The first floor takes off with a living room and a dining room joined to create a spacious formal living area. The kitchen is planned for practical use, and serves the breakfast area and dining room well. Step down to the adjacent sunken family room and enjoy the raised-hearth fireplace that will remove the chill from those cold winter nights. A centrally located powder room is easily accessed from all areas of the first floor.

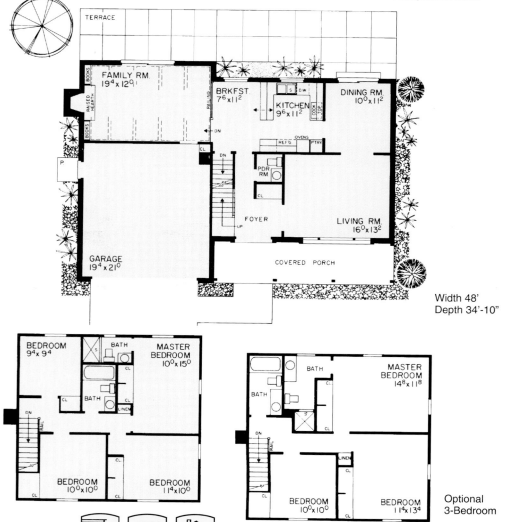

Width 48'
Depth 34'-10"

Optional 3-Bedroom

Additional products and services available. See page 4.

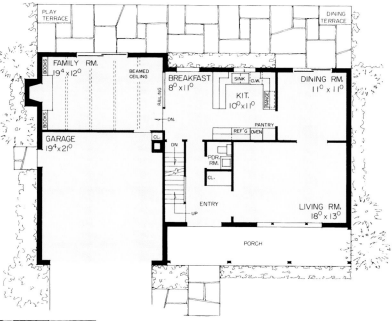

PLAY TERRACE

DINING TERRACE

FAMILY RM.
19⁴ x 12⁰

BEAMED CEILING

BREAKFAST
8⁰ x 11⁰

KIT.
10⁰ x 11⁰

DINING RM.
11⁰ x 11⁰

SINK · D.W. · RANGE

RAILING

DN.

BOOKS

GARAGE
19⁴ x 21⁰

PANTRY

REF'G · OVEN

DN

CL.

CL.

PDR. RM.

CL.

ENTRY

UP

LIVING RM.
18⁰ x 13⁰

PORCH

Width 50'
Depth 34'-10"

BED RM.
10⁴ x 9⁴

BATH

SHOWER

MASTER BED RM.
11⁰ x 15⁰

CL.

CL.

BATH

CL.

DN

LIN

CL.

CL.

BED RM.
9⁴ x 10⁰

CL.

BED RM.
14⁴ x 10⁰

DESIGN HH1957

First Floor:	1,042 sq. ft.
Second Floor:	780 sq. ft.
Total:	1,822 sq. ft.

As You Like It

Three for the price of one! Details are included with this plan for each of the three exteriors pictured. The floor plan remains essentially the same with the exception of slight changes to the window location.

Designed for comfortable living, the beamed-ceilinged family room will quickly become a favorite gathering place. A railing divides the sunken family room from the kitchen and the breakfast room which offers an ideal place for casual dining. For more formal pursuits, the nearby dining room blends well with the living room to create an area spacious enough to accommodate a host of guests. The second floor contains four bedrooms, one a master bedroom with a private bath.

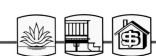

Additional products and services available. See page 4.

33

DESIGN HH1850

Main Level:	1,456 sq. ft.
Lower Level:	728 sq. ft.
Total:	2,184 sq. ft.

Split The Difference

Enjoy the view from the outdoor deck located on the upper level of this Colonial split-level home. The kitchen connects with the breakfast area and formal dining room, both featuring passage to the deck through sliding glass doors. Overlooking the rear grounds is a restful master bedroom, featuring a dressing room, a built-in vanity and a private bath. Two family bedrooms, a bath and a linen closet complete the sleeping area.

A fireplace in the family room warmly greets you on the lower level with space to accommodate family activities. If needed, the study could serve as an additional bedroom. A full bath and laundry room complete this level.

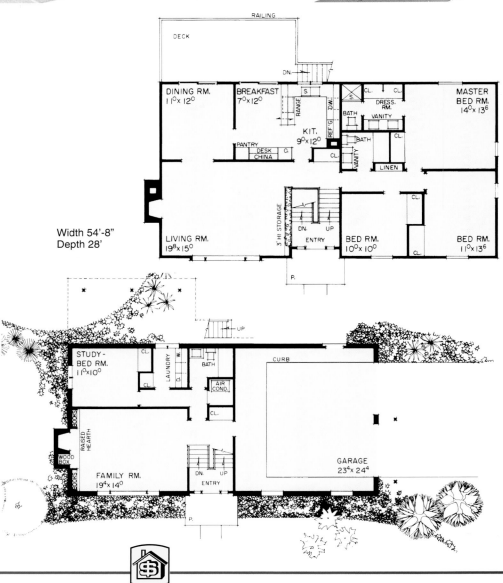

Width 54'-8"
Depth 28'

Additional products and services available. See page 4.

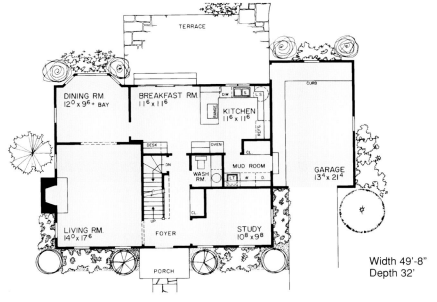

DINING RM.
12⁰ x 9⁶ + BAY

BREAKFAST RM.
11⁶ x 11⁶

KITCHEN
11⁶ x 11⁶

TERRACE

GARAGE
13⁴ x 21⁴

MUD ROOM

WASH RM.

DESK

OVEN

RANGE

LIVING RM.
14⁰ x 17⁶

FOYER

STUDY
10⁸ x 9⁸

PORCH

Width 49'-8"
Depth 32'

DRESSING ROOM

BATH

BATH

SHELVES

LINEN

BEDROOM
13⁰ x 12⁴

MASTER BEDROOM
14⁰ x 17⁶

BEDROOM
13⁰ x 12⁴

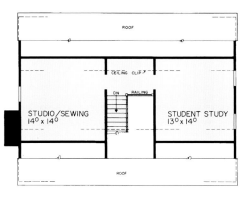

ROOF

CEILING CLG.

RAILING

STUDIO/SEWING
14⁰ x 14⁰

STUDENT STUDY
13⁰ x 14⁰

ROOF

DESIGN HH2659

First Floor:	1,023 sq. ft.
Second Floor:	1,008 sq. ft.
Third Floor:	476 sq. ft.
Total:	2,507 sq. ft.

A Federal Treasure

Simplicity at its best! A reserved, yet elegant exterior houses an amenity-filled, three-story plan. The foyer opens to a quiet study on the right and a formal living room on the left. Dinner guests will enjoy bay-windowed views of the rear grounds from the formal dining room. A breakfast room joins with the kitchen for sharing casual meals.

The second floor contains the sleep area. A relaxing master, bedroom is highlighted with built-in shelves and a private bath. Two family bedrooms and a shared bath round out this floor.

Budding students will appreciate the peace and quiet the third-floor student study furnishes; while artists and seamstresses value the creative space in the studio/sewing room.

DESIGN HH3503

First Floor:	1,748 sq. ft.
Second Floor:	1,748 sq. ft.
Third Floor:	1,100 sq. ft.
Total:	4,596 sq. ft.

Slender And Graceful

Though well-suited for a narrow lot, this brick home features generous space for elegant living. The formal living areas provide the utmost in comfort. A welcoming fireplace beckons entry to the living room through a columned passageway. Here, shelves and bookcases flank the entry to the adjacent dining room. An amenity-filled kitchen combines with the family kitchen which features a bay window and a fireplace.

The second floor contains two family bedrooms, a full bath and a sumptuous master suite. Here, a fireplace, a bay-windowed sitting area and a pampering master bath fulfill your dreams for a restful retreat. The third floor finds an additional treasure: a guest bedroom and a full bath, plus a library/playroom.

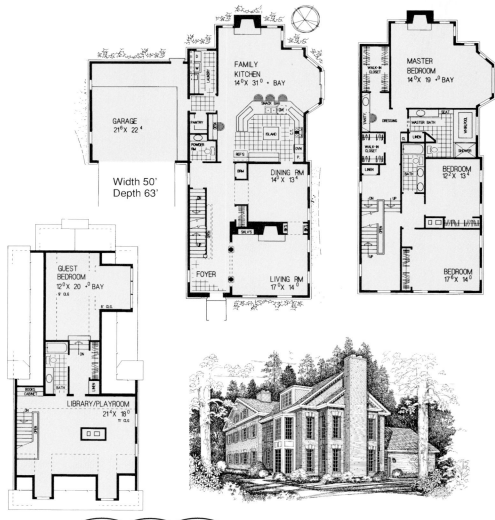

Additional products and services available. See page 4.

Photo by Andrew D. Lautman

Width 64'
Depth 64'

DESIGN HH2662

First Floor:	1,735 sq. ft.
Second Floor:	1,075 sq. ft.
Third Floor:	746 sq. ft.
Total:	3,556 sq. ft.

A Tale Of Two Styles

Influences from Georgian and Federal architecture blend harmoniously to bring out the best in this gracious home. Formal rooms with entertaining in mind come to the forefront with an elegant parlor to the left of the foyer and a grand dining room to the right.

The U-shaped kitchen unites with the warm and inviting gathering room for informal times. Two wings on opposite ends of the plan—one a study, the other a breakfast room—create symmetry. Each has unique bowed windows and a cheerful fireplace.

Five bedrooms provide sleep accommodations. The second floor contains two family bedrooms, a full bath and a master bedroom. Two additional bedrooms and a shared bath comprise the third floor.

Additional products and services available. See page 4.

37

This home, as shown in the photograph, may differ from the actual blueprints. For more detailed information, please check the floor plans carefully.

Photo by Andrrew D. Lautman

DESIGN HH2889

First Floor:	2,349 sq. ft.
Second Floor:	1,918 sq. ft.
Total:	4,267 sq. ft.

Georgian Elegance

It's easy to imagine our spirited, patriotic forefathers meeting in a home such as this. The pediment gable with cornice work and dentils, and the beautifully proportioned columns identify this home as an elegant Georgian.

Enter a large receiving hall bound by grand living and dining rooms and graced by a curving, double staircase. Beyond the living room is a study with access to the rear terrace. Informal family get-togethers will be enjoyed in the spacious gathering room. It is warmed by a centered fireplace bordered by windows on each side. An efficient kitchen features an island cooktop and shares space with the breakfast room.

The second floor holds three family bedrooms, two full baths and an outstanding master suite that personifies elegance and romance.

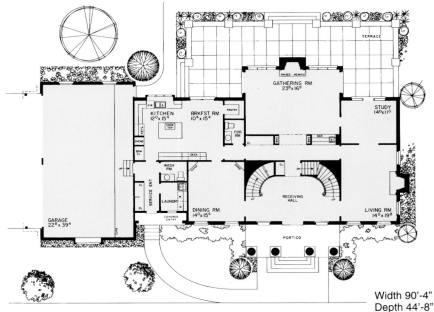

Width 90'-4"
Depth 44'-8"

Additional products and services available. See page 4.

This home, as shown in the photograph, may differ from the actual blueprints. For more detailed information, please check the floor plans carefully.

Photo by Laszlo Regos

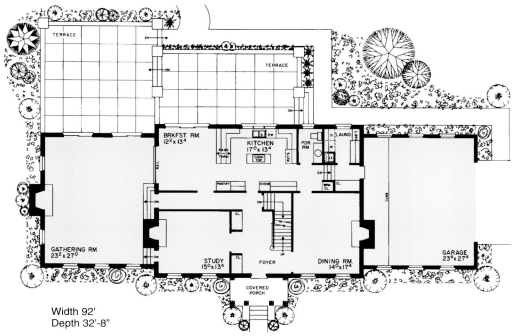

Width 92'
Depth 32'-8"

DESIGN HH2683

First Floor:	2,126 sq. ft.
Second Floor:	1,882 sq. ft.
Total:	4,008 sq. ft.

Revolutionary Design

This historical Georgian home has roots in the 18th Century.

Inside, the sophisticated step-down gathering room fills an entire wing, artfully designed to accommodate family gatherings or entertaining on a grand scale. Guests and family alike will appreciate the study and dining room located on either side of the foyer. Each of these rooms is warmed by a fireplace. The breakfast room and the kitchen are drenched in sunlight from the sliding glass door and the triple window above the sink.

On the second floor three bed-rooms and a full bath are crowned by a superb master suite. A deluxe bath, a fireplace and a sunken lounge with a dressing room promise moments of relaxation.

Additional products and services available. See page 4.

39

DESIGN HH3337

First Floor:	2,167 sq. ft.
Second Floor:	1,992 sq. ft.
Total:	4,159 sq. ft.

Spirited Southern Colonial

This graceful Southern Colonial home invites you to savor the smell of sweetly scented magnolias from its three terraces and second-floor balcony.

In the dining room, dessert and after-dinner conversation is enhanced by the companionable crackle of the fireplace. For more reflective moments, light a fire in the study, where you can ponder the answers to life's questions. Yet a third fireplace blazes merrily in the spacious step-down gathering room, welcoming family and friends. A snack bar efficiently unites the kitchen with a bay-windowed breakfast room.

Three family bedrooms and a full bath share the second floor with the master bedroom. Designed to depart from the ordinary, the master suite features a romantic fireplace, a large exercise room and a pampering bath.

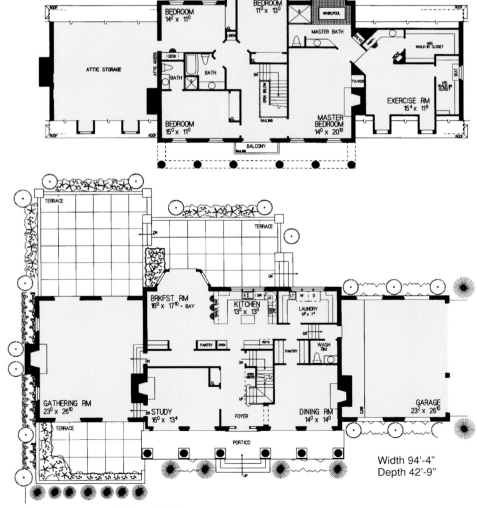

Width 94'-4"
Depth 42'-9"

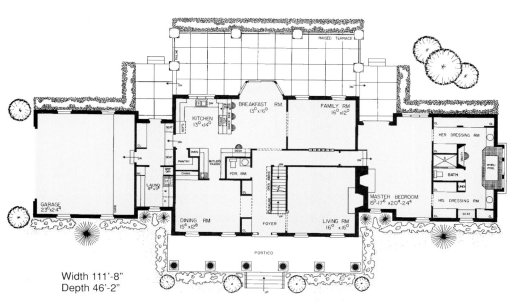

Width 111'-8"
Depth 46'-2"

DESIGN HH3303

First Floor:	2,563 sq. ft.
Second Floor:	1,496 sq. ft.
Total:	4,059 sq. ft.

Sophisticated Southern Style

Stately columns and one-story wings represent a style that epitomizes the grandeur of a time when charm and grace were ever-present.

Upon entering the formal living and dining rooms, it is at once apparent that upscale amenities are reflected throughout. To the rear of the plan, the kitchen, the bay-windowed breakfast room and the family room join to provide unlimited flexibility and appeal.

A private wing is dedicated to the master bedroom. Relax and relish the rosy glow cast from the fireplace's dying embers. The luxurious bath is second to none, featuring His and Hers dressing rooms, plenty of closet space and a pampering whirlpool tub.

The second floor includes four family bedrooms—each with a walk-in closet—that share two full baths.

DESIGN HH2665

First Floor:	1,152 sq. ft.
Second Floor:	1,152 sq. ft.
Total:	2,304 sq.ft.
(Excludes Guest Suite and Galleries)	

George Washington Slept Here

The origin of this house dates back to 1787 and George Washington's Mount Vernon. Galleries connect flanking wings—which may be added later—to create a large formal courtyard for this historic mini-estate.

On the first floor, a keeping room, a dining room, a breakfast room and a formal living room allow plenty of space for social gatherings. Four bedrooms—one a master suite–and two full baths are found on the second floor.

One wing accommodates guest quarters with a full bath, a lounge area and an upstairs studio. The other wing contains a garage with a storage/hobbies room situated above. The guest bedroom/lounge with an upstairs study may be optionally designed as a game room with a spiral staircase and a loft.

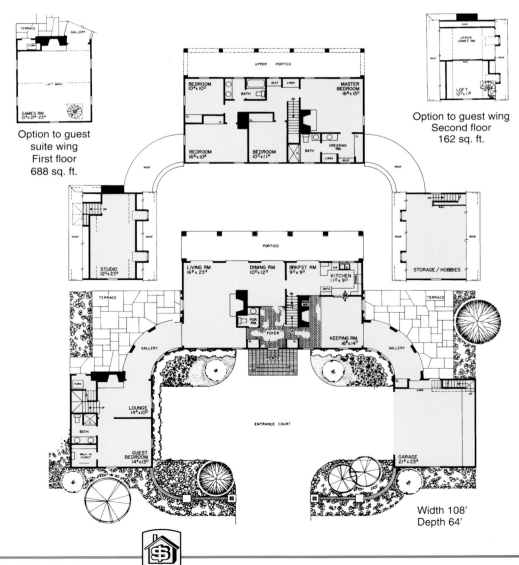

Option to guest suite wing First floor 688 sq. ft.

Option to guest wing Second floor 162 sq. ft.

Width 108'
Depth 64'

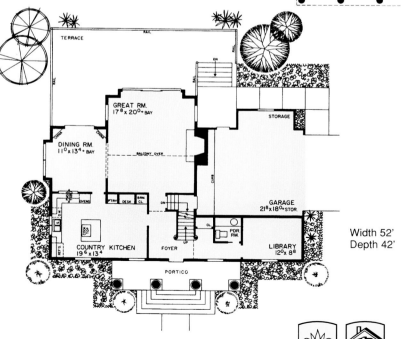

Width 52'
Depth 42'

DESIGN HH2668

First Floor:	1,206 sq. ft.
Second Floor:	1,254 sq. ft.
Total:	2,460 sq. ft.

Gracious Southern Manor

This elegant mini-manor displays a grand, columned portico reminiscent of those that warmly received visitors arriving in horse-drawn carriages for Sunday barbecue.

The fine hospitality for which the South is so well-known is demonstrated throughout the plan. The grand foyer leads to a library on the right and a welcoming country kitchen on the left. A spacious L-shaped kitchen and a nearby dining room assure space to visit with friends and family, and catch up on local events. The great room features a warming fireplace and a rear wall of glass with sliding doors opening onto the terrace.

Upstairs, three family bedrooms share a full bath. The master bedroom offers room to stretch and is highlighted by a walk-in closet and a pampering bath.

Additional products and services available. See page 4.

43

DESIGN HH3333

First Floor:	1,584 sq. ft.
Second Floor:	1,344 sq. ft.
Total:	2,928 sq. ft.

Southern Comfort

A columned porch and balcony furnish a gracious entrance to this captivating Southern Colonial adaptation. The foyer opens to a spacious living room with a centered fireplace and an adjoining dining room sized to accommodate a lavish soiree. A U-shaped kitchen shares space with a sunny, bay-windowed morning room and features a pass-through to the nearby family room located close enough to enjoy the aroma of freshly baked bread. A fireplace bids a warm welcome.

The upstairs sleeping area includes three family bedrooms and a master suite. Relax and unwind in the master bedroom, or retreat to the master bath which features a soothing whirlpool tub, a separate shower and a double-bowl vanity. His and Hers walk-in closets round out the suite.

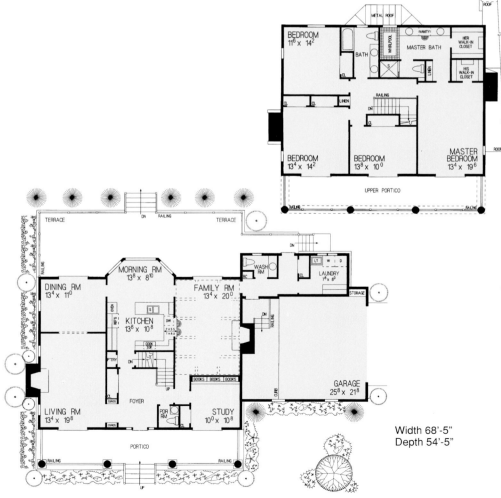

Width 68'-5"
Depth 54'-5"

Additional products and services available. See page 4.

Photo by Andrew D. Lautman

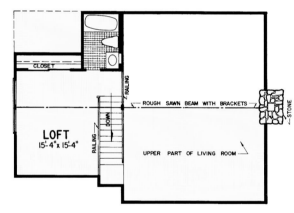

Width 36'
Depth 38'

DESIGN HH4061

First Floor:	1,008 sq. ft.
Second Floor:	323 sq. ft.
Total:	1,331 sq. ft.

Diamond In The Rough

If you've never taken time to whittle a piece of wood or catch fireflies in a jar, this home presents the perfect setting to do just that. A rocking-chair-perfect front porch spans the entire front of this rustic farmhouse for enjoying the outdoors.

Inside, open planning combines a spacious living room and dining room. A massive stone fireplace provides the central focus and will serve handily for popping corn and chasing the chill from frosty winter nights. An efficient, U-shaped kitchen is conveniently placed to serve these areas. A bedroom, a bath and a laundry room complete the first floor.

The second floor contains a full bath and a loft with plenty of space for the children or guests to bunk.

Additional products and services available. See page 4.

45

DESIGN HH3460

Square Footage: 1,389

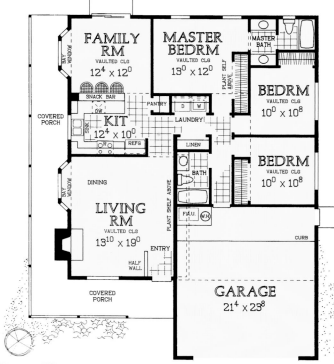

Double The Charm

Decisions, decisions. This quaint farmhouse offers two elevations in its blueprint package. You can't lose, because both are winning choices! Though rooflines and porches are different, the floor plan is primarily the same.

Good times will be shared in the formal living room/dining room combination warmed by a fireplace. The kitchen, which separates the formal area from the casual area, features a snack bar that divides the work area from the family room. Sliding glass doors provide easy access to the back yard.

Located to the rear of the plan is the master bedroom which includes a private bath and a shelf for showing off plants, antiques or family treasures. Two family bedrooms share a hall bath. A laundry room with linen storage handily serves all areas.

Width 44'-8"
Depth 54'-6"

Additional products and services available. See page 4.

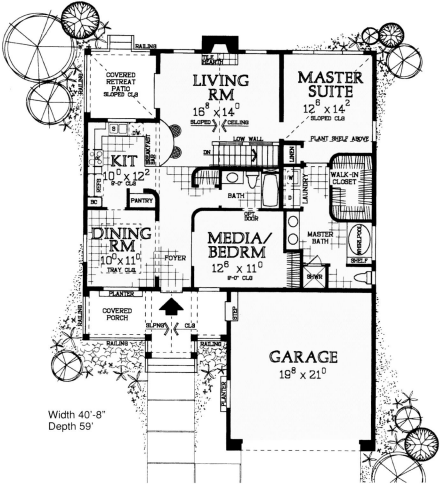

Width 40'-8"
Depth 59'

DESIGN HH3442

Square Footage: 1,273

Unique Entry Speaks Volumes

A covered porch and an inviting entry bid a warm-hearted welcome to this charming one-story farmhouse. Inside, the foyer introduces the dining room on the left. Nearby, a convenient step-saving kitchen enjoys a window overlooking a covered patio retreat, a pantry and a breakfast bar. A centered fireplace and a sloped ceiling enhance the spacious living room which easily accommodates formal and informal gatherings.

The master suite provides a wall of windows that face the rear grounds. Other amenities include a huge walk-in closet, space for a washer and dryer, and a master bath highlighted by a tranquil whirlpool tub and a separate shower. A media room—or if you prefer, a bedroom—and a full bath complete the plan.

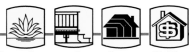

DESIGN HH3466

Square Footage:	1,800

Contemporay Farmhouse Style

Not only does this covered porch supply room to rock, it takes full advantage of outdoor living opportunities with an entertainment terrace and a built-in barbecue grill.

Inside, a foyer opens to a dining room on the left and a living room with a warming hearth on the right. Livability is enhanced in both with plant shelves and built-ins. A clever bar area separates the kitchen work area from the breakfast nook which opens onto the entertainment terrace.

Rest and relax in the secluded master suite, split from the secondary bedroom for utmost privacy. A luxurious master bath displays a large walk-in closet, a pampering tub, a separate shower and a double-bowl vanity.

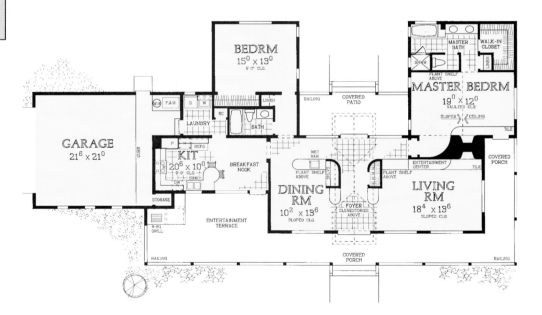

Width 89'
Depth 46'-2"

Additional products and services available. See page 4.

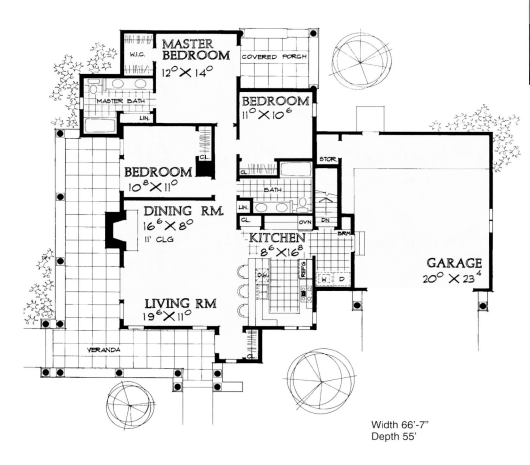

Width 66'-7"
Depth 55'

DESIGN HH3465

Square Footage: 1,410

L-Shaped Veranda

There is nothing quite like the sound of rain falling softly on a metal roof. This one is supported by an L-shaped veranda and graceful, tapered columns.

Inside, the living room and dining room join to create a 36-foot area perfect for formal occasions or quiet family evenings by the fireside. Busy cooks will appreciate the U-shaped kitchen open to the conversation area. Separated only by a snack bar, it facilitates baking chocolate chip cookies while watching a favorite movie.

Two family bedrooms—one with direct access to the veranda—share a bath and a nearby linen closet. The master bedroom enjoys a private covered porch. A walk-in closet and a master bath with a large linen closet and a double-bowl vanity complete the suite.

Additional products and services available. See page 4.

49

DESIGN HH3461

First Floor:	1,391 sq. ft.
Second Floor:	611 sq. ft.
Total:	2,002 sq. ft.

High-Class Country Style

A Palladian window set in a dormer provides a classic twist and a nice introduction to this 1½-story farmhouse. The two-story foyer draws on natural light and a pair of columns that frame the living room to set a comfortable, yet elegant mood. While the living room presents a grand space for entertaining, the dining room accommodates a full-course dining experience as easily as a family supper. The kitchen is a delight with its island cooktop and shares the warmth from the nearby family room and a warming fireplace.

Moonlight filters through a bay window casting a luminous glow on the master bedroom. A luxurious master bath with a whirlpool tub invites indulgence and will soon be a favored retreat. Three family bedrooms and a full bath share the second floor.

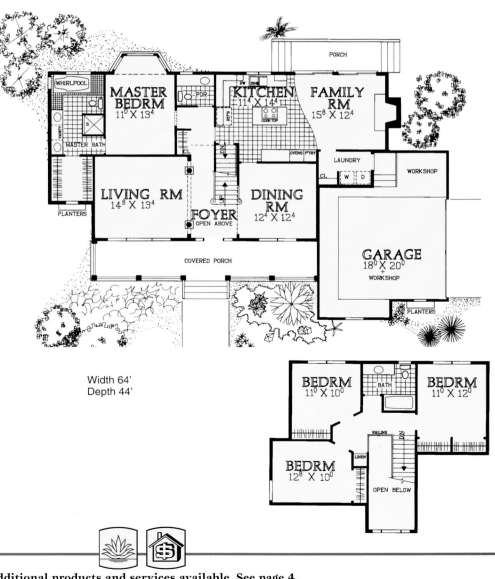

Width 64'
Depth 44'

Additional products and services available. See page 4.

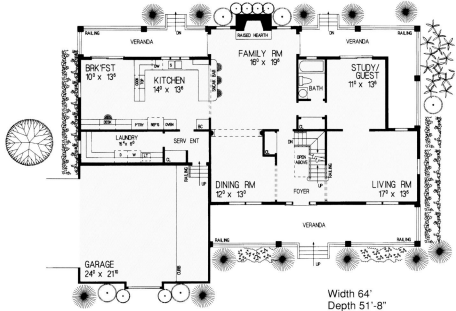

Width 64'
Depth 51'-8"

DESIGN HH3307

First Floor:	1,765 sq. ft.
Second Floor:	1,105 sq. ft.
Total:	2,870 sq. ft.

Country Crickets In Stereo

With a veranda on the front of this farmhouse, and two on the rear, you'll have your choice of seats for an unforgettable country concert. Nothing compares to the sound of light breezes blowing through fields or the cricket songs heard at twilight.

Enter the foyer which opens to the living room on the right and the dining room on the left. Columns graciously frame the entry to the family room. Here, a raised-hearth fireplace adds warmth to family gatherings. A snack bar connects the kitchen and breakfast room for the best in casual living. A study/guest room and adjacent bath complete the first floor.

Upstairs, two family bedrooms share a full bath. The master bedroom features a large walk-in closet and a thoughtfully appointed bath where you can bathe yourself in luxury.

DESIGN HH2776

First Floor:	1,134 sq. ft.
Second Floor:	874 sq. ft.
Total:	2,008 sq. ft.

New England Country Charm

Board-and-batten siding delivers all the country charm of a New England farmhouse. The large front covered porch is sized to accommodate a porch swing at each end—a wonderful way to enjoy the beautiful warm-weather months.

Immediately to the left of the front entrance is the corner living room. The bay-windowed dining room offers unobstructed views of the back yard and is easily served by the U-shaped kitchen nearby. A fire blazing merrily in the raised-hearth fireplace yields a warm welcome into the family room which also supplies access to the rear terrace. A powder room and laundry room complete the first floor.

The second floor houses two family bedrooms, a full bath and a master bedroom highlighted by a private bath and a walk-in closet.

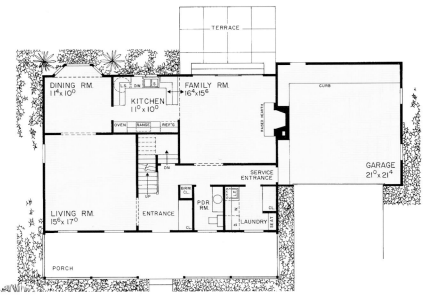

Width 61'-4"
Depth 38'

Additional products and services available. See page 4.

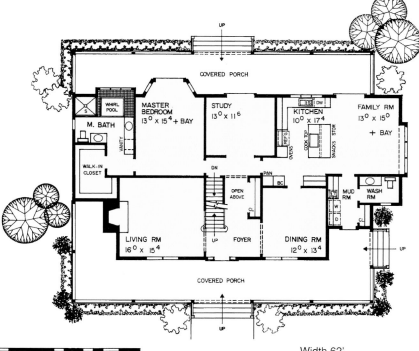

Width 62'
Depth 48'-8"

DESIGN HH3396

First Floor:	1,829 sq. ft.
Second Floor:	947 sq. ft.
Total:	2,776 sq. ft.

Quiet Country Style

Rustic charm abounds in this pleasant country farmhouse. Covered porches to the front and rear provide a wealth of outdoor living potential for the entire family.

The interior features well-proportioned rooms that begin with the formal dining room and the inviting living room flanking the foyer. To the rear is an efficient L-shaped kitchen with an island cooktop and a snack bar. A few steps away, a family room connects with the breakfast nook for informal gatherings and casual meals. A private study is adjacent to the first-floor master suite. The master bedroom puts the bay window to good use as a reading alcove. An amenity-filled master bath features a large walk-in closet, a relaxing whirlpool tub and a separate shower.

The second floor holds three family bedrooms—two with dormer windows—and a full bath.

Additional products and services available. See page 4.

53

DESIGN HH3398

First Floor:	1,533 sq. ft.
Second Floor:	1,288 sq. ft.
Total:	2,821 sq. ft.

Farmhouse Fashion

Covered porches wrap this lovely farmhouse with warmth and comfort. Inside, an open, airy floor plan allows sunlight to brighten living areas. A corner fireplace extends a warm welcome in the living room. Formal meals may be savored in the dining room, while the nearby kitchen provides a snack bar for light eating and an attached breakfast room for cozy meals and leisurely coffee breaks. The spacious family room—enhanced by a lively corner fireplace—offers a relaxing informal environment. Passage to the rear covered porch is obtained through the breakfast room and the family room.

The second floor contains the sleeping area—two family bedrooms, a full bath and a well-appointed master suite. The master bedroom provides ample space to stretch with a private master bath that enjoys a large walk-in closet, a rejuvenating whirlpool tub and a separate shower.

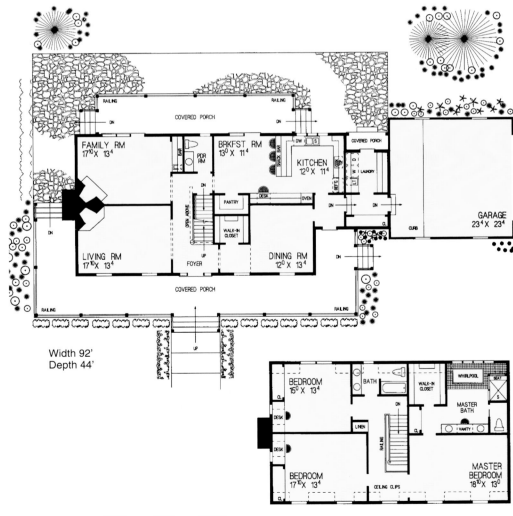

Width 92'
Depth 44'

Additional products and services available. See page 4.

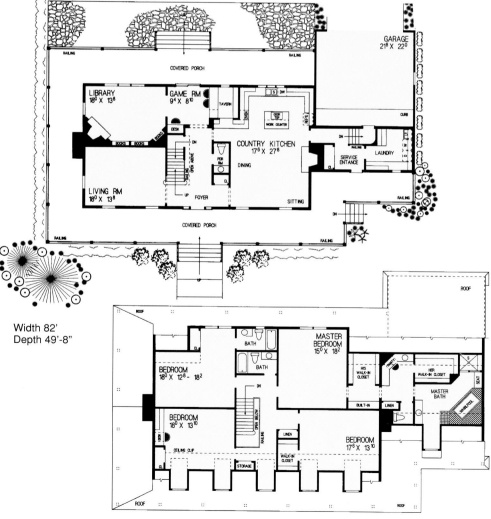

Width 82'
Depth 49'-8"

DESIGN HH3399

First Floor:	1,716 sq. ft.
Second Floor:	2,102 sq. ft.
Total:	3,818 sq. ft.

The Heart Of Country

Finally, a wraparound porch that lets you "Waltz Across Texas" and then some! Inside, an expansive living room provides space for formal entertaining, while the remainder of the first floor is dedicated to an informal lifestyle. A huge, U-shaped country kitchen incorporates space for an island work center, a cozy fireplace, a dining area and a sitting area.

Separating the kitchen from the library is a game room and an attached tavern. Light a fire in the corner fireplace, select a novel from the built-in bookcase and stretch out in front of the library window.

Upstairs, two family bedrooms share a hall bath and a third possesses a private bath. The sumptuous master bedroom surrounds you with luxury. Special features include His and Hers walk-in closets and a master bath with a corner whirlpool.

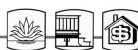

Additional products and services available. See page 4.

55

DESIGN HH2694

First Floor:	2,026 sq. ft.
Second Floor:	1,386 sq. ft.
Total:	3,412 sq. ft.

Cream-Of-The-Crop Farmhouse

This two-story farmhouse faithfully recalls the 18th-Century homestead of Secretary of Foreign Affairs, John Jay. The ambiance of its historic past blends well with the amenity-filled floor plan.

After a formal meal, enjoy a recital in the living room's music alcove or lively conversation punctuated by the crackle of the cozy fireplace. Quieter, solitary moments may be spent in the bookshelf-lined library. A huge country kitchen sports a third fireplace and provides the hub for informal get-togethers.

Upstairs are three sizable bedrooms including a master suite. The master bedroom is designed with comfort and privacy in mind. A dramatic bath is enhanced by a wealth of closet space, a spacious dressing room and a whirlpool tub.

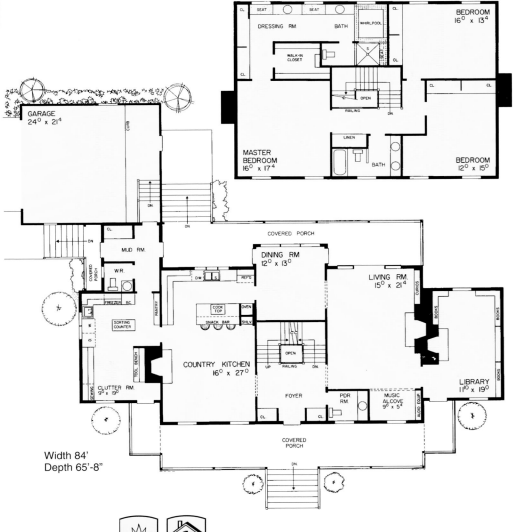

Width 84'
Depth 65'-8"

Additional products and services available. See page 4.

Width 70'
Depth 34'

DESIGN HH2908

First Floor:	1,427 sq. ft.
Second Floor:	1,153 sq. ft.
Total:	2,580 sq. ft.

A Slice Of Americana

Early American influence supplies this farmhouse with a warmth that withstands the test of time. A covered front porch with pillars and rails, double chimneys and a bay-windowed building attachment are pleasing details of a bygone era.

The foyer introduces the formal living area to the left. Here, a large living room with a fireplace bids a hearty welcome and extends warmth into the dining room nearby. A U-shaped kitchen overlooking the rear terrace easily serves this area as well as the attached breakfast room. The central focus of this design is the first-floor attachment containing a family room that connects the main house to a two-car garage.

The second floor is comprised of three bedrooms, a full bath and a master bedroom with a dressing room and a private bath.

Additional products and services available. See page 4.

57

This home, as shown in the photograph, may differ from the actual blueprints. For more detailed information, please check the floor plans carefully.

Photo by Andrew D. Lautman

DESIGN HH2946

First Floor:	1,581 sq. ft.
Second Floor:	1,344 sq. ft.
Total:	2,925 sq. ft.

All-American Country

Small-town hospitality, the pleasures of casual conversation and the good grace of pleasant company are all essential elements for a fine country lifestyle. And what better place to gather with family and friends than on a wraparound porch or rear terrace?

Inside, a fireplace provides the focus for the formal living room. A connecting dining room supplies passage to the rear terrace for dessert.

Sunlight floods the bay-windowed breakfast room shared by the kitchen. The family room is sized to comfortably house even the largest casual gatherings. A mud room, a laundry room and a large workshop complete the first floor.

Upstairs, three secondary bedrooms share a full bath. A master bedroom enhanced by His and Hers walk-in closets, a dressing room and a private bath round out the plan.

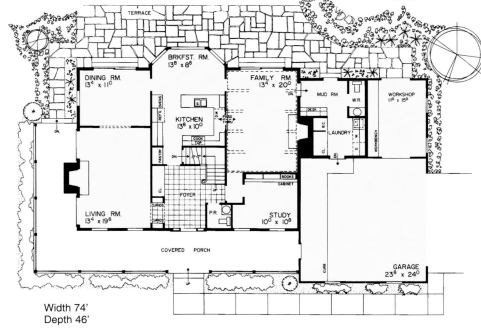

Width 74'
Depth 46'

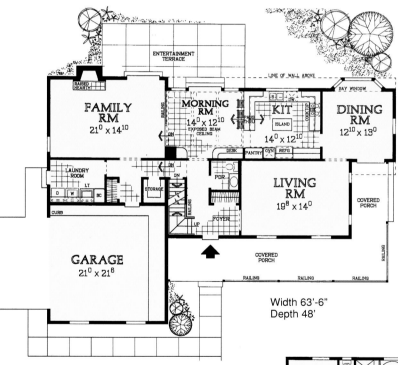

ENTERTAINMENT TERRACE

LINE OF WALL ABOVE

RAISED HEARTH

FAMILY RM 21⁰ x 14¹⁰

MORNING RM 14⁰ x 12¹⁰ EXPOSED BEAM CEILING

BAY WINDOW

KIT 14⁰ x 12¹⁰ ISLAND

DINING RM 12¹⁰ x 13⁰

DESK PANTRY OVN REFG

LAUNDRY ROOM D W BC LT

STORAGE

PDR

LIVING RM 19⁸ x 14⁰

COVERED PORCH

CURB

RAILING

FOYER

UP

GARAGE 21⁰ x 21⁶

COVERED PORCH

RAILING RAILING RAILING

Width 63'-6"
Depth 48'

ROOF

ATTIC 39⁰ x 29⁰ (APPROX. HEADROOM 32" x 12")

ROOF

DN

ROOF

BEDRM/ STUDY 10⁴ x 11¹⁰

SHWR WHIRLPOOL

MASTER BATH

BATH LIN

WALK-IN CLOSET

MASTER SUITE 16⁴ x 14¹⁰

DN

BEDRM 12² x 10⁶

BEDRM 14⁶ x 10⁶

UP TO ATTIC

DESIGN HH3325

First Floor:	1,595 sq. ft.
Second Floor:	1,112 sq. ft.
Total:	2,707 sq. ft.

Create-A-Farmhouse

Horizontal clapboard siding, varying roof planes and finely detailed window treatments set the country tone for this engaging family farmhouse.

Combined living and dining rooms function exceptionally well together. A plethora of windows in the living room provide an abundance of natural light to this area. For informal occasions, a spacious family room and a breakfast room extend a wealth of livability. A raised-hearth fireplace graces the family room and large glass doors provide natural illumination and direct access to the entertaining terrace. The U-shaped kitchen utilizes a work island supplemented by plenty of cabinet and counter space.

Sleeping accommodations consist of four bedrooms, including a master bedroom suite with a walk-in closet and an additional long wardrobe closet. The rear bedroom will make a fine study, guest room or fourth bedroom.

Additional products and services available. See page 4.

59

DESIGN HH3462

First Floor:	1,395 sq. ft.
Second Floor:	813 sq. ft.
Total:	2,208 sq. ft.

A Country Dream Come True

Front and rear covered porches surround this family farmhouse to ensure endless country comfort while varied roof planes add visual appeal.

Inside, distinct formal and informal living zones provide the best accommodations for any occasion. The columned foyer opens to both the dining and living rooms. A central kitchen services the large family room with an island work counter and a snack bar. For everyday chores, a laundry room is conveniently located, also providing access to the garage.

On the first floor you'll find the master suite. It employs complete privacy and luxury with its double closets and master bath. Upstairs, three family bedrooms—one with a built-in desk—a full bath and a linen closet extend fabulous livability.

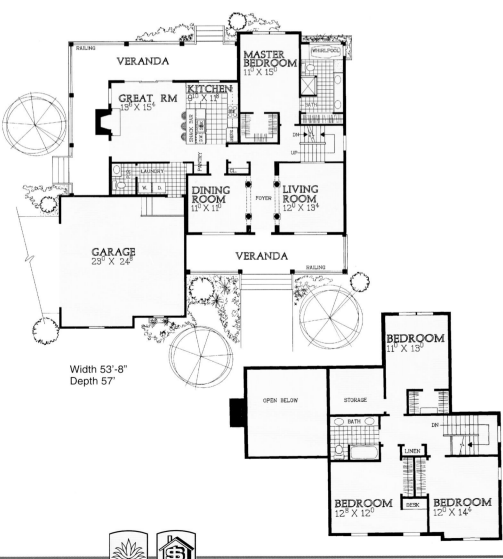

Width 53'-8"
Depth 57'

Additional products and services available. See page 4.

Photo by Carl Socolow

This home, as shown in the photograph, may differ from the actual blueprints.
For more detailed information, please check the floor plans carefully.

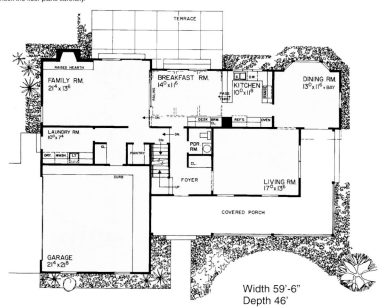

Width 59'-6"
Depth 46'

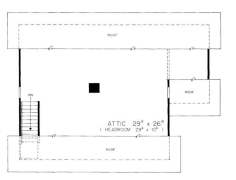

DESIGN HH2774

First Floor:	1,366 sq. ft.
Second Floor:	969 sq. ft.
Total:	2,335 sq. ft.
Third Floor Attic:	969 sq. ft.

Picture-Perfect Farmhouse

The characteristics of this inviting country farmhouse paint a picture of perfection that captures the essence of down-home hospitality.

For large socials, the spacious living room and adjoining dining room furnish an entertaining showplace. A U-shaped kitchen with a pass-through to the breakfast room is conveniently located to serve both formal and informal living areas. The step-down family room sports a beam ceiling, a raised-hearth fireplace and rear-terrace access.

The second floor holds three family bedrooms—or if you prefer, two bedrooms and a study—and a full bath. The master bedroom also resides upstairs and is highlighted by a built-in vanity, a dressing room and a full bath. The third-floor attic may be completed as the need for additional space arises.

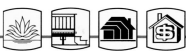

Photo by Bob Greenspan

DESIGN HH3309

First Floor:	1,375 sq. ft.
Second Floor:	1,016 sq. ft.
Total:	2,391 sq. ft.

A Victorian Farmhouse Masterpiece

A gazebo located on the front veranda yields the perfect place for geranium baskets while rising to the challenge of presenting a unique elevation.

The rear of the plan houses a family room that will become a favorite place for informal gatherings. From the casual breakfast room, pass through sliding glass doors to the rear veranda. Or if you prefer, use the formal dining room that opens onto the front veranda. Additional outdoor entrance is supplied from the formal living room to the gazebo for afternoon tea.

On the second floor, a study contributes space for quiet, reflective moments. The sleeping area consists of two secondary bedrooms that share a hall bath. The romantic master bedroom provides ample space for privacy. A master bath invites relaxation with a soothing whirlpool tub.

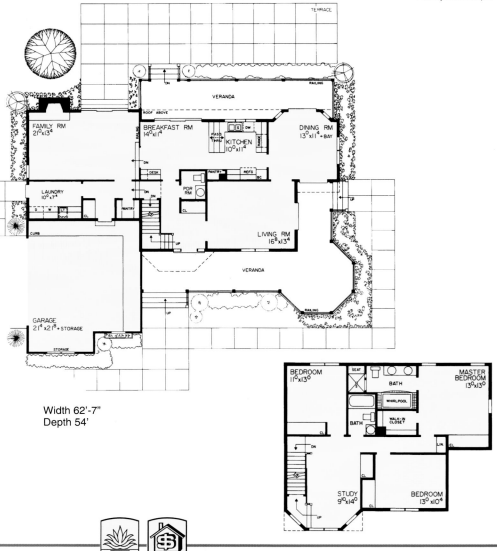

Width 62'-7"
Depth 54'

Additional products and services available. See page 4.

This home, as shown in the photograph, may differ from the actual blueprints. For more detailed information, please check the floor plans carefully.

Photo by Bob Greenspan

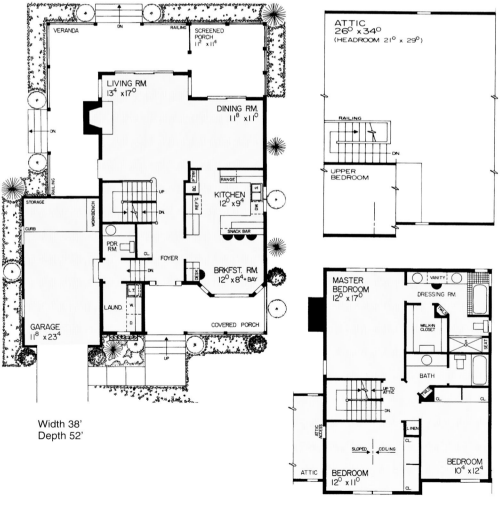

Width 38'
Depth 52'

DESIGN HH2974

First Floor:	911 sq. ft.
Second Floor:	861 sq. ft.
Total:	1,772 sq. ft.

A Dash Of Victorian

Though designed to fit on a narrow lot, this Victorian farmhouse makes no compromise when it comes to captivating exterior styling. Thoughtful planning simplifies the interior and greatly increases livability.

Upon entering, the foyer introduces a cheerful bay-windowed breakfast room that overlooks the front porch. Located nearby is a step-saving kitchen which also serves the attached snack bar and formal dining room with equal ease. A cheerful fireplace situated in the living room not only removes the chill from frosty fall evenings, but invites the leisurely gathering of friends and family.

Upstairs, two family bedrooms share a hall bath. The master bedroom provides a restful retreat. Amenities in the master bath include a large walk-in closet, a dressing room, a double-bowl vanity and a separate tub and shower.

DESIGN HH3382

First Floor:	1,366 sq. ft.
Second Floor:	837 sq. ft.
Third Floor:	363 sq. ft.
Total:	2,566 sq. ft.

Delicate Queen Anne Victorian

This enchanting three-story home boasts delicately turned rails and decorated columns on its covered front porch and second-floor balcony.

A sizable entry opens to an inviting living room to the right, and a banquet-size dining room on the left. A unique, bay-shaped family kitchen provides a grand, open space. The countertop borders one wall and features an above-sink window that overlooks the rear veranda and gazebo. An open eating area centrally located shares comfortable space with a raised-hearth fireplace flanked by windows nearby.

The second floor contains a secondary bedroom, a full bath and an outstanding master suite. A guest bedroom featuring a walk-in closet and a private bath completes the third floor.

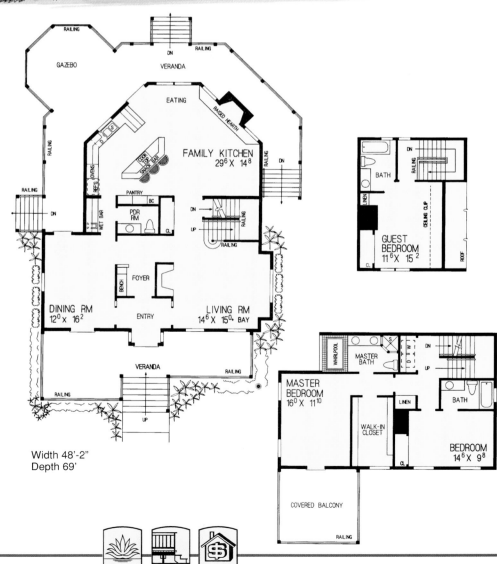

Width 48'-2"
Depth 69'

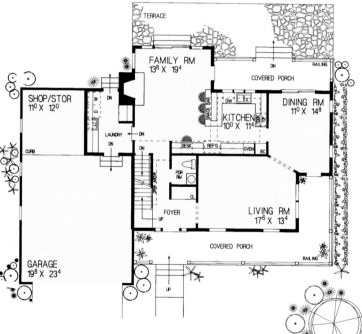

Width 56'
Depth 44'

DESIGN HH3385

First Floor:	1,096 sq. ft.
Second Floor:	900 sq. ft.
Total:	1,996 sq. ft.

A Folk Victorian Tale

Fish scale shingles and decorative stickwork, pleasing details of a bygone era, are found on the exterior of this stunning Folk Victorian home. An abundance of windows throughout create a light-filled interior. The formal living room and dining room blend to provide a grand L-shaped space that extends to the front and rear.

Carefree, casual times will be shared in the family room just steps away from the kitchen and the cookie jar. Here, a built-in desk provides space for meal planning and a handy snack bar for family members on the go.

Four bedrooms occupy the second floor. The master suite features twin lavatories, a window seat and three closets. One of the three family bedrooms has its own private balcony and could easily serve as a study.

Photo by Andrew D. Lautman

DESIGN HH2973

First Floor:	1,269 sq. ft.
Second Floor:	1,227 sq. ft.
Total:	2,496 sq. ft.

Victorian Drama

A circle-head window takes center stage over the front covered porch while smaller versions double the dramatic impact of the two-story turret.

Enter the first-floor study, settle into your favorite antique chair, and inhale the aroma of fine English leather. Later, family games and conversation may be enjoyed in front of the friendly fireplace in the bay-windowed family room. A U-shaped kitchen is centered between the adjoining breakfast room and the formal dining room to easily serve both. Completing the grand first floor is a formal living room, a powder room and a mud room.

The second floor contains three bedrooms, a full bath and a luxurious master bedroom. Special features include His and Hers walk-in closets and a lavish master bath.

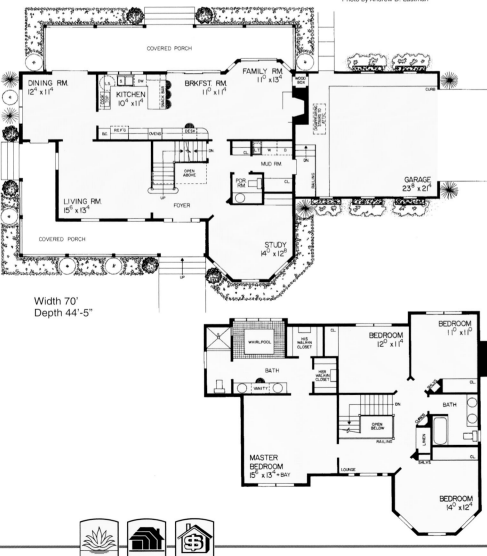

Width 70'
Depth 44'-5"

Additional products and services available. See page 4.

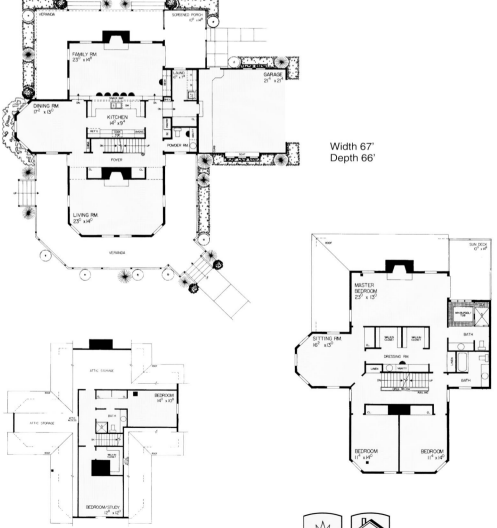

Width 67'
Depth 66'

DESIGN HH2970

First Floor:	1,538 sq. ft.
Second Floor:	1,526 sq. ft.
Third Floor:	658 sq. ft.
Total:	3,722 sq. ft.

Iced With Gingerbread Trim

This charming Victorian is reminiscent of a time when letter writing was an art and the scent of lavender hung lightly in the air. However, the floor plan moves quickly into the present with a contemporary floor plan. A veranda wraps around the living room providing entrance from each side. Centered for dramatic effect is a warmly welcoming fireplace. The central hub of the first floor is occupied by a kitchen that efficiently serves the dining room, family room and living room with equal ease.

Located on the second floor are two family bedrooms, a full bath and an opulent master suite. Amenities include a romantic fireplace, a bay-windowed sitting room, a pampering master bath and a private sun deck. The third floor holds two bedrooms—one a possible study—and a full bath.

Additional products and services available. See page 4.

67

DESIGN HH2953

First Floor:	2,995 sq. ft.
Second Floor:	1,831 sq. ft.
Total:	4,826 sq. ft.

Gracious Victorian Estate

Business cards have replaced Victorian calling cards and living rooms have replaced parlors, but this magnificent estate home promises charm and grace that is always in style. The impressive two-story foyer provides a direct view into the great room with a large central fireplace. To the left of the foyer is a bookshelf-lined library and to the right is a dramatic, octagonal-shaped dining room. An island cooktop completes a convenient work triangle in the kitchen and a pass-through connects this room with the Victorian-style morning room.

A sumptuous first-floor master suite opens to the rear covered porch. A through-fireplace warms the bedroom, sitting room and dressing room, which includes His and Hers walk-in closets. Four bedrooms, three baths and a lounge with a fireplace are located on the second floor.

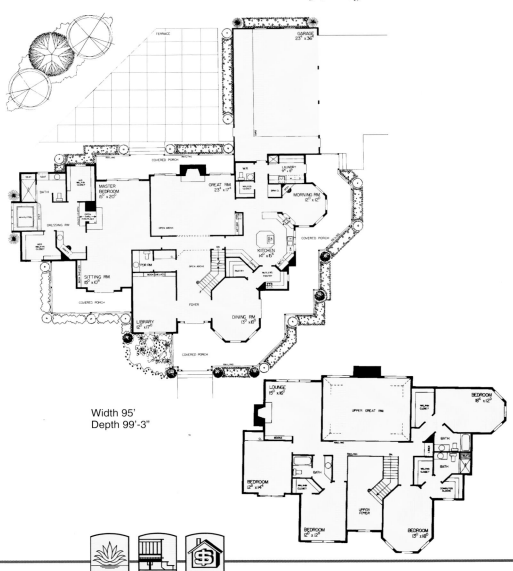

Width 95'
Depth 99'-3"

Additional products and services available. See page 4.

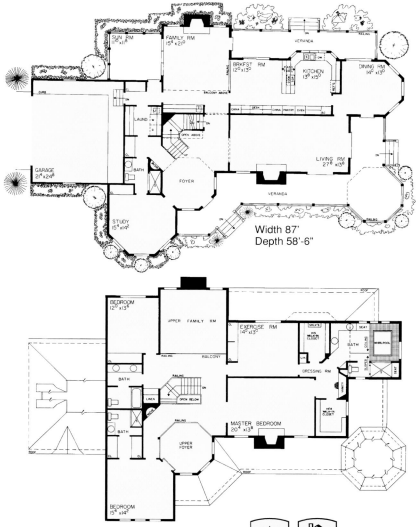

Width 87'
Depth 58'-6"

DESIGN HH3304

First Floor:	2,102 sq. ft.
Second Floor:	1,971 sq. ft.
Total:	4,073 sq. ft.

New Gilded Age

Say hello to the "new" golden era. From verandas—both front and rear—to the stately turrets and impressive chimney stack, Victorian style is exquisitely displayed. Besides the grand living room, formal dining room and two-story family room, there is a room-to-relax private study. A gourmet kitchen with built-ins has a pass-through counter to the breakfast room.

The master suite located on the second floor is extraordinary. A fireplace casts a romantic glow onto the large master bedroom. Space for a ballet barre or an entire aerobics class is found in the exercise room nearby. After a tough workout, head for the master bath's relaxing whirlpool spa. His and Hers walk-in closets round out the suite. Two additional bedrooms, each with a full bath, are contained on the second floor.

Additional products and services available. See page 4.

69

DESIGN HH3502

First Floor:	2,086 sq. ft.
Second Floor:	2,040 sq. ft.
Total:	4,126 sq. ft.

Rock-Solid Farmhouse

Nothing compares with the style and texture of stone. This lovely farmhouse is reminiscent of the solid, comfortable homes once so prevalent on homesteads throughout America.

Enter the foyer from the columned front porch. A formal living room is located on the left and a library on the right. The formal dining room connects directly to the living room and indirectly to the island kitchen through a butler's pantry. Beam ceilings highlight the family room and breakfast room which are both open to the kitchen. A covered veranda accessed from the breakfast room leads to a side yard.

On the second floor are three bedrooms—one a master suite—and a guest room with a private bath. The master bedroom features a fireplace and a fine bath with a whirlpool tub. The two secondary bedrooms share a full bath.

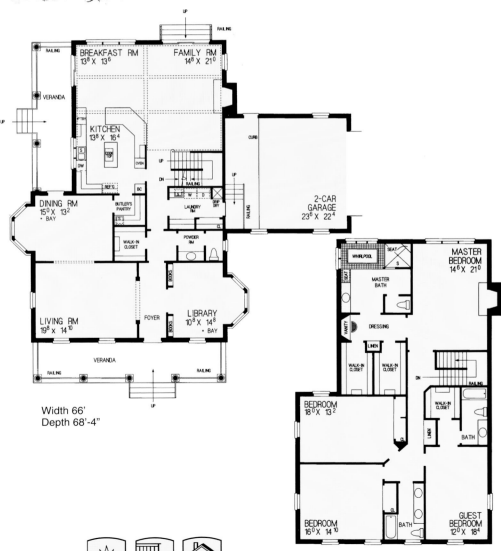

Width 66'
Depth 68'-4"

Additional products and services available. See page 4.

Width 63'-4"
Depth 54'-10"

DESIGN HH2962

Square Footage: 2,112

Live Like Royalty

Your Tudor home is your castle, and in today's hectic times this truth is more important than ever before. Open planning, a sloped ceiling and a wall of sliding glass doors allow sunlight to brighten the formal living room and dining room combination. The L-shaped kitchen with its island range and views of the rear terrace is open to the spacious breakfast room. Here, passage to the rear terrace is provided through yet another set of sliding glass doors.

A master suite invites relaxation with a spacious bedroom and a restful private bath. Amenities include a huge walk-in closet, a whirlpool tub and a separate shower. An adjacent study easily converts to a nursery or a third bedroom. A secondary bedroom, a full bath, a powder room and a laundry room complete the wonderful interior.

Additional products and services available. See page 4.

71

DESIGN HH3314

Square Footage:	1,951

Timeless Tudor Textures

A rustic exterior enhanced by the details of distinguished Tudor style blend harmoniously to bring out the best of both. The living area is located on the left side of the plan, the sleeping area on the right. Windows frame each side of the welcoming fireplace, providing the focal point for the gathering room. An adjacent dining room joins the screened porch—the combined living area enhances indoor/outdoor livability. A snack bar brings the kitchen and multi-windowed breakfast room together.

Special features in the master bedroom include a sloped ceiling, two walk-in closets, an amenity-filled bath and access to the rear veranda. Two family bedrooms, a full bath and an abundance of linen storage complete the sleeping zone.

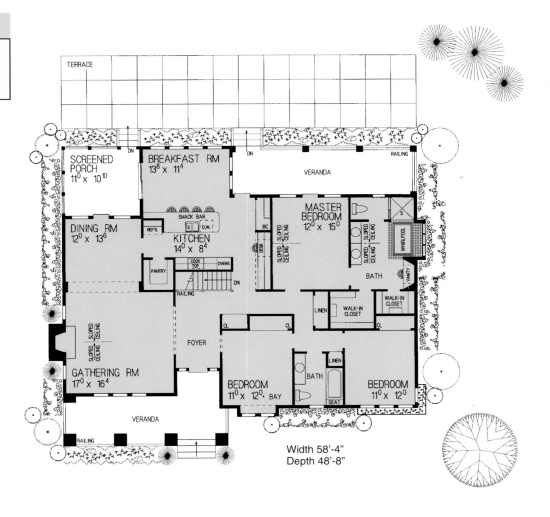

Width 58'-4"
Depth 48'-8"

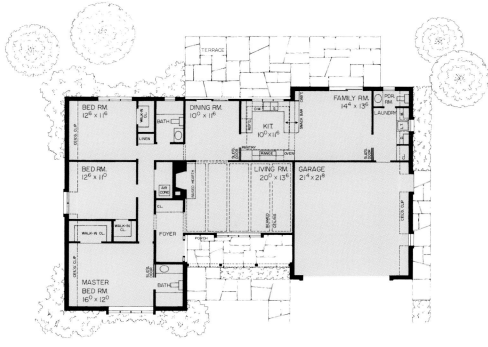

Width 64'-10"
Depth 43'-11"

Optional
basement
plan

DESIGN HH2206

Square Footage:	1,769

Royal Treatment

Old World styling, New World convenience! Half-timbered stucco, brick and diamond lites lend cottage character to this one-story Tudor home.

Inside, the foyer opens to a beamed-ceilinged living room where a warming fireplace extends a cheerful greeting to family and friends alike. An abundance of windows makes the kitchen bright and cheerful. Situated between the family room and the dining room, the kitchen also enjoys access to the rear terrace from either side.

The left portion of the plan houses the sleeping wing. A private bath and a walk-in closet enhance the master bedroom. Two family bedrooms—each with a walk-in closet—share a full bath.

DESIGN HH2802

Square Footage:	1,729

A King And A Princess

Henry VIII and Snow White have something in common—a love for the distinctive charm furnished by Tudor design. A covered porch serves as a fitting introduction to an amenity-filled floor plan. The gathering room gains a great deal of attention with its rustic appeal and outside passage to the rear terrace. The efficient kitchen features a snack bar for quick, easy meals. Located nearby, a breakfast room with a bumped-out bay welcomes casual meals while the living room overlooking the terrace and covered dining porch is perfect for special occasions.

The master bedroom provides ample space for privacy and its own separate entrance to the rear terrace. Two family bedrooms—one with a bay window, and one that converts to a study—share a full bath.

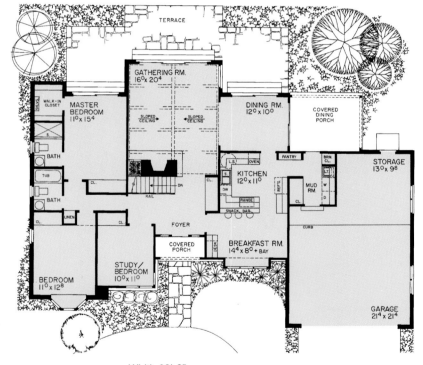

Width 68'-2"
Depth 48'-10"

Optional
non-basement

Additional products and services available. See page 4.

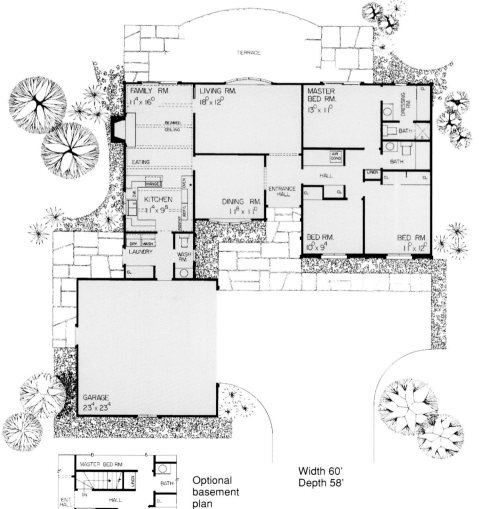

DESIGN HH2606

Square Footage:	1,499

Tudor With A Twist

Designed for a comfortable lifestyle, this compact one-story home offers the perfect blend of Tudor flavor and contemporary flair. A generous entrance hall opens straight ahead to a spacious living room naturally lit by a large bowed window. For more informal get-togethers, the beamed-ceilinged family room with its cozy fireplace will welcome family and friends. A U-shaped kitchen unites with the formal and informal living areas, easily serving each one.

Enjoy the relaxing environment furnished in the master bedroom. Features include a dressing room, a private bath and terrace access. Two family bedrooms located at the front of the plan share a full bath nearby.

Optional basement plan

Width 60'
Depth 58'

DESIGN HH2964

First Floor:	1,441 sq. ft.
Second Floor:	621 sq. ft.
Total:	2,062 sq. ft.

Deeply Rooted In Royalty

Elegant appeal is provided by the varying rooflines, stucco and brick details of royal Tudor style.

Inside, a two-story foyer soars to great heights. Every room to the rear of the plan opens onto the rear terrace. This is excellent news for those who enjoy the nightly wonder of watching the sun melt away as the moon rises. A fireplace extends a gracious welcome into the spacious living room, connecting to the formal dining room for a grand entertaining flow. An adjacent U-shaped kitchen is enhanced with a snack bar and a casual breakfast room.

The first-floor master bedroom is generously proportioned for room to stretch. A private bath features a walk-in closet and a whirlpool tub. The second floor holds two family bedrooms—one with a walk-in closet—a full bath and a walk-in linen closet.

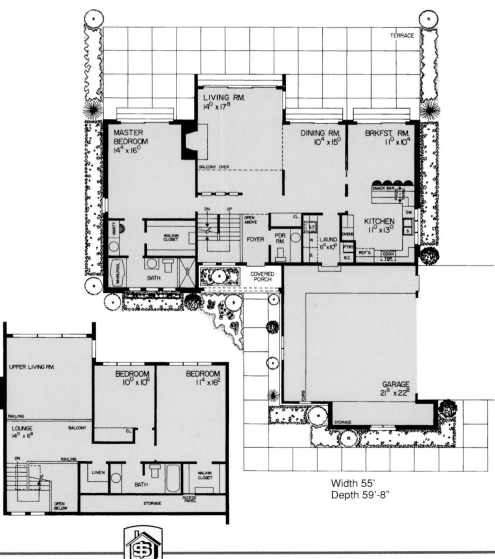

Width 55'
Depth 59'-8"

Additional products and services available. See page 4.

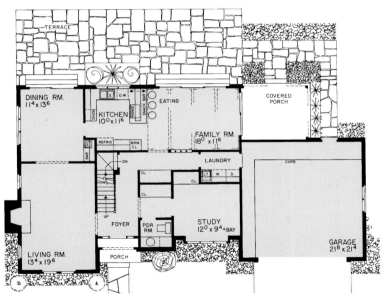

Width 63'
Depth 34'-8"

DESIGN HH2854

First Floor:	1,261 sq. ft.
Second Floor:	950 sq. ft.
Total:	2,211 sq. ft.

A Wealth Of Tudor Style

The flair of Old England has been captured in this noble Tudor design. Interior livability will efficiently serve the various needs of the family. A foyer leads to a spacious living room on the left and a quiet study on the right. The kitchen is designed for the busy gourmet who enjoys companionship while cooking. A snack bar separates the eating area and family room which opens onto a covered porch. Special occasions are enjoyed in the formal dining room enhanced with a wet bar.

Upstairs, the master bedroom is distinguished by an impressive dressing room and a private bath. An adjoining nursery easily converts to a lounge or study. Two family bedrooms and a full bath complete the second floor.

Additional products and services available. See page 4.

77

DESIGN HH3331

First Floor:	1,115 sq. ft.
Second Floor:	690 sq. ft.
Total:	1,805 sq. ft.

The Majesty Of Tudor

Thoughtful planning supplies a wealth of livability in this compact Tudor home.

During the day, sunlight floods the two-story gathering room with warmth while evenings find the fireplace blazing merrily, bidding a warm welcome to family and friends. The dining room opens onto a deck, providing outdoor dining options. A corner oven, a pantry and a window overlooking the back yard contribute to the appeal of the efficient kitchen located nearby.

Quietly set apart, the master bedroom offers a private retreat. The full bath adjoins the master bedroom and conveniently furnishes separate entrance from the hall. The second floor holds two family bedrooms, a full bath and a lounge.

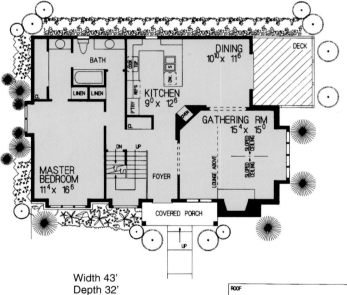

Width 43'
Depth 32'

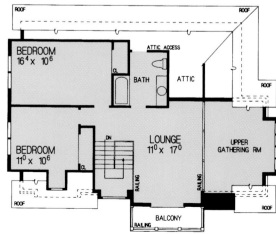

   Additional products and services available. See page 4.

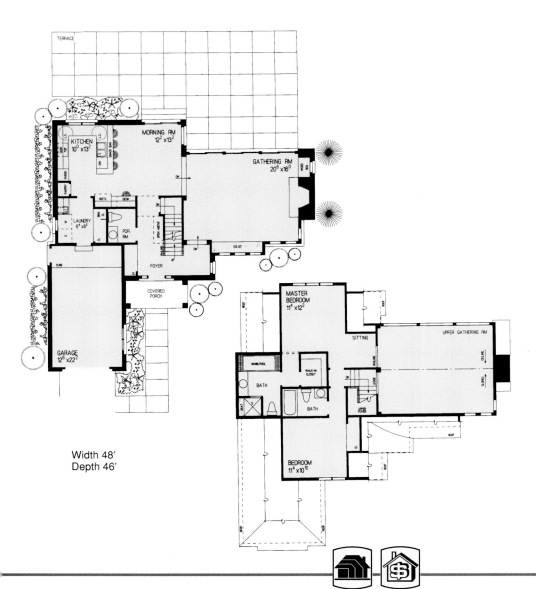

Width 48'
Depth 46'

DESIGN HH2491

First Floor:	1,060 sq. ft.
Second Floor:	580 sq. ft.
Total:	1,640 sq. ft.

A Prince Of A Plan

The trim size of this charming Tudor home belies a great deal of livability. Straight ahead from the foyer is a sunlit morning room that affords a cozy place to begin each day. A snack bar for on-the-go meals connects the efficient kitchen. Generous expanses of glass bring light and space to the large step-down gathering room. A window seat, a warming fireplace with a built-in wood box and terrace access highlight this area. A powder room and a laundry room complete the first floor.

Upstairs, quality appointments and elegant details grace the master bedroom. Amenities include a walk-in closet and a relaxing master bath with a pampering whirlpool tub. A family bedroom and a full bath share the second floor.

Additional products and services available. See page 4.

79

This home, as shown in the photograph, may differ from the actual blueprints. For more detailed information, please check the floor plans carefully.

Photo by Nick Kelsh

DESIGN HH2855

First Floor:	1,372 sq. ft.
Second Floor:	1,245 sq. ft.
Total:	2,617 sq. ft.

Fit For A King

Outstanding quality is evident throughout this impressive two-story Tudor home. From the foyer, a large living room with a fireplace is located to the right and a spacious step-down family room is found to the left. Outdoor entertainment is encouraged by the covered porch.

The breakfast room is open to the kitchen which easily serves the adjacent dining room for formal occasions. Guests will enjoy unobstructed views from two expansive walls of windows. The mud room and the wash room conveniently serve the two-car garage which features space for a hobby room or storage.

The second floor contains three bedrooms and a full bath, along with a spacious master bedroom suite. Here, special features include a dressing room with a built-in seat and a private bath.

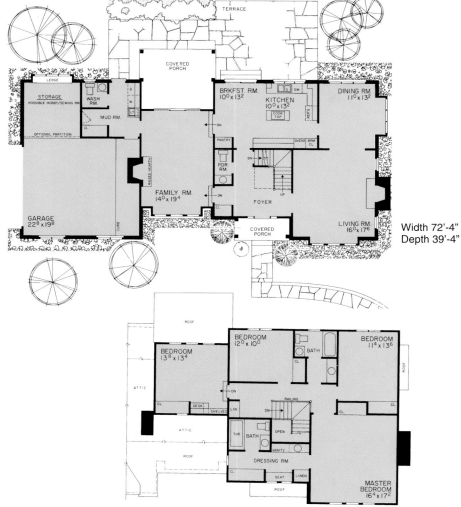

Width 72'-4"
Depth 39'-4"

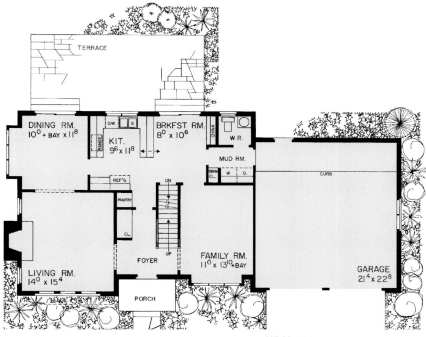

Width 60'
Depth 28'-10"

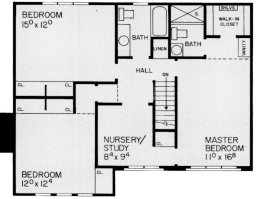

DESIGN HH2800

First Floor:	999 sq. ft.
Second Floor:	997 sq. ft.
Total:	1,996 sq. ft.

Tailor-Made Tudor Design

This English Tudor-style home reflects the craftsmanship that lifts this design above others. Along with its outstanding exterior, it contains a terrific floor plan. Flanking the foyer is a comfortable living room with a cozy fireplace and a spacious family room. The U-shaped kitchen is conveniently located between the formal dining room and a breakfast room with a built-in china cabinet. Both of these rooms feature sliding glass doors that open onto the rear terrace. A wash room and a mud room are located near the two-car garage.

Two bedrooms, a bath and a master bedroom are conveniently located on the second floor. A walk-in closet, a built-in vanity, a private bath and an adjoining nursery/study grace the master suite.

DESIGN HH3342

First Floor:	1,467 sq. ft.
Second Floor:	715 sq. ft.
Total:	2,182 sq. ft.

Long Live Tudor Style!

Stone, stucco and brick lend the distinguished details that identify this contemporary home's Tudor style.

The foyer opens onto a living room with a second-floor balcony overlook and a warming fireplace. A connecting dining room is perfect for hosting intimate dinner parties. Nearby, the kitchen shares space with a sunny breakfast room enhanced with a bumped-out bay. Sliding glass doors provide passage to the rear terrace.

Two bedrooms—one an optional study—share a full bath on the first floor. The master bedroom is located on the second floor for privacy. Among the outstanding features are His and Hers walk-in closets and a luxurious bath with dual vanities, a pampering whirlpool tub and a separate shower. A studio completes the upstairs sleeping area.

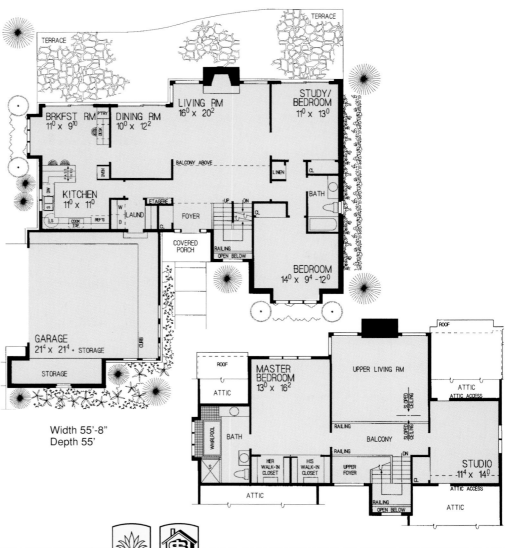

Width 55'-8"
Depth 55'

Additional products and services available. See page 4.

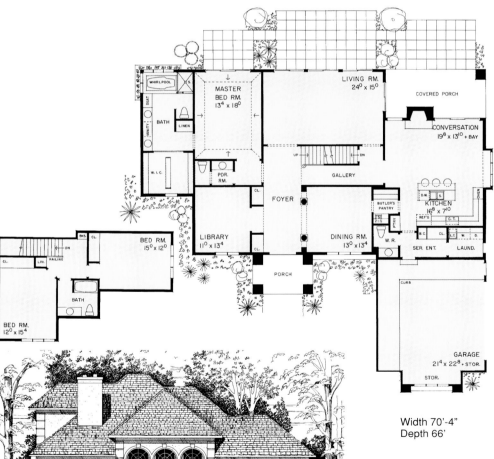

Width 70'-4"
Depth 66'

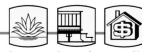

DESIGN HH3558

First Floor:	2,328 sq. ft.
Second Floor:	603 sq. ft.
Total:	2,931 sq. ft.

Enveloped In European Charm

Sophisticated living combined with European flair await you in this wonderful 1½-story home. An elegant formal living room and dining room are ideal for entertaining, as is the stunning conversation room. Here, a wall of glass surrounds the warming fireplace and opens onto a covered porch, making it a favorite spot for family gatherings. The large island kitchen—connected to the dining room through a butler's pantry—is a gourmet's dream come true.

A library provides space for quieter pursuits. Sharing this wing is the master suite. The spacious master bath features a huge walk-in closet, dual vanities with a built-in seat, linen storage, a relaxing whirlpool tub and a separate shower. Two large bedrooms and a full bath are found on the second floor.

Additional products and services available. See page 4.

83

DESIGN HH3569

Square Footage:	1,972

Compact Luxury And Style

A graceful entry opens this impressive one-story European-style home. The foyer introduces an open gathering room/dining room combination with access to a covered dining porch offering terrific opportunities for indoor/outdoor pursuits. In the kitchen, such features as an island cooktop and a built-in desk add to the home's livability.

A front-facing study could easily convert into a bedroom for guests—a full bath is directly accessible from the rear of the room. Taking advantage of front and side views is a corner bedroom. The spacious master bedroom accesses the rear terrace and also sports a bath with a double-bowl vanity and a relaxing whirlpool tub.

A laundry room and a powder room complete this gracious plan.

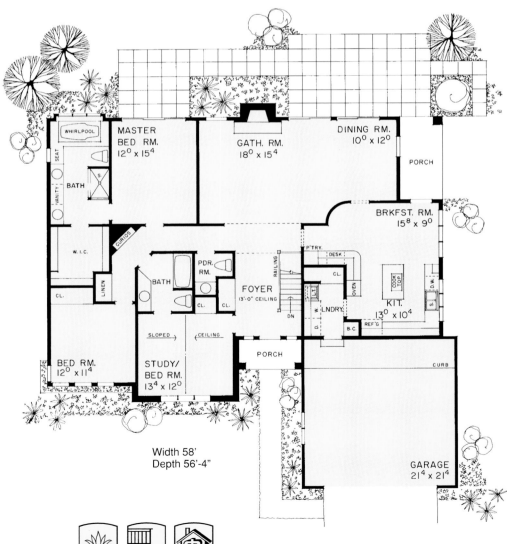

Width 58'
Depth 56'-4"

Additional products and services available. See page 4.

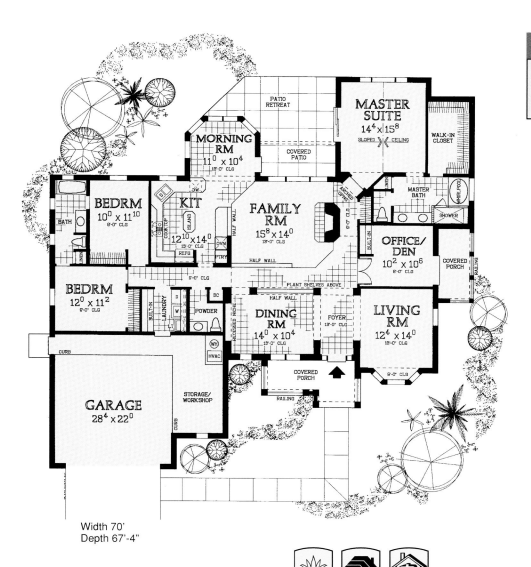

Width 70'
Depth 67'-4"

Square Footage: 2,520

Echoes Of European Style

Europe's culture inspires the best in fine arts—chefs, dancers, painters—and as you see demonstrated in this home, architecture. This lovely one-story home opens to formal areas well-situated for entertaining—a bay-windowed living room to the right and a dining room with a recessed niche to the left. A large family room opens to a rear covered patio and retreat perfect for enjoying starry nights, and is warmed in the winter months by a welcoming hearth. The island kitchen is joined with a sundrenched morning room for casual meals.

An arched opening leads into the secluded master suite. The master bedroom invites sophisticated luxury compliments of a sloped ceiling and a lavish master bath with a whirlpool tub for ultimate relaxation. On the other side of the home, two family bedrooms share a full bath.

DESIGN HH3559

Square Footage:	2,916

The European Mini-Estate

This European-inspired plan features a host of intricate details that represent the finer things in life.

The combined living and dining rooms to the rear provide a showplace for entertaining as well as a very special conversation room that departs from the ordinary. Angled for interest, this room is bordered on three sides by an abundance of glass and sports a centered fireplace. The kitchen is separated from the living areas by a snack bar counter. A media room to the front of the plan provides space for state-of-the-art electronics.

Three bedrooms, including the master suite, grace the sleeping wing located on the right. The master bedroom is most impressive with sliding glass doors to the rear terrace. The shower—sunken down one step—is highlighted with glass block. A garden whirlpool tub rounds out the sumptuous suite.

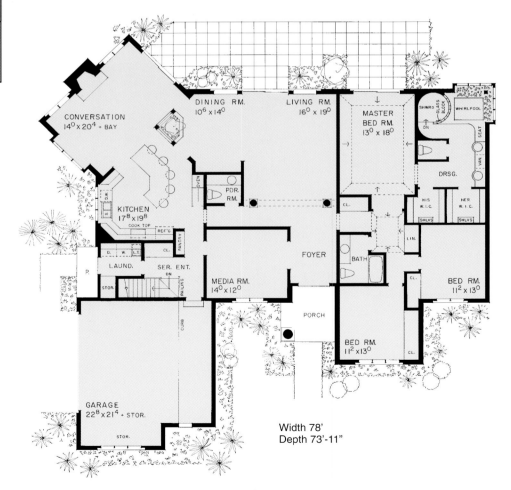

Width 78'
Depth 73'-11"

Additional products and services available. See page 4.

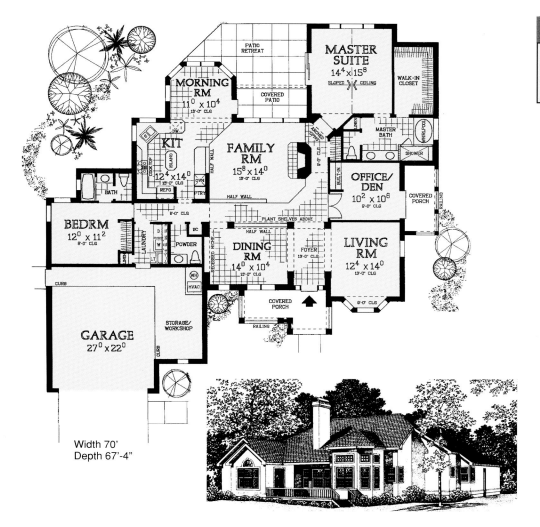

Width 70'
Depth 67'-4"

Square Footage: 2,312

Old World Elegance

The essence of Old World style is captured in this exceptional one-story home. Inside, the plan caters to comfortable living. Thoughtful design provides plenty of room for both formal and informal entertaining: a living room, a dining room, a family room, and a bay-windowed morning room that opens to a grand rear patio. An office or den with a private porch and built-in bookshelves will be favored by electronics connoisseurs.

Sleeping areas are split for privacy with the master suite on one side of the home and a secondary bedroom and a full bath on the other. The romantic master suite features a vaulted ceiling and deck access. Amenities in the lavish master bath include a compartmented toilet, a separate shower and whirlpool tub, a double-bowl vanity and an enormous walk-in closet.

DESIGN HH2779

Square Footage: 3,225

One-Story Of France

The French are experts when it comes to style, and their European architectural influence is illustrated here by the hip roof and corner quoins that grace this lovely home.

Generously proportioned rooms are found throughout. A grand entry opens to a banquet-sized dining room on the left and a large parlor on the right. A gathering room located to the rear is bordered on each side by covered porches accessed through sliding glass doors. The island kitchen easily serves the neighboring snack bar and nook. A large butler's pantry contains a sink and facilitates passage for serving the dining room.

The master bedroom has private access to the rear terrace. Special features of the master bath include a dressing room and a large walk-in closet. Two family bedrooms and a study—or if you prefer, a third bedroom—share a full bath.

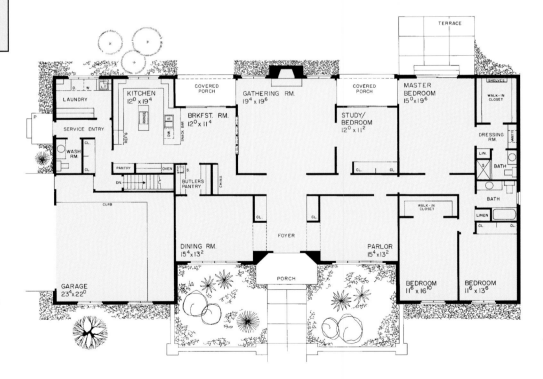

Width 92'-8"
Depth 46'-8"

Additional products and services available. See page 4.

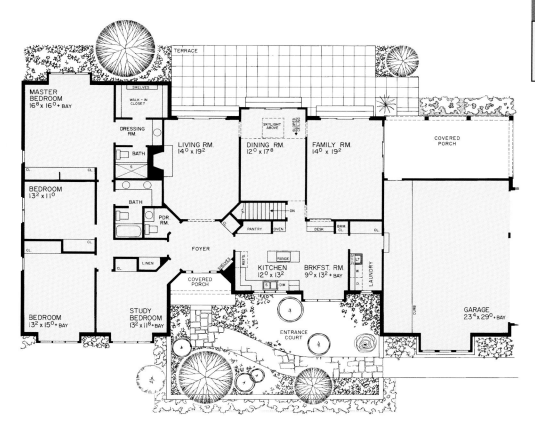

Width 91'-8"
Depth 52'

DESIGN HH2851

Square Footage:	2,739

Elegant French Chateau

European design elements such as decorative wrought iron, a grand entrance court and a hip roof characterize this home as a classically French-inspired chateau.

Beyond the covered porch, an octagonal foyer introduces a charming floor plan. The formal living room, graced by a fireplace, and the dining room provide commanding views of the rear grounds. A handsome family room overlooks the rear terrace as well and opens onto a covered porch that extends outdoor livability. An L-shaped kitchen with an island range attaches to a sunny breakfast room.

Three family bedrooms—one doubles as a study—share a full bath. The peaceful master bedroom is located to the rear for privacy. Highlights include a graceful bumped-out bay, a dressing room with a walk-in closet and a private bath.

DESIGN HH3459

First Floor:	1,392 sq. ft.
Second Floor:	1,178 sq. ft.
Total:	2,570 sq. ft.

Soar To New Heights

Classic details, including graceful columns, enhance the stucco exterior of this lovely European-style home artfully designed for a narrow lot.

A two-story foyer introduces a soaring two-story living room with its own porch. The adjacent dining room features a bumped-out nook and a china alcove. Nearby, an L-shaped island kitchen easily serves the formal and informal living areas. Kitchen amenities include a large pantry and a built-in desk. The family room sports an abundance of built-ins, a warming fireplace and patio access.

Three family bedrooms, including two with balcony access, share a private bath. The quiet master bedroom promises room to relax. A unique master bath features a walk-in closet, a compartmented toilet, a corner whirlpool tub and a separate shower.

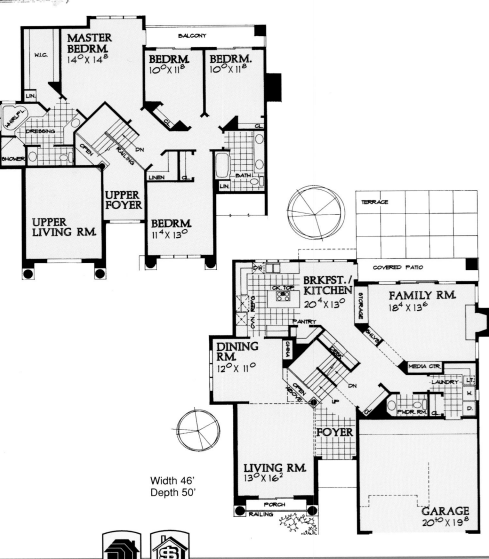

DESIGN HH3463

First Floor:	1,163 sq. ft.
Second Floor:	1,077 sq. ft.
Total:	2,240 sq. ft.

The Sky's The Limit

Fine family living and European style take off in this grand volume plan. The tiled foyer leads to a stately living room with sliding glass doors to the terrace and columns separating it from the dining room. Additional accents include a corner bookshelf and access to a covered porch. For casual living, look no further than the family room/breakfast room combination. The interesting kitchen supplies an island counter in the midst of its accommodating, angled layout.

On the second floor, the master bedroom draws attention to itself by offering a fireplace, access to a deck and a spoiling bath. A smart addition, the study niche in the hallway shares the outside deck. Two family bedrooms and a bath wrap up the sleeping facilities.

TERRACE

COVERED PORCH

FAMILY RM
13⁰ X 13⁺⁰

BRKFST.
9⁰ X 7⁰

LIVING RM
13⁴X13

DINING RM
12²X13⁰

STOR

FOYER

KITCHEN

ISLAND

D.W.

PTRY.

BATH

RANGE

REF'G

LAUND

AC

WH

COVERED PORCH

GARAGE
21⁴ X 19⁺⁰

DECK

MASTER BEDROOM
13⁰X16⁺⁰

UPPER LIVING RM
13⁴X13⁰

WALK-IN CLOSET

BOOKS

LIN

MASTER BATH

PLANT LEDGE

RAILING

DECK

SHOWER

WHIRLPL

DN

BALCONY

UPPER FOYER

BATH

BEDRM
12⁰X 11⁰

CL

BEDRM
11⁰X 11⁴

Width 36'
Depth 63'

Additional products and services available. See page 4.

91

DESIGN HH2940

First Floor:	4,786 sq. ft.
Second Floor:	1,842 sq. ft.
Total:	6,628 sq. ft.

Too Grand To Giftwrap

All you ever wanted in a home—and then some—is found in this fabulous Norman manor. A two-story gathering room is two steps down from the adjacent lounge with an impressive wet bar and a semi-circular music alcove. The highly efficient galley-style kitchen overlooks the family room fireplace and a spectacular windowed breakfast room.

The impressive first-floor master suite is second to none. A romantic fireplace and a sitting area surrounded by glass is just the beginning. Separate His and Hers walk-in closets and baths share space with the soothing whirlpool tub. The second floor features a balcony that overlooks the gathering room below. Four secondary bedrooms, each with a private bath, complete the upstairs.

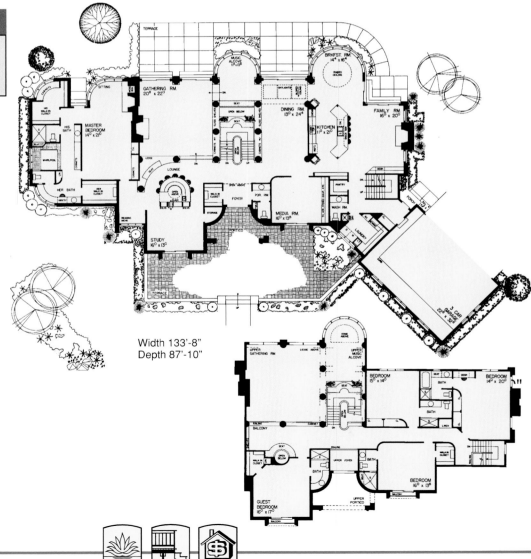

Width 133'-8"
Depth 87'-10"

Additional products and services available. See page 4.

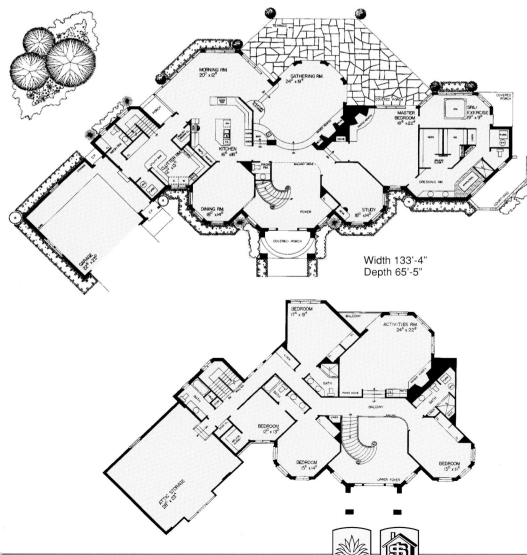

Width 133'-4"
Depth 65'-5"

DESIGN HH2968

First Floor:	3,736 sq. ft.
Second Floor:	2,264 sq. ft.
Total:	6,000 sq. ft.

Nothing But The Best

Elegant Norman style makes this extraordinary home a masterpiece in design. The distinctive covered entry to this stunning manor, flanked by twin turrets, leads to a gracious foyer with impressive fan lights.

The plan opens from the foyer to a formal dining room, a master study and a step-down gathering room. Numerous amenities found in the spacious kitchen include an island work station and a built-in desk. The adjacent morning room and the gathering room with a wet bar and raised-hearth fireplace are bathed in light and are open to the terrace for outdoor entertaining.

Luxury abounds in a master suite filled with a wealth of amenities that include a spa/exercise room, huge His and Hers walk-in closets and a lavish master bath. Four bedrooms upstairs and an activities room complete the plan.

Additional products and services available. See page 4.

93

DESIGN HH3380

First Floor:	3,350 sq. ft.
Second Floor:	1,203 sq. ft.
Total:	4,553 sq. ft.

Azure Seas Or Massive Trees

Details on this grand manor are reminiscent of a Mediterranean villa. However, this home is equally stunning resting on a bluff overlooking the sea, or gracing the end of a grand, tree-lined drive.

Inside, an elegant foyer boasts a curved double staircase. Flanking the entry is a baronial dining room and a distinguished library. A huge step-down gathering room is graced by a fireplace and columns. The gourmet kitchen serves the breakfast room and, through the butler's pantry, the formal dining room.

The master bedroom, located on the first floor for privacy, provides unsurpassed luxury and style. Twin walk-in closets, a dressing room and an inviting whirlpool tub embellish the amenity-filled master bath. Four secondary bedrooms and two full baths are contained on the second floor.

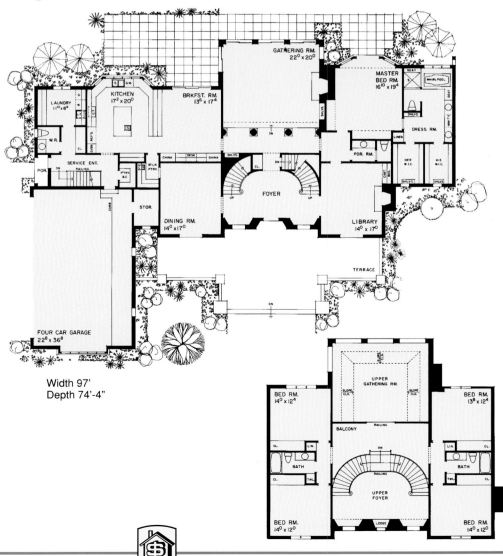

Width 97'
Depth 74'-4"

94

Photo by Andrew D. Lautman

This home, as shown in the photograph, may differ from the actual blueprints.
For more detailed information, please check the floor plans carefully.

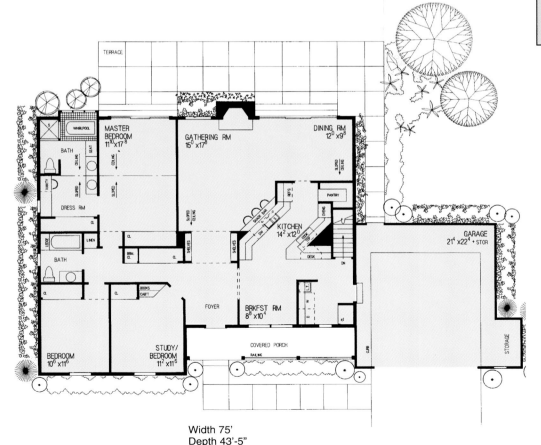

Width 75'
Depth 43'-5"

DESIGN HH2947

Square Footage: 1,830

And The Winner Is...

Something special defines winners. If this home entered the Olympics, it would take the Gold Medal—included in the Academy Awards, it would sweep the Oscars—or take the state fair's blue ribbon. Don't you deserve the best in life? Of course you do, and this home is designed with you in mind.

A deluxe floor plan awaits beyond the covered front porch. Enjoy casual meals in the sunny breakfast room served by the uniquely shaped, galley-style kitchen. Here, the snack bar is shared with the spacious gathering room and fireplace. A dining room with terrace access is situated for formal dinners.

The large master bedroom is enhanced with sliding glass doors to the rear terrace, a sloped ceiling and a luxurious master bath. Two additional bedrooms—one doubles as a study—are located at the front of the home and share a hall bath.

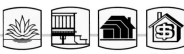

Additional products and services available. See page 4.

95

DESIGN HH3348

Square Footage:	2,549

A Lesson In Tradition

After fighting snarled traffic and waiting in long lines, there is nothing more pleasing than a small child's face watching from the front windows, waiting to welcome you home. The kitchen and breakfast room are only steps away from the garage, simplifying the task of carrying packages into the house. Every get-together will be a special occasion in the spacious family room sporting a beam ceiling and a raised-hearth fireplace. For more formal functions a dining room combines with the living room.

Sleep facilities are contained in the left wing of the house. Three family bedrooms, or two and a study, share a full bath. The luxurious master bedroom is highlighted by a bay window and a wealth of closets. A built-in vanity introduces a lavish master bath with a pampering whirlpool tub.

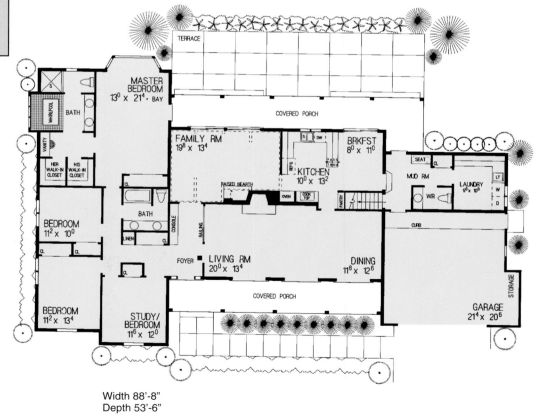

Width 88'-8"
Depth 53'-6"

Additional products and services available. See page 4.

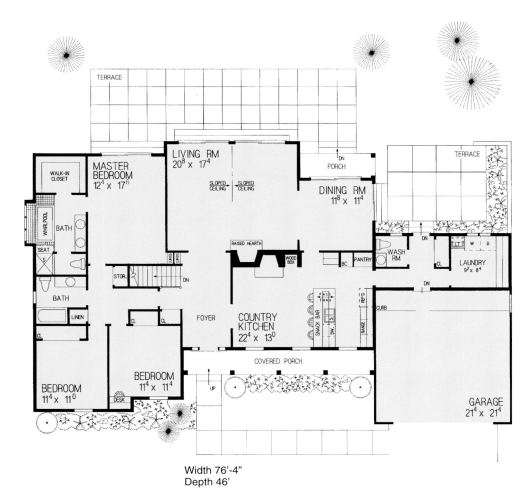

Width 76'-4"
Depth 46'

Square Footage: 2,168

Home For The Holidays

This traditional home's varying rooflines and decoratively arched covered front porch invite a festive trimming of Christmas lights. Early fall may find a row of smiling jack-o-lanterns on the covered porch, and early spring, Easter eggs may be hidden nearby.

The foyer opens to a huge country kitchen and a fireplace that bids a warm welcome. Situated for formal and informal serving convenience and companionship while cooking is an efficient kitchen. The formal living area combines a large living room and a dining room for an extraordinary entertaining space. Access to the rear terrace and covered porch extend outdoor livability.

Two family bedrooms, one with a built-in desk, share a full bath. The master bedroom opens to the terrace via sliding glass doors and is enhanced by a master bath displaying a walk-in closet, a relaxing whirlpool tub and a separate shower.

Additional products and services available. See page 4.

97

DESIGN HH1920

Square Footage: 1,600

Hula Hoops And Hide-And-Seek

One look at this traditional home suggests carefree childhoods and the "wonder years" that bring about the evolution of young adults. It would be difficult to find a better home in which to raise children.

An entry hall opens to a large living room designed for variety in furniture placement. Nearby, a dining room opens onto the rear terrace and shares space with a U-shaped kitchen that overlooks the backyard. A step-down family room provides a gathering place where family memories will be created and shared. Sliding glass doors afford passage to a terrace where barbecues and picnics may be enjoyed.

Two family bedrooms—each with a walk-in closet—share a full bath. The master bedroom located to the front of the home features a walk-in closet and a private bath.

Width 60'
Depth 42'

Additional products and services available. See page 4.

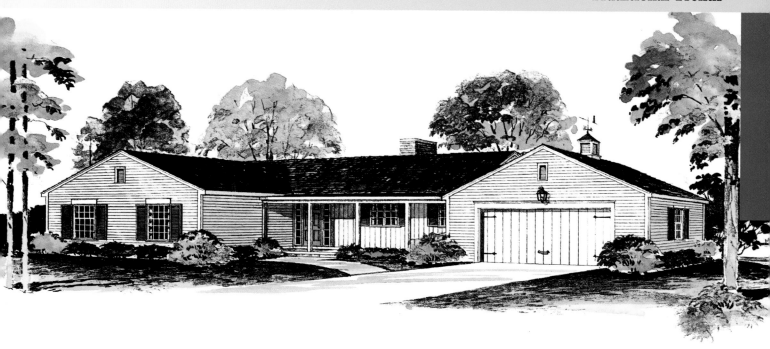

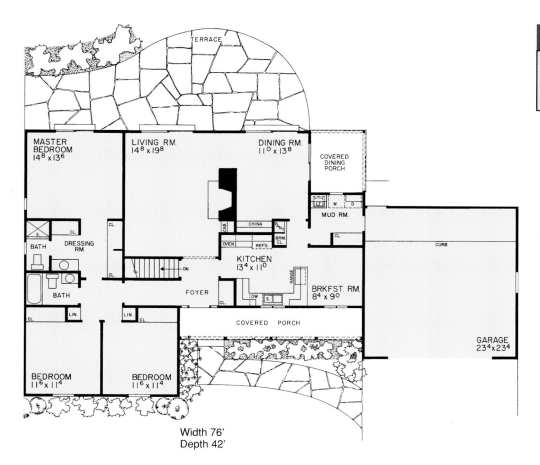

TERRACE

MASTER BEDROOM
14⁸ x 13⁶

LIVING RM.
14⁸ x 19⁸

DINING RM.
11⁰ x 13⁸

COVERED DINING PORCH

MUD RM.

BATH

DRESSING RM.

CL.

CHINA

PAN.

BRM. CL.

CL.

BATH

OVEN

REF'G.

CURB

KITCHEN
13⁴ x 11⁰

DN

RANGE

FOYER

BRKFST. RM.
8⁴ x 9⁰

GARAGE
23⁴ x 23⁴

DW

S.

CL.

LIN.

LIN.

CL.

BEDROOM
11⁶ x 11⁴

BEDROOM
11⁶ x 11⁴

COVERED PORCH

Width 76'
Depth 42'

DESIGN HH2672

Square Footage:	1,717

Traditionally Yours

Here's a home you'll love to come home to! The inviting appearance of this traditional home is enhanced by its covered porch, multi-pane windows, narrow clapboard and vertical wood siding.

Inside, a U-shaped kitchen is situated to efficiently serve the casual breakfast room and a formal dining room that sports a built-in china cabinet. From this area, sliding glass doors open onto the rear terrace or the covered dining porch, providing two fine options for outdoor dining. An adjacent living room also opens to the terrace and is warmed by a comfortable fireplace.

Two family bedrooms located at the front of the plan share a hall bath. The private master bedroom features a dressing room and a private bath.

Additional products and services available. See page 4.

99

DESIGN HH2505

Square Footage:	1,366

A Traditional Trio

This lovely one-story home offers traditional design with a twist: three distinctively different exterior options to choose from. So whether you favor the clean lines of contemporary style or the down-home warmth of country design, your preference is included.

A grand entry opens onto a gathering room with a raised hearth and a connecting dining room. Both rooms offer passage to the rear terrace with the dining room supplying entry to a dining terrace as well. A galley-style kitchen is designed to save steps and efficiently serve the bay-windowed eating nook and the formal living area. Sleep facilities include two family bedrooms, a full bath and a master bedroom that enjoys a walk-in closet and a private bath.

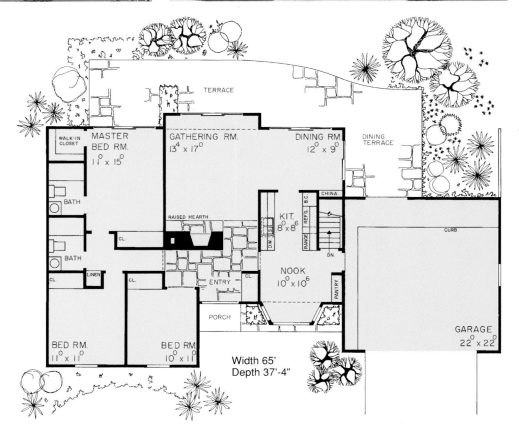

Additional products and services available. See page 4.

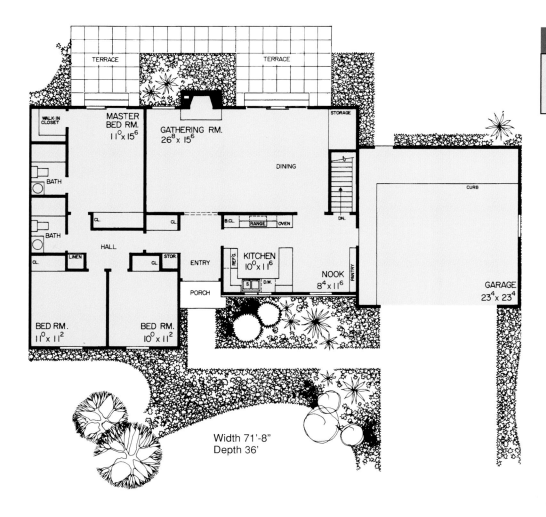

TERRACE

TERRACE

WALK-IN CLOSET

MASTER BED RM.
11^0 x 15^6

GATHERING RM.
26^8 x 15^6

STORAGE

DINING

BATH

BATH

CL.

CL.

B.CL. | RANGE | OVEN

DN.

HALL

LINEN

CL.

CL.

STOR.

ENTRY

REFG. | KITCHEN 10^0 x 11^6

CURB

BED RM.
11^0 x 11^2

BED RM.
10^0 x 11^2

PORCH

S | D.W.

NOOK
8^4 x 11^6

PANTRY

GARAGE
23^4 x 23^4

Width 71'-8"
Depth 36'

DESIGN HH2597

Square Footage: 1,515

Family Traditions

The contrast of vertical and horizontal lines, a sheltered front porch and an illuminating welcome from the coach lamp combine to create a superior ranch exterior.

Functional floor planning is designed with families in mind. Beyond the porch is an entry that leads to all living areas. Located on the right is a U-shaped kitchen that looks out to the front yard and shares space with the eating nook. To the rear of the plan is a combined gathering room and dining room that spans over 26 feet. Accenting this area is a cozy fireplace, sliding glass doors to the terrace and a large storage area.

Two family bedrooms are located to the front of the plan and share a full bath. A spacious master bedroom features a private bath and exclusive entry via sliding glass doors to the rear terrace.

DESIGN HH3340

Square Footage: 1,611

A Home For All Seasons

Imagine this charming traditional home framed in fall leaves, blanketed in winter snow, and enhanced with a riot of color, compliments of spring and summer flowers. No matter what the season, this plan provides a wealth of livability.

Overlooking the rear terrace, the living room and dining room combine to create a wall of glass and unobstructed views beyond the skylit covered porch. Sliding glass doors furnish access. An adjacent kitchen features a built-in planning desk and a snack bar that separates the sunny breakfast room.

A clustered sleeping area promotes peace and quiet. Two family bedrooms—one doubles as a study—share a nearby bath. The restful master bedroom is highlighted by a sloped ceiling, a huge walk-in closet and a private bath.

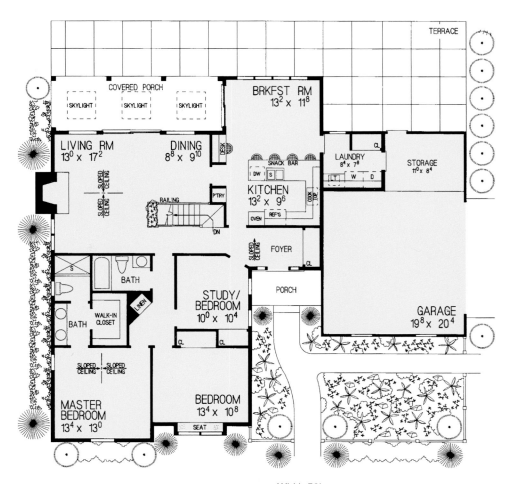

Width 58'
Depth 52'-6"

Additional products and services available. See page 4.

Width 67'-4"
Depth 62'

DESIGN HH3334

First Floor:	2,193 sq. ft.
Second Floor:	831 sq. ft.
Total:	3,024 sq. ft.

A Traditional Classic

Classic traditional style and an amenity-filled floor plan unite to form a winning combination. From the foyer, step down into a two-story gathering room. A warming, raised-hearth fireplace and sliding glass doors opening to a wraparound deck grace this area. Tucked behind the garage is an efficient kitchen. Smartly located, it serves the bayed breakfast room and the formal dining room—via a butler's pantry—with equal ease. Entry to the deck is furnished from the breakfast room and dining room as well.

The master bedroom occupies space on the first floor for privacy. Here, a cozy fireplace and a moonlit bay window cast a romantic glow. His and Hers walk-in closets, a dressing room and a relaxing bath round out the suite. A study, a powder room and a laundry room complete the plan.

DESIGN HH3351

First Floor:	1,794 sq. ft.
Second Floor:	887 sq. ft.
Total:	2,681 sq. ft.
Bonus Room:	720 sq. ft.

Home-Grown Traditions

Home-grown comfort is the key to the appeal of this traditionally styled home. Upon entering the foyer, a living room formally greets you with a warming fireplace. A connecting dining room with a bumped-out bay will accommodate formal dinner parties and is easily served by an adjacent kitchen. A U-shaped countertop serves to separate the casual family room which provides passage to the back yard.

The luxuriously appointed master bedroom is located on the first floor for privacy. Highlighting the suite is a sumptuous master bath with a whirlpool tub and a study for quiet, reflective moments. A nearby powder room allows for effortless conversion of the study into a guest bedroom. Three family bedrooms—one with a walk-in closet—share a full bath on the second floor.

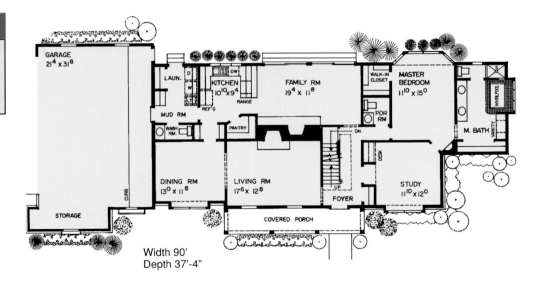

Width 90'
Depth 37'-4"

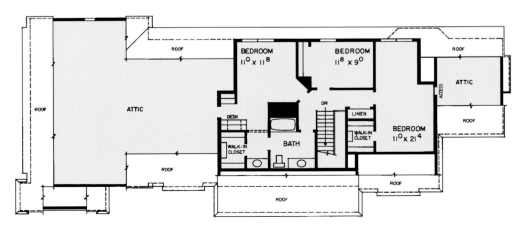

Additional products and services available. See page 4.

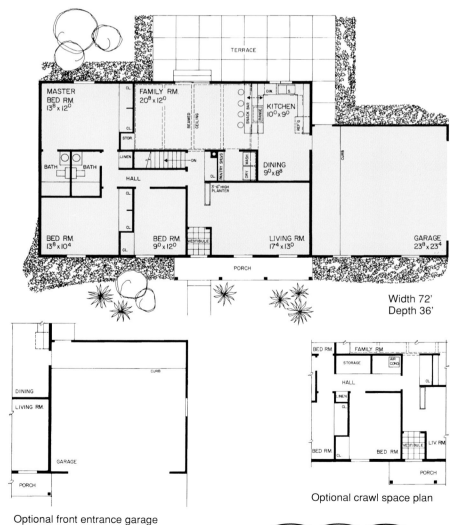

TERRACE

MASTER BED RM. 13⁸ x 12⁰

FAMILY RM. 20⁸ x 12⁰

KITCHEN 10⁰ x 9⁰

BEAMED CEILING

SNACK BAR

RANGE

D.W. S

REF'G

CL

CL

STOR.

LINEN

BATH BATH

HALL

DN

PANTRY SHELVS

DRY WASH

DINING 9⁰ x 8⁸

3'-6" HIGH PLANTER

CURB

BED RM. 13⁸ x 10⁴

CL

CL

CL

BED RM. 9⁰ x 12⁰

VESTIBULE

LIVING RM. 17⁴ x 13⁰

GARAGE 23⁸ x 23⁴

PORCH

Width 72'
Depth 36'

DINING

LIVING RM.

CURB

GARAGE

PORCH

Optional front entrance garage

BED RM.

FAMILY RM.

STORAGE

AIR COND.

HALL

LINEN

CL

CL

BED RM.

BED RM.

VESTIBULE

LIV. RM.

PORCH

Optional crawl space plan

DESIGN HH2810

Square Footage:	1,536

Traditional Style Comes To Life

A sheltering covered porch furnishes a delightful introduction to this traditional one-story home. The vestibule opens to a spacious living room graced by a built-in planter. Straight ahead is a beamed-ceilinged family room with sliding glass doors that open onto the terrace. An adjacent kitchen supplies a snack bar for quick meals and an eating nook for casual dining.

Two family bedrooms are found at the front of the plan and share a hall bath. The master bedroom is located nearby and features its own private bath.

Plans for an alternate garage are included for those that prefer a front-loading garage instead of the side-loading garage shown.

This home, as shown in the photograph, may differ from the actual blueprints. For more detailed information, please check the floor plans carefully.

Photo by Andrew D. Lautman

DESIGN HH2878

Square Footage:	1,521

A Traditional Story

It's difficult to believe that such a great deal of livability could be contained in less than 1,600 square feet! But this traditionally-styled home is efficiently designed to make optimum use of a compact floor plan, proving it can be done.

Located directly back from the foyer is a spacious gathering room further opened by a sloped ceiling and warmed by a cheerful fireplace. An adjacent dining room opens onto the rear terrace via sliding glass doors for al fresco dining. A U-shaped kitchen is situated close to the formal dining room and easily serves the adjoining breakfast room, also with the aid of a pass-through.

Two secondary bedrooms—or if you prefer, one and a study—share a full bath. The comfortable master bedroom is graced with a large walk-in closet, a dressing room and a private bath.

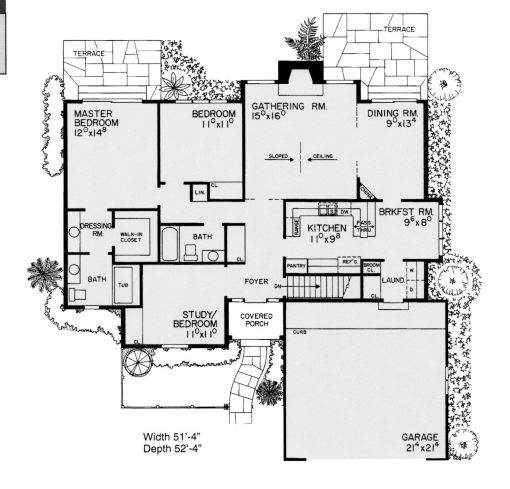

Width 51'-4"
Depth 52'-4"

Additional products and services available. See page 4.

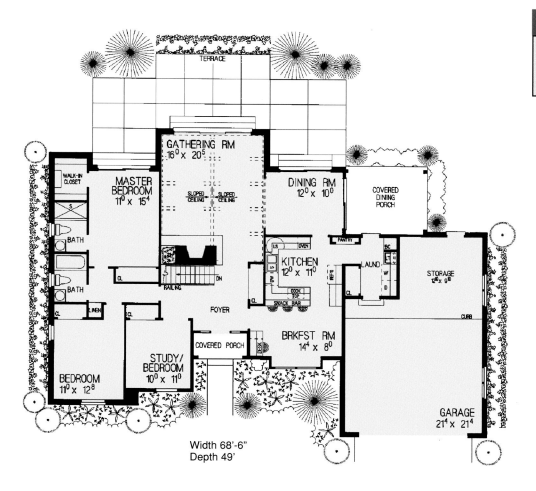

Width 68'-6"
Depth 49'

DESIGN HH3345

Square Footage:	1,738

Come Home To Tradition

Jack Benny hid it well. The timing that lay behind his melancholy expression was the hallmark of his comic genius. What does this tell us? Expect the unexpected. Expect this quaint traditional home to offer an unexpected amount of living space.

A sunny breakfast room with a bumped-out bay moves to the forefront. Centered to save steps, the kitchen serves a snack bar for quick meals as well as the adjacent formal dining room and covered dining porch. The gathering room is opened further by a sloped ceiling and a wall of sliding glass doors that access the rear terrace for complete outdoor enjoyment.

Two bedrooms, one that may also serve as a study, are found in the left wing of the home. The master bedroom features a large walk-in closet and a private master bath.

Additional products and services available. See page 4.

107

DESIGN HH2707

Square Footage: 1,267

An Early American Legacy

Our ancestors were responsible for a legacy that went far beyond the Declaration of Independence. Here, a charming Early American adaptation serves as a picturesque traditional home with a contemporary twist. Those in search of an efficient, economical-to-build home need look no further.

The centrally located living room is spacious and enjoys a raised-hearth fireplace. Eating space is reserved in the L-shaped kitchen. A nearby dining room overlooks the rear grounds, providing excellent views and setting a captivating scene for formal occasions.

A corner family bedroom shares a full bath with an additional bedroom that serves equally well as a study. The spacious master bedroom is highlighted by a private master bath and a separate entrance onto the terrace.

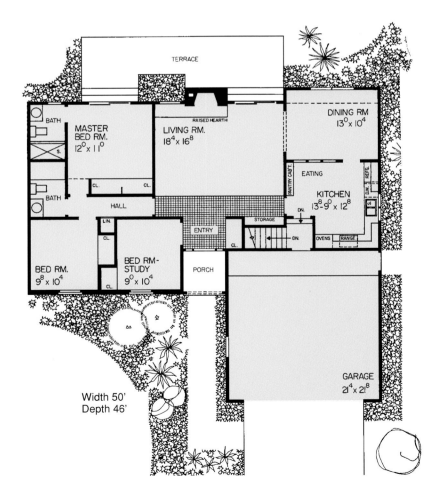

Width 50'
Depth 46'

Additional products and services available. See page 4.

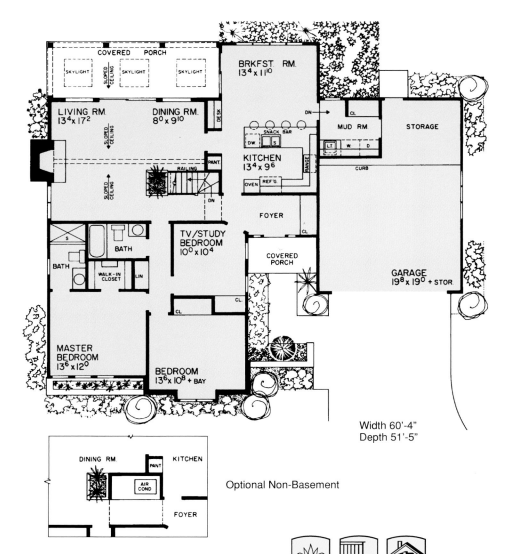

COVERED PORCH

SKYLIGHT | SLOPED CEILING | SKYLIGHT | SKYLIGHT

BRKFST. RM.
13⁴ x 11¹⁰

LIVING RM.
13⁴ x 17²

DINING RM.
8⁰ x 9¹⁰

DESK

SLOPED CEILING

SLOPED CEILING

SNACK BAR

DW | S

PANT.

RAILING

KITCHEN
13⁴ x 9⁶

RANGE

OVEN | REF'G.

DN

CL

MUD RM. | STORAGE

LT | W | D

CURB

DN

FOYER

CL

TV/STUDY
BEDROOM
10⁰ x 10⁴

S

BATH

BATH

WALK-IN CLOSET | LIN

COVERED PORCH

CL

GARAGE
19⁸ x 19⁰ + STOR.

CL

MASTER
BEDROOM
13⁶ x 12⁰

BEDROOM
13⁶ x 10⁸ + BAY

Width 60'-4"
Depth 51'-5"

DINING RM. | KITCHEN

PANT

AIR COND

FOYER

Optional Non-Basement

DESIGN HH2805

Square Footage:	1,547

Traditional Warmth And Comfort

Listen closely. Do you hear it? It's the sound of cool mountain spring water cascading over rocks. A home such as this may be at its best nestled between 100-year-old trees close to a creek. Of course, those that choose an urban lifestyle may disagree. Whatever the landscape, this traditional plan will be at home.

The living/dining room combination connects to span the width of the skylit covered porch. A breakfast room will be a favored spot for planning daily activities or enjoying a leisurely, unhurried meal.

To the left of the foyer is a media/TV room that triples as a quiet study or a third bedroom. A secondary bedroom with a bumped-out bay and a master bedroom complete the sleeping area. Generous details such as a private bath and a huge walk-in closet round out the suite.

Additional products and services available. See page 4.

109

DESIGN HH3376

Square Footage:	1,999

Traditional Textures

The warmth of stone and the dignity of wood siding dress this lovely traditional home in style. Inside, a gathering room with a cheerful fireplace is framed by windows that flood the area with sunlight. The dining room supplies entrance to the rear terrace and connects to the gathering room to create a grand space for entertaining. A kitchen unites with a bayed breakfast room for casual meals and conversation.

To the left of the foyer is a bayed media room that easily converts to an additional bedroom. A family bedroom is steps away from a full bath. Stretch out in the master bedroom which sports a bumped-out bay, a dressing area and an amenity-filled master bath with a whirlpool tub.

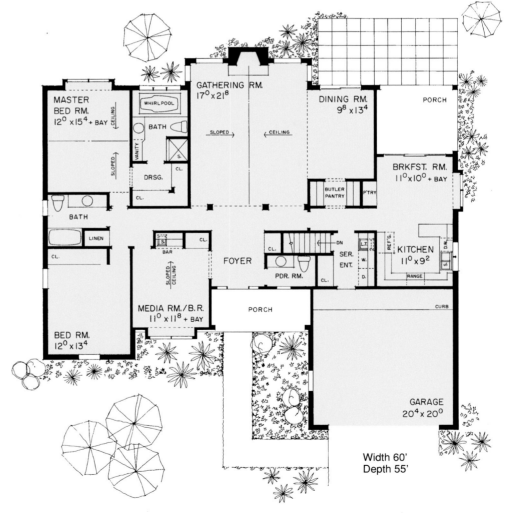

GATHERING RM.
17⁰ x 21⁸

MASTER BED RM.
12⁰ x 15⁴ + BAY

WHIRLPOOL

BATH

SLOPED → ← CEILING

DINING RM.
9⁸ x 13⁴

PORCH

DRSG.

CL.

BATH

LINEN

BAR

BUTLER PANTRY

P'TRY

BRKFST. RM.
11⁰ x 10⁰ + BAY

FOYER

CL.

SER. ENT.

DN

KITCHEN
11⁰ x 9²

RANGE

PDR. RM.

MEDIA RM./B.R.
11⁰ x 11⁸ + BAY

PORCH

BED RM.
12⁰ x 13⁴

CURB

GARAGE
20⁴ x 20⁰

Width 60'
Depth 55'

Additional products and services available. See page 4.

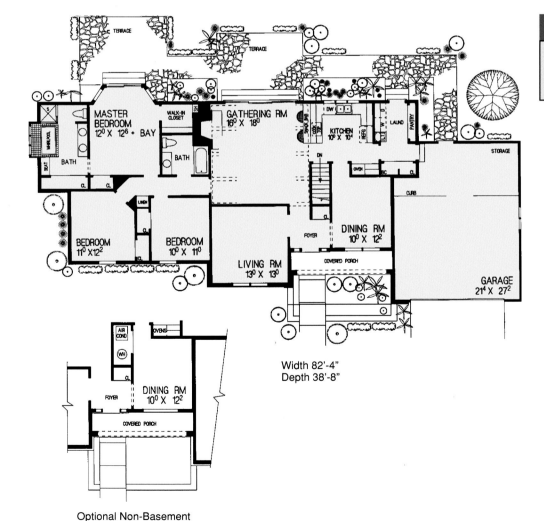

Width 82'-4"
Depth 38'-8"

Optional Non-Basement

DESIGN HH3350

Square Footage: 1,777

Traditional Style Set In Stone

A variety of details and textures spruce up the exterior of this engaging one-story traditional home. The excitement continues on the interior as well.

Formal living areas open from the foyer with a living room on the left and a dining room on the right. Family get-togethers will be enjoyed in a gathering room enhanced by a beam ceiling, a fireplace, sliding glass doors to the rear terrace and a snack bar that defines the kitchen.

The grand master bedroom is a delightful retreat. Amenities include a relaxing bath with a garden whirlpool tub, a large walk-in closet and a private terrace accessed from the bayed area. A laundry room located near the garage completes the plan.

DESIGN HH3357

Square Footage:	2,913

Tradition with a Contemporary Twist

Initially, peanut butter and jelly may seem like an odd combination. But certain pairings are meant to be. So it is with this home's traditional details united with the clean lines of contemporary style.

The interior also shares an abundance of combinations that fit like a glove. For example, a formal living area joins the dining room, furnishing terrace access from both. In the eating area a snack bar connects the kitchen with the country kitchen and the attached greenhouse. Doing double duty as a study is the media room.

Two family bedrooms share a location at the front of the plan as well as a full bath. The spacious master bedroom merges with a sumptuous master bath featuring double lavatories, a soothing whirlpool tub and a shower.

Width 82'-8"
Depth 74'

Additional products and services available. See page 4.

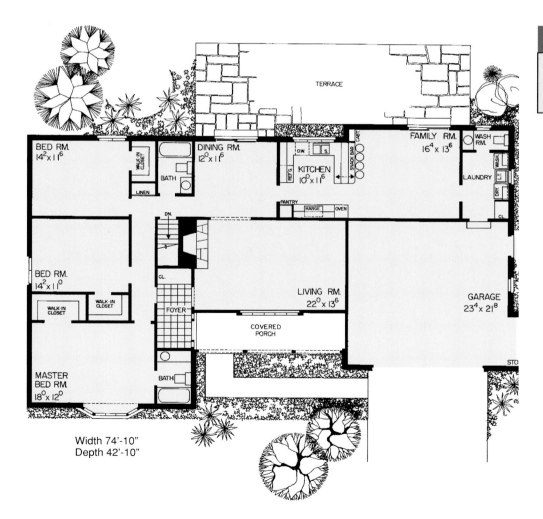

Width 74'-10"
Depth 42'-10"

BED RM.
14²x11⁶

WALK-IN CLOSET

DINING RM.
12⁰x11⁶

BATH

LINEN

TERRACE

D.W.

KITCHEN
10⁰x11⁶

REF'G

PANTRY

RANGE OVEN

SNACK BAR

FAMILY RM.
16⁴x13⁶

WASH RM.

WASH

LAUNDRY

DRY

CL

DN.

BED RM.
14²x11⁰

WALK-IN CLOSET

WALK-IN CLOSET

CL.

FOYER

LIVING RM.
22⁰x13⁶

COVERED PORCH

GARAGE
23⁴x21⁸

STO

MASTER BED RM.
18⁰x12⁰

BATH

DESIGN HH2603

Square Footage:	1,949

Touched By Tradition

Traditions such as a child's game of hide and seek and barbecues on the Fourth of July are welcomed by this brick traditional-style home.

A covered porch opens to a living room warmed by a fireplace and spacious enough to accommodate a family reunion. The rear terrace is entered through sliding glass doors in the connecting formal dining room. A U-shaped kitchen overlooks the rear terrace and joins the family room with a handy snack bar.

Two family bedrooms, each with a walk-in closet, share a full bath. The large master bedroom provides comfort and style with a bay window. A walk-in closet and a master bath are features that enhance the livability of the suite.

DESIGN HH3458

First Floor:	1,617 sq. ft.
Second Floor:	725 sq. ft.
Total:	2,342 sq. ft.

Eye-Catching Gables

With all the romance of the 18th Century, The House of Seven Gables captures the imagination and reveals the trends of a time past. Our "House of Five Gables" is captivating in its own right and weaves a fine tale of traditional styling. Its interesting rooflines are the first attraction, but brick and horizontal siding and radial head windows lend an extra measure of charm. Sidelites and a transom light up the entry and add a touch of elegance.

The 1½-story floor plan incorporates four bedrooms and both formal and informal living areas. The spacious family room has a high ceiling and a dramatic view of the balcony. In the U-shaped kitchen, a snack bar caters to quick, on-the-run meals. The basement allows additional space for a hobby room, recreational space or guest bedrooms.

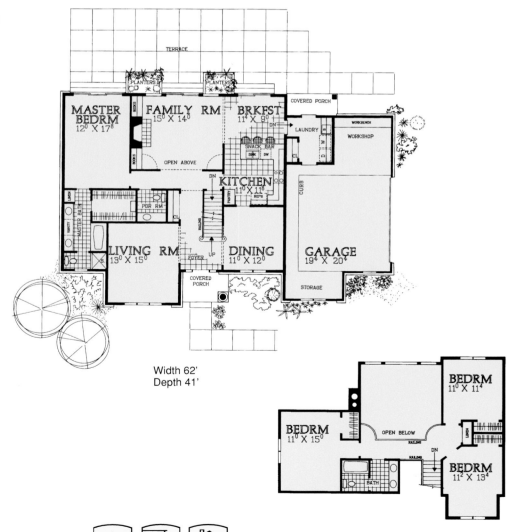

Width 62'
Depth 41'

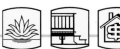

Additional products and services available. See page 4.

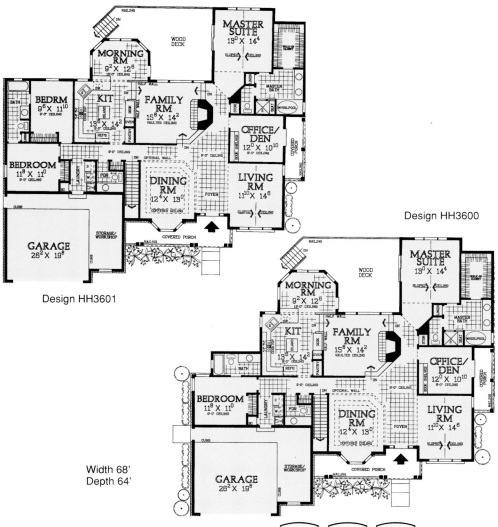

Design HH3601

Width 68'
Depth 64'

Design HH3600

DESIGN HH3600/HH3601

Square Footage: 2,258/2,424

Country Design With Three Or Four Bedrooms

Would-be country squires beware! This home is impossible to resist! Three gables, a railed front porch and a large Palladian window at the living room are enhanced by contrasting horizontal siding and brick.

The floor plan includes formal spaces for entertaining the boss and casual areas where the family can get cozy. The family room is particularly appealing with access to a rear wood deck and is warmed in the cold months by a welcoming hearth.

Bedrooms are split. The master suite sits to the right of the plan and has a walk-in closet and fine bath. A nearby office or den has a private porch. One family bedroom is on the other side of the home and also has a private bath. If needed, the plan can also be built with a third bedroom sharing the bath (Design HH3600).

DESIGN HH3355

Square Footage:	1,387

Cottage In The Woods

Talk about charm! This one-story cottage is the very essence of it. Mixed materials on the exterior include stone and horizontal and vertical siding. (The proverbial white picket fence is almost TOO perfect and encloses a sunny courtyard entrance.)

Though it's just under 1,400 total square feet, the floor plan for this treasure offers three bedrooms (or two with a study) and a sizable gathering room with a fireplace and sloped ceiling. The galley kitchen provides a pass-through snack bar and has a planning desk and attached breakfast room. A rear terrace that spans the entire rear of the home calls to those with a yen for outdoor fun.

Besides two smaller bedrooms with a full bath, there's an extravagant master suite with a large dressing area, double vanity and raised whirlpool tub.

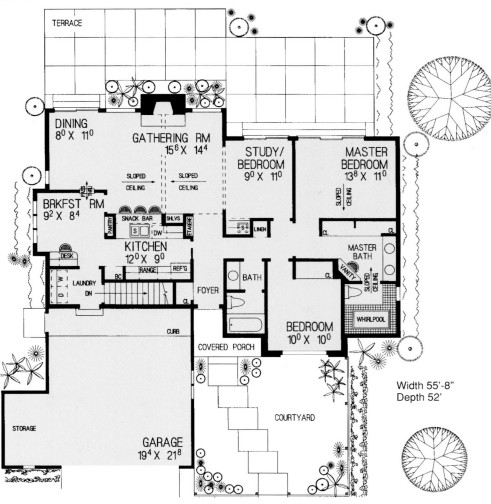

Width 55'-8"
Depth 52'

Additional products and services available. See page 4.

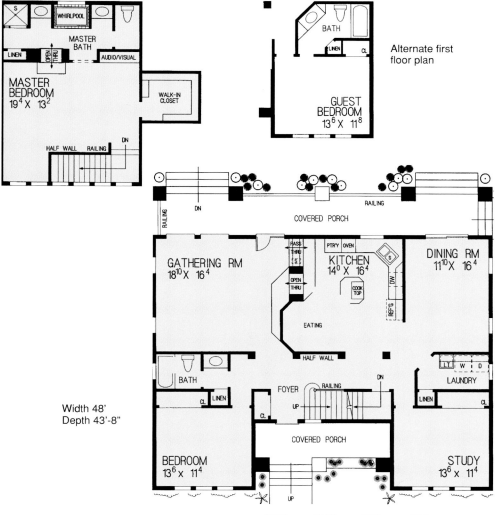

MASTER BATH

WHIRLPOOL

LINEN | OPEN THRU | AUDIO/VISUAL

MASTER BEDROOM
19^4 X 13^2

WALK-IN CLOSET

HALF WALL | RAILING | DN

BATH

LINEN | CL

Alternate first floor plan

GUEST BEDROOM
13^6 X 11^8

Width 48'
Depth 43'-8"

RAILING

DN

COVERED PORCH

RAILING

GATHERING RM
18^{10} X 16^4

PASS THRU

OPEN THRU

PTRY | OVEN

KITCHEN
14^0 X 16^4

COOK TOP

DW

REF'G

DINING RM
11^{10} X 16^4

EATING

HALF WALL

BATH

CL | LINEN

FOYER | RAILING

UP

DN

LAUNDRY

LT | W | D

LINEN | CL

CL

BEDROOM
13^6 X 11^4

COVERED PORCH

UP

STUDY
13^6 X 11^4

DESIGN HH3318

First Floor:	1,557 sq. ft.
Second Floor:	540 sq. ft.
Total:	2,097 sq. ft.

Bungalow Built For Two (Or More!)

Comfortable from East Coast to California, the bungalow style is revived with a livable floor plan in this special traditional plan. Stone detailing at the entrance contrasts with horizontal and vertical wood siding. A shed dormer above the entrance lends light to the second floor, the stairwell and the entry.

Living areas are to the rear: a gathering room with through-fireplace and pass-through to the kitchen and a formal dining room with porch access. To the front of the plan are a family bedroom and bath and a study. The study can also be planned as a guest bedroom with a bath.

Upstairs, the master of the house is pampered with a totally private suite. Special treats are the through-fireplace to the bath and a gigantic walk-in closet. The bath contains a separate shower, whirlpool tub and compartmented toilet.

Additional products and services available. See page 4.

117

This home, as shown in the photograph, may differ from the actual blueprints. For more detailed information, please check the floor plans carefully.

Photo by Andrew D. Lautman

DESIGN HH3316

First Floor:	1,111 sq. ft.
Second Floor:	886 sq. ft.
Total:	1,997 sq. ft.

Traditional Craftsman Style

Noted at its inception for being one of the most distinctive styles of the time, the Craftsman home became a symbol of architectural diversity. The recessed dormer is typical of this unique style.

This plan offers three bedrooms and plenty of living space. The screened porch leads to a rear terrace as does the breakfast room. A living room/dining room combination adds spaciousness to the floor plan. Columns define these two areas. Other welcome amenities include: boxed windows in the breakfast room and dining room, fireplace in the living room and a planning desk and pass-through snack bar in the kitchen.

Everyone will have a bedroom of their own—on the second floor. The master suite was made for the spoiled child in all of us: large bath, whirlpool tub, walk-in closet and more.

Width 34'-1"
Depth 50'

Additional products and services available. See page 4.

COVERED PORCH

MASTER BEDRM
13⁴ x 18⁰

FAMILY ROOM
15⁴ x 11⁶

LINEN

MASTER BATH

BREAKFAST ROOM
15⁴ x 11⁸

DESK

KIT.
13⁰ x 11⁴

SINK

DW

WET BAR

DINING RM
13⁴ x 11⁰

5' HIGH SHELVES

UP   DW

OPEN ABOVE

LIVING RM
13⁴ x 11⁴

PDR

FOYER

COVERED PORCH

Width 35'-4"
Depth 66'

BEDRM
15⁴ x 11⁸

BEDRM
11⁶ x 11⁰

BATH

LINEN

DN

DESIGN HH3497

First Floor:	1,581 sq. ft.
Second Floor:	592 sq. ft.
Total:	2,173 sq. ft.

Two-Story Bungalow For Narrow Sites

You remember homes like this in the neighborhood where you grew up. Their natural warmth and inviting front porches made you vow you'd live in one just like it when you grew up. This two-story narrow-lot tamer has all the charm of those neighborhood homes—updated with a spectacular floor plan.

The formal living area opens directly off the foyer. A fireplace and a tall wall of shelves grace this area. Straight ahead is a U-shaped kitchen with a snack bar, a planning desk and easy access to the formal dining room. A wet bar makes entertaining easy. The family room opens to a covered porch and offers corner windows for light.

Split-bedroom planning puts the master bedroom on the first floor. Upstairs secondary bedrooms offer ample closet space and access to a shared bath.

DESIGN HH3315

First Floor:	2,918 sq. ft.
Second Floor:	330 sq. ft.
Total:	3,248 sq. ft.

Shingled Bungalow With Two Verandas

Picture this house at the seaside. Picture it in a flower-filled country meadow. It even works in an urban setting, set back from a shady, tree-lined street. If you picture this home as your own, you won't be disappointed.

Picture your family in the living and dining area, which encompasses an area over 36' wide. Amenities include a wet bar, a raised-hearth fireplace and full windows to the rear veranda. A U-shaped kitchen with a snack bar attaches to a comfortable breakfast room. A second-floor lounge is a bonus space.

Picture yourself in the master suite—cozy by the fire, relaxing in the whirlpool bath, organized in the huge walk-in closet. Secondary bedrooms are perfect for children or guests and share a full bath with dual vanities.

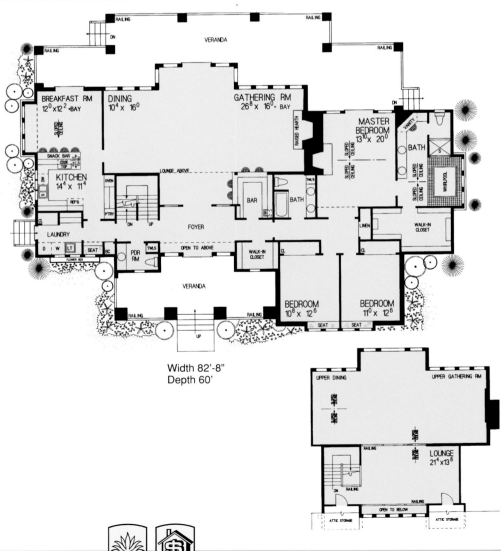

Width 82'-8"
Depth 60'

Additional products and services available. See page 4.

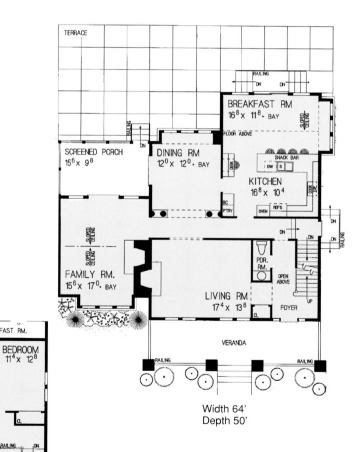

TERRACE

BREAKFAST RM
16⁸ x 11⁸ + BAY

SCREENED PORCH
15⁶ x 9⁸

DINING RM
12⁰ x 12⁰ + BAY

KITCHEN
16⁸ x 10⁴

SNACK BAR

FAMILY RM.
15⁶ x 17⁰ + BAY

POR. RM.

LIVING RM
17⁴ x 13⁸

FOYER

VERANDA

RAILING

Width 64'
Depth 50'

UPPER BREAKFAST RM.

BEDROOM
12⁰ x 10⁰

BATH

BEDROOM
11⁴ x 12⁸

LINEN

BATH

OPEN BELOW

VANITY

WALK-IN CLOSET

MASTER BEDROOM
12⁴ x 16⁰

DESIGN HH3313

First Floor:	1,482 sq. ft.
Second Floor:	885 sq. ft.
Total:	2,367 sq. ft.

Cottage-Style Bungalow

Shingled and pillared, this substantial-looking home promises cozy nights by the fire and sunny days on the veranda. A family-styled home, its Craftsman heritage appeals to the historian as well as the designer.

The first floor is designed for comfort. It features a formal living room and dining room as well as a family room with a sloped ceiling and fireplace. The kitchen is as well-appointed as Julia Child would require and connects to a sunny breakfast room with a bay window.

Porches abound from the covered veranda at the entry to the screened porch off the family room. A clever porte cochere heralds a side entry to the central hall.

Peace and quiet take precedence upstairs. The master bedroom is adorned with a super bath and large walk-in closet. Family bedrooms sit to either side of a compartmented bath.

DESIGN HH3319

Square Footage: 2,274

Bungalow Gone Contemporary

Want a cottage-style plan with a more contemporary look? The design of this home—with vertical siding and a grand entrance—combines elements of both traditional and contemporary styling for a captivating exterior. All the standard features of Craftsman are here: wide pillars of stone, varied roof heights, a front covered porch.

The design separates the master suite from family bedrooms and puts casual living to the back in a family room. The gathering room and dining room are centrally located and have access to a rear terrace, as does the master suite. Sleeping arrangements involve two family bedrooms found to the front of the plan and a master suite at the opposite end of the home. A home office or study is accessed from the entry foyer as well as the master suite.

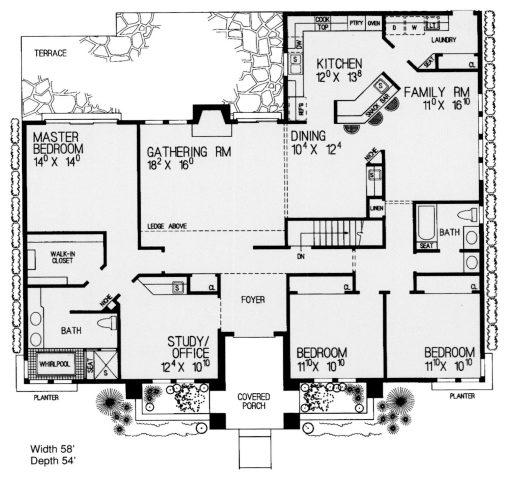

TERRACE

MASTER BEDROOM
14⁰ X 14⁰

GATHERING RM
18² X 16⁰

LEDGE ABOVE

WALK-IN CLOSET

NICHE

BATH

WHIRLPOOL

PLANTER

STUDY/OFFICE
12⁴ X 10¹⁰

COOK TOP PTRY OVEN D W LT LAUNDRY

KITCHEN
12⁰ X 13⁸

SNACK BAR

FAMILY RM
11⁰ X 16¹⁰

DINING
10⁴ X 12⁴

NICHE

LINEN

DN

BATH
SEAT

FOYER

BEDROOM
11¹⁰ X 10¹⁰

BEDROOM
11¹⁰ X 10¹⁰

COVERED PORCH

PLANTER

Width 58'
Depth 54'

Additional products and services available. See page 4.

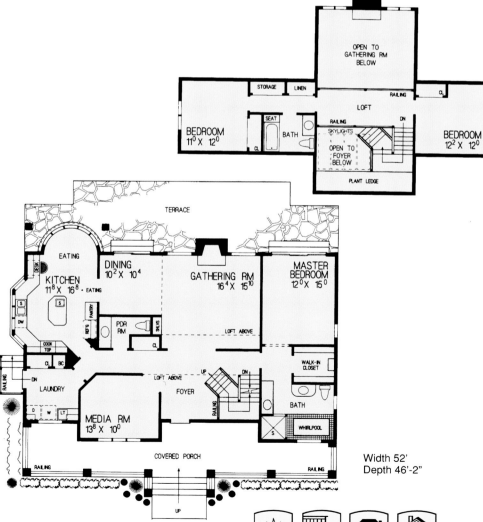

OPEN TO
GATHERING RM
BELOW

STORAGE LINEN

RAILING CL

LOFT

SEAT

BATH RAILING DN

SKYLIGHTS

BEDROOM
11⁰ X 12⁰

OPEN TO
FOYER
BELOW

BEDROOM
12² X 12⁰

PLANT LEDGE

TERRACE

EATING

KITCHEN
11⁸ X 16⁸ EATING

DINING
10² X 10⁴

GATHERING RM
16⁴ X 15¹⁰

MASTER
BEDROOM
12⁰ X 15⁰

DESK

S

S

REF'S

PANTRY

PDA
RM

SILVS

DW

LOFT ABOVE

COOK
TOP

CL BC

UP DN

LOFT ABOVE

WALK-IN
CLOSET

RAILING

DN LAUNDRY

FOYER

RAILING

BATH

D W LT

MEDIA RM
13⁸ X 10⁰

WHIRLPOOL

S

COVERED PORCH

RAILING RAILING

UP

Width 52'
Depth 46'-2"

DESIGN HH3321

First Floor:	1,636 sq. ft.
Second Floor:	572 sq. ft.
Total:	2,208 sq. ft.

Amenity-Laden Bungalow

You'll love what we've done on the inside of this cottage! The covered porch at the front opens at the entry to a foyer with an angled staircase. To the left is a media room; to the rear is the gathering room with fireplace. Attached to the gathering room is a formal dining room with rear-terrace access. The kitchen features a curved casual eating area and an island work station.

The right side of the first floor is dominated by the master suite. It has access to the rear terrace and a luxurious bath. Upstairs are two family bedrooms.

When you're done applauding the interior, take a moment to appreciate the superior Craftsman styling on the exterior. The covered porch is most notable with strong pillars and a spindled railing. The deep roofline signals authentic styling.

DESIGN HH3568

First Floor:	1,882 sq. ft.
Second Floor:	1,763 sq. ft.
Total:	3,645 sq. ft.

Baronial Estate

An early morning fox hunt. Afternoon tea. If you have a taste for the grand manner, there's much about this plan that will appeal to you.

Inventive floor planning makes royal living comfortable. An angled wing encloses the sunken living room and a roomy study. The dining room, with its window bay, introduces the other half of the house. Here, the resident gourmet will appreciate the kitchen with its ample counter space and island cooktop. The breakfast room remains open to the kitchen and, through a pair of columns, the family room.

The second floor offers excellent sleeping quarters with four bedrooms. The master suite spoils its occupants with a sloped ceiling, balcony and fireplace. A huge walk-in closet and a divine bath finish off the room. Three additional bedrooms include one with a private bath.

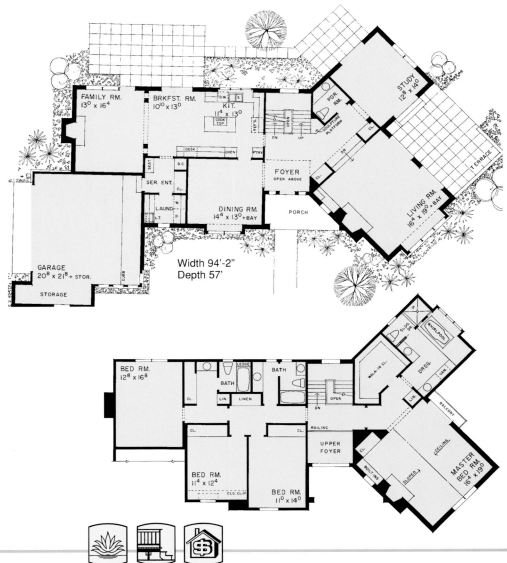

Width 94'-2"
Depth 57'

Additional products and services available. See page 4.

DESIGN HH3360

Main Level:	2,673 sq. ft.
Lower Level:	1,389 sq. ft.
Total:	4,062 sq. ft.

Traditional For Sloping Lots

Expanding families and empty-nesters take a good look at this plan! Not only does it accommodate an otherwise impossible lot, but it is completely livable on the main level with expansion capabilities at the lower level.

The foyer is raised slightly and leads to a large gathering room/dining room combination at the rear of the home. A curved wet bar serves this area. The kitchen features a U-shaped counter area (one wing is a pass-through snack bar) and a casual breakfast area. A media room (or guest room) has handy space for video equipment.

Bedrooms include the lavish master suite and a secondary bedroom on the main level and a third bedroom on the lower level. A huge activities room with a summer kitchen dominates the additional space at the lower level.

Width 60'
Depth 72'

Additional products and services available. See page 4.

125

DESIGN HH2565

Square Footage: 1,540

Three Exterior Styles

Smaller is often better. There's only the two of you. Maybe your family is grown and you're looking toward retirement. Maybe you're just starting out and don't need a five-bedroom Brady-Bunch home yet. With three distinct exterior styles to choose from—all included in the blueprint package—this unique one-story can work for you. It may function as either a two- or three-bedroom home. The living room is huge and features a fine, raised-hearth fireplace and a beamed ceiling. The kitchen revolves around a center island cooktop and a breakfast nook.

The stairway to the basement is handy and may lead to a future recreation area. In addition to the two full baths, there is an extra wash room.

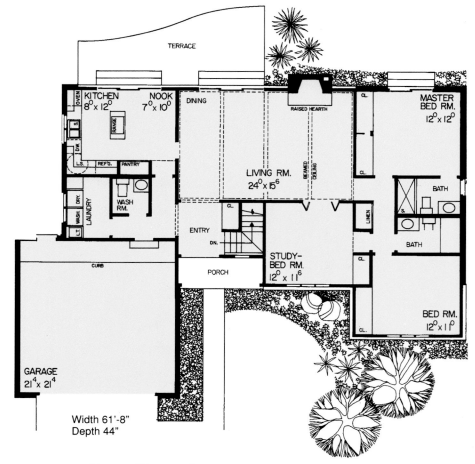

Width 61'-8"
Depth 44"

Additional products and services available. See page 4.

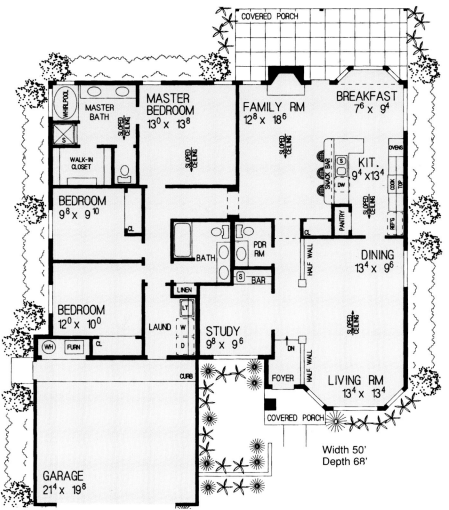

Width 50'
Depth 68'

DESIGN HH3422

Square Footage:	1,932

The Good Life

Casual lifestyles call for homes with open floor plans, attention to amenities and plenty of style. The Floridian style works perfectly within these parameters. This home's easy elegance gives you enough formality to host an evening dinner party, yet surrounds you with comfort the remainder of the time.

An entry garden can be filled with your favorite flowers or made into a patio with potted plants. The entry opens to the formal dining and living areas with half-wall definition. A study across the hall doubles as a home office. The family room is open to the breakfast room and kitchen and is warmed on cool evenings by a glowing fire in the hearth.

Bedrooms cater to the owners—a grand master bath has features for pampered living. The secondary bedrooms share a full bath with double-bowl vanity.

DESIGN HH3416

Square Footage:	1,375

Mother-In-Law Suite

"Sure it's small," you say to yourself, "but it's got everything I'm looking for in a home and even has a separate space for the kids when they come to visit." The facade is unassuming and clean-lined (and the little courtyard is so private, it will be a secret to any who never venture beyond the front walk).

Inside there are two fine bedrooms—one a master suite with a whirlpool tub. The media room gives you space where you can spread out your work or snuggle in for a home video and no one can bother you. The living room and dining room are spacious enough for having a few friends over from time to time, warming their bones by the fire and their hearts with good conversation.

The mother-in-law suite connects to the house, but has a separate entry and its own unique space. It seems larger that it is because of the sloped ceiling. A fireplace makes it just like home!

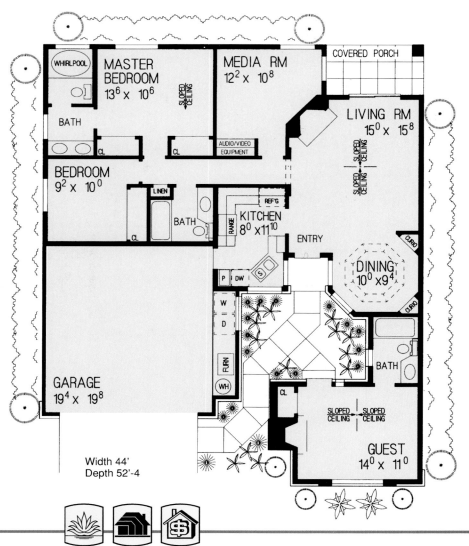

Width 44'
Depth 52'-4

Additional products and services available. See page 4.

DESIGN HH3419

Square Footage:	1,965

Stucco With A Touch Of Tudor

By combining the well-defined look of Floridian styling with just a hint of Tudor detailing, we've created a truly unique exterior that works well in any area—but was designed for the Florida lifestyle. Brick accents and wood detailing make the difference in this plan.

The day-to-day living spaces in this home are kept to the left of the plan: large family room with fireplace, hard-working kitchen, and dandy breakfast room. Formal areas are focused at the center of the plan and overlook the rear covered porch.

Four bedrooms (in such a modest square footage!) are all to the right of the home. The master suite has a hexagonal bath with a compartmented shower and toilet and a whirlpool tub. The walk-in closet means easy access for the owner. The family bedrooms have access to a good-sized bath in the hall.

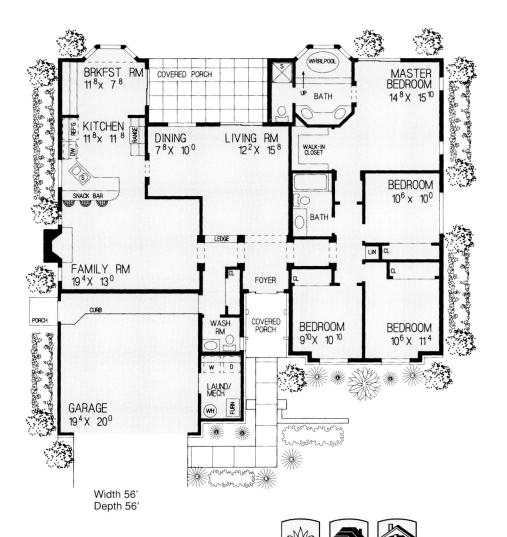

Width 56'
Depth 56'

DESIGN HH3478

Square Footage:	1,898

Maximum Livability, Compact Plan

Two-bedroom homes are not easy to find. When they are as spacious feeling and well-designed as this one, they are not to be ignored. Stucco is the material of choice for the exterior—true to authentic Floridian design.

The living and dining rooms combine for a spacious area with sloped ceilings, flat arches and shelves above for plants, decorative pots or family treasures. The kitchen shares space with the bayed breakfast nook, providing accessibility to the back yard through sliding glass doors. The adjacent family room has a fireplace, creating a living area ideal for informal gatherings.

Sleeping quarters consist of the master suite, a secondary bedroom and a study that may be used as a third bedroom if needed. The master bedroom boasts a whirlpool tub and a large walk-in closet.

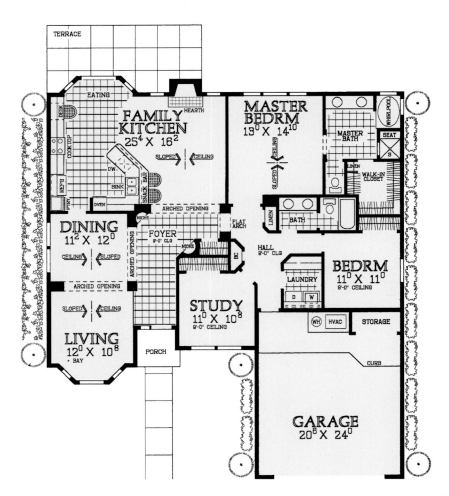

Width 51'-6"
Depth 59'-6"

Additional products and services available. See page 4.

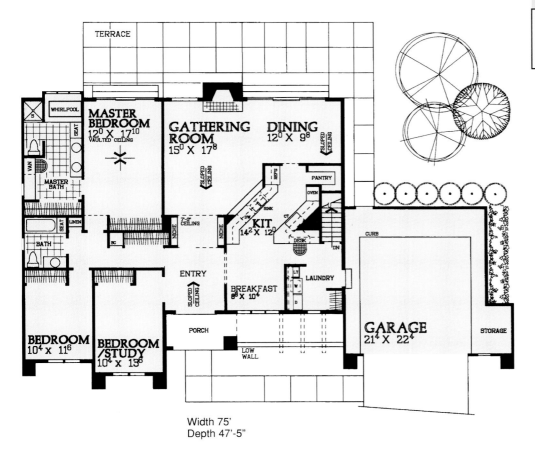

TERRACE

MASTER BEDROOM
12⁰ X 17¹⁰
VAULTED CEILING

WHIRLPOOL

MASTER BATH

VAN

LINEN

BATH

BEDROOM
10⁴ X 11⁶

BEDROOM /STUDY
10⁴ X 13⁶

GATHERING ROOM
15⁰ X 17⁸
SLOPED CEILING

DINING
12⁰ X 9⁸
SLOPED CEILING

NICHE

7'-0" CEILING

NICHE

KIT
14² X 12⁰

PANTRY

OVEN

SINK

DESK

ENTRY
SLOPED CEILING

BREAKFAST
8⁸ X 10⁴

LAUNDRY

PORCH

LOW WALL

CURB

GARAGE
21⁴ X 22⁴

STORAGE

Width 75'
Depth 47'-5"

DESIGN HH3480

Square Footage:	1,845

Arched Support

Why did Old World architects carry on such a love affair with arches? The reason is plain to see in this striking Spanish design—because they're spectacular! Besides the arched entry that reveals an open patio defined by a low wall, the arch pattern is carried through in the circle-head windows.

A combination gathering room/dining room with an adjacent angled kitchen accommodates both family occasions and formal dinner parties. A walk-in pantry in the kitchen allows you to take advantage of grocery specials by stocking up. The handy laundry room leads directly to a two-car garage where a large storage area handles gardening equipment.

The master suite is roomy and features sliding glass doors to the rear terrace. One family bedroom and a study are also available. Move the entry of the study to the hall to make it a comfortable bedroom.

DESIGN HH3415

Square Footage:	2,406

Bigger Than It Looks

The surprise of this house is that the rear of it extends so that it is actually deeper than it is wide. This helps to make the master bedroom suite very private and also gives it access to the wonderful covered terrace.

Two living areas are found in this plan. The formal spaces greet visitors right up front and just a step down from the entry foyer. The family room, on the other hand, is tucked away to the rear and melds with the kitchen and breakfast area for one big happy family retreat. (Imagine fires in the hearth and sunny breakfasts on Sundays.)

Four bedrooms mean never having to share private space. The master suite has an oversized walk-in closet and is large enough for even a California-king-sized bed with all the trimmings.

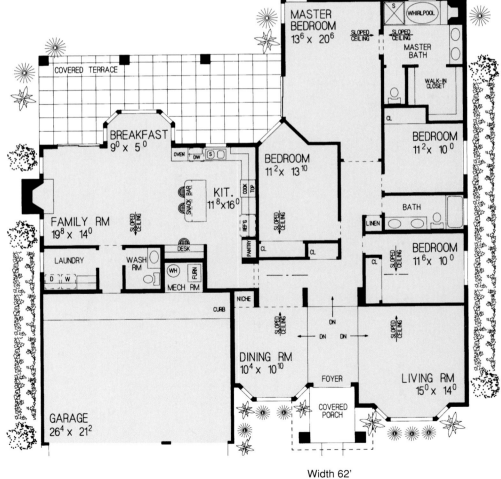

Width 62'
Depth 64'

Additional products and services available. See page 4.

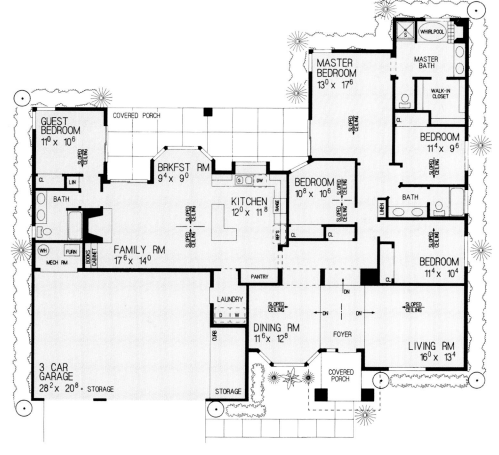

MASTER BEDROOM 13⁰ x 17⁶

MASTER BATH

WHIRLPOOL

WALK-IN CLOSET

GUEST BEDROOM 11⁰ x 10⁶

COVERED PORCH

BEDROOM 11⁴ x 9⁶

BRKFST RM 9⁴ x 9⁰

KITCHEN 12⁰ x 11⁸

BEDROOM 10⁸ x 10⁶

BATH

LIN

BATH

LINEN

FAMILY RM 17⁶ x 14⁰

MECH RM

BOOKS CABINET

BEDROOM 11⁴ x 10⁴

PANTRY

LAUNDRY

DN

3 CAR GARAGE 28² x 20⁸ · STORAGE

DINING RM 11⁶ x 12⁸

FOYER

DN DN

LIVING RM 16⁰ x 13⁴

STORAGE

COVERED PORCH

Width 70'
Depth 63'

DESIGN HH3411

Square Footage:	2,441

Sunlit Stucco

This is a home full of sunlight. It's a home where friends can gather to celebrate and the family can relax. It could be the home you choose to build. From dramatic entry to covered rear porch, it speaks of style and comfort.

Cleverly designed for overnight or even long-term guests, this design splits five bedrooms with four on the right side of the plan and a guest suite to the left. Separating the two areas is a family room and kitchen/breakfast combination—enough room for the largest of families. Formal entertaining is reserved for the sunken living room and dining room to the front of the house. Each contains a sloped ceiling.

The three-car garage guarantees that you'll never again be scrambling for space for cars, lawn mowers and all the paraphernalia of daily life.

Additional products and services available. See page 4.

133

DESIGN HH3639

First Floor:	2,137 sq. ft.
Second Floor:	671 sq. ft.
Total:	2,808 sq. ft.

Floridian In A Grand Style

If first impressions really make the most important statements—this home makes it in grand style. The two-story entry-way and double doors to the reception foyer make a first impression that can't be beat.

Inside, formal living areas grab your attention with a dining room and an elegant living room that opens to a covered entertainment area outside. The family room—with a fireplace—features open views to the kitchen and breakfast nook. The nearby "recipe corner" includes a built-in desk. The laundry room is fully functional with a laundry tub and a broom closet.

On the left side of the plan, the master bedroom suite has a full, private bath and a lanai perfect for a spa. A large den could easily double as a study. Two bedrooms and a full bath are located upstairs.

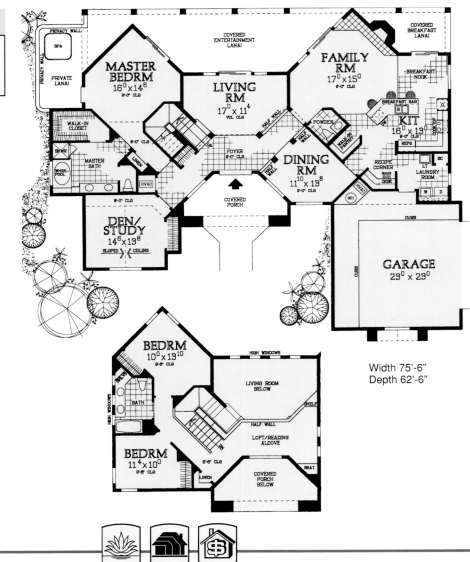

Width 75'-6"
Depth 62'-6"

Additional products and services available. See page 4.

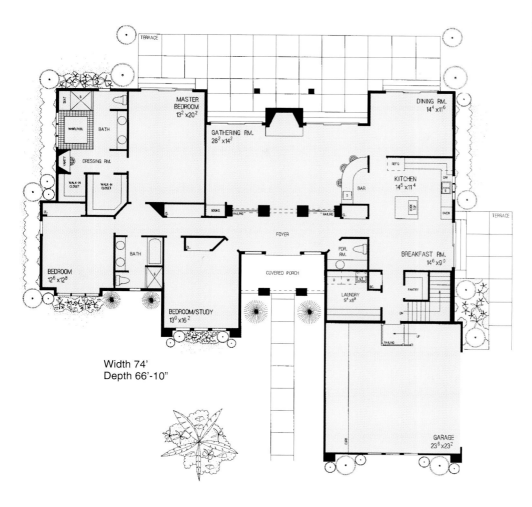

Width 74'
Depth 66'-10"

DESIGN HH2950

Square Footage:	2,559

Better Than The Fabled Fountain Of Youth

Though Ponce de Leon searched for years in the area around what we now know as Florida, he never found the fabled fountain of youth. If he had found a Floridian home as appealing as this, we're sure he'd have given up his search and settled down in comfort!

The common living areas—gathering room, formal dining room, and breakfast room—are offset by a quiet study that could be used as a bedroom or guest room. A lovely hearth warms the gathering room and complements the curved snack-bar eating area.

A master suite features two walk-in closets, a double vanity and a whirlpool spa. Sliding glass doors open to the wide rear terrace. The two-car garage provides a service entrance; close by is a laundry area and a pantry.

Additional products and services available. See page 4.

135

DESIGN HH3413

Square Footage:	2,517

Delightful Details

Just because a home isn't palatial, that doesn't mean it has to be lacking in all the special details that make it delightful to live in. This Floridian one-story features so many unique elements, you'll wonder how we packed them all in!

Note, for instance, the central gallery—perpendicular to the raised entry hall—running almost the entire width of the house. An L-shaped, angled kitchen serves the breakfast room and family room in equal fashion. For formal occasions, you'll appreciate the living and dining rooms. Each has a bay window and sloped ceiling; the living room also has a warming hearth.

Sleeping areas are found in four bedrooms, including an optional study with a wet bar and an exquisite master suite. The master is conveniently separated from the family bedrooms—for privacy and quiet.

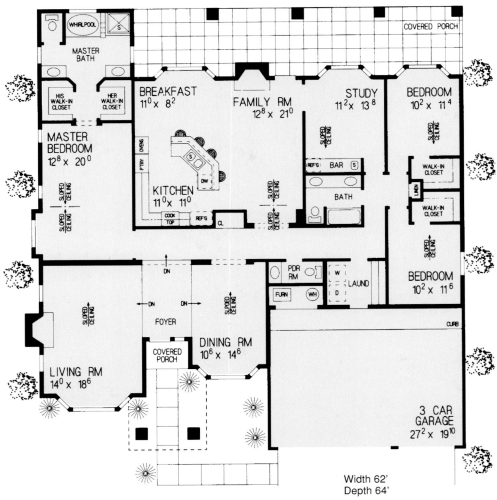

Additional products and services available. See page 4.

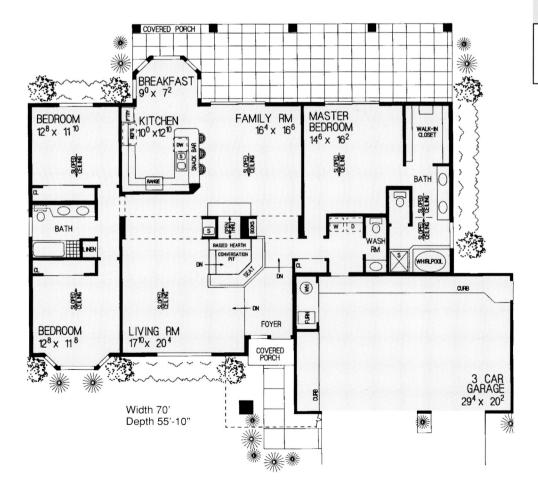

Width 70'
Depth 55'-10"

DESIGN HH3421

Square Footage: 2,145

Three-Car Garage

No one in your family will ever complain again about a lack of garage space if you build this stucco one-story. In fact, there's so much about this plan to love, you'll want to investigate the great floor plan as well.

Split-bedroom planning puts the master suite on the opposite side of the house from two family bedrooms. And what a master bedroom! Sloped ceilings in both the bedroom and bath, sliding glass doors to the rear covered porch, a huge walk-in closet and a whirlpool tub!

Gourmets can rejoice at the abundant work space in the U-shaped kitchen and will appreciate the natural light afforded by the large bay window in the breakfast room. A formal living room has a sunken conversation area with a cozy fireplace as its focus. The rear covered porch can be reached through sliding glass doors in the family room.

Additional products and services available. See page 4.

137

DESIGN HH3429

First Floor:	1,739 sq. ft.
Second Floor:	1,376 sq. ft.
Total:	3,115 sq. ft.

Stucco Design With Multi Gables

Beautiful stucco styling is enhanced further by the many gables and long, sloping roof-lines on this two-story home. It's a larger home—perfect for families or those with extended families who are living in.

Formal living areas (the living room and dining room) have a casual counterpoint in the family room and glassed-in breakfast room. The kitchen is a hub for both areas and also serves the dining room. A first-floor study has an adjacent bath, making it a convenient guest or mother-in-law suite when needed.

The second floor has three bedrooms and an activities room with an audio/video center for the kids. The master suite is raised from its entry by two steps, as is the huge master bath. A bayed sitting room lends special interest to this already sumptuous suite.

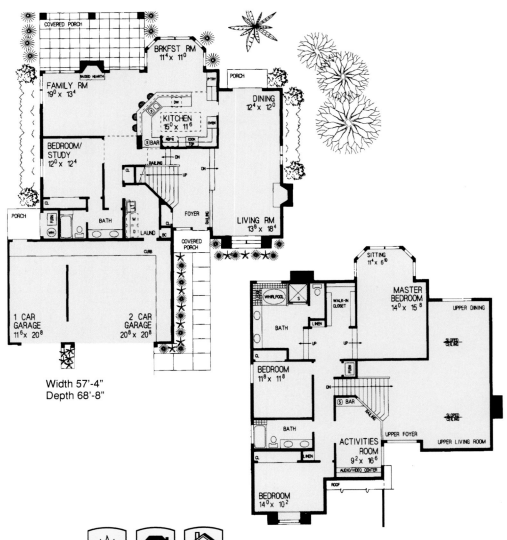

Width 57'-4"
Depth 68'-8"

This home, as shown in the photograph, may differ from the actual blueprints. For more detailed information, please check the floor plans carefully.

Photo by Andrew D. Lautman

Width 57'
Depth 64'

DESIGN HH3414

First Floor:	2,024 sq. ft.
Second Floor:	1,144 sq. ft.
Total:	3,168 sq. ft.

Wide Open Spaces

Love the allure of wide open spaces? Longing for a home that won't fence you in? Wrought in sunny stucco and planned for two stories, this Florida-style design gives you all the room you seek.

The two-story entry connects directly to a formal living/dining area—note the bay window, fireplace and sloped ceiling in this formal space. A curved staircase leads around to the family room (another fireplace!) and open kitchen with bayed breakfast room. The covered patio just beyond opens this area even further.

Split-bedroom planning puts the master suite on the first floor for supreme privacy. His and Hers walk-in closets, a whirlpool tub and dual vanities spell luxury for the owner's retreat. Upstairs are three family bedrooms, a guest room with a deck and two full baths.

Additional products and services available. See page 4.

139

DESIGN HH3323

First Floor:	1,923 sq. ft.
Second Floor:	838 sq. ft.
Total:	2,761 sq. ft.

Windows On the World

A home is not just what's good on the inside. It includes all of the surrounding landscape and even far-off views. This exciting Floridian allows you to take in all the views from any direction with huge, full-story windows both upstairs and down.

Take a step down from the foyer and go where your mood takes you: a gathering room with a fireplace and an alcove for reading or quiet conversations, a media room for enjoying the latest technology, or to the dining room with sliding glass doors to the terrace. The kitchen has an island range and eating space. Also on the first floor is a large master suite that includes a sitting area with terrace access, a walk-in closet and a whirlpool.

An elegant spiral staircase leads to two family bedrooms that share a full bath and a guest bedroom with a private bath.

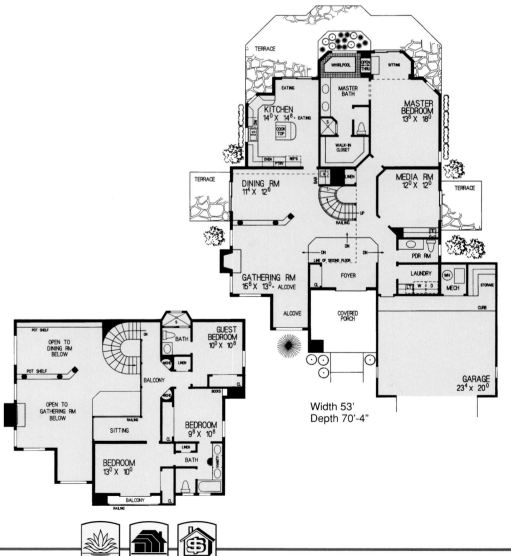

Width 53'
Depth 70'-4"

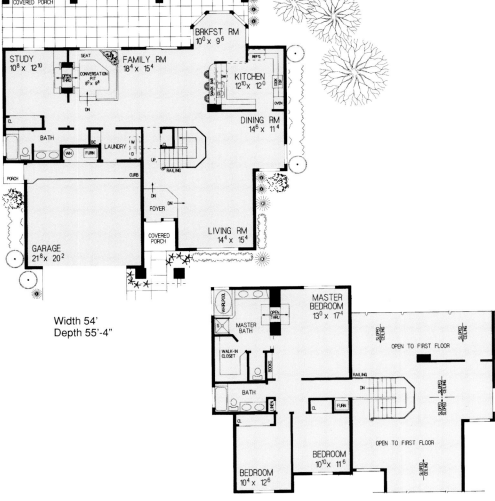

Width 54'
Depth 55'-4"

DESIGN HH3424

First Floor:	1,625 sq. ft.
Second Floor:	982 sq. ft.
Total:	2,607 sq. ft.

Living In The Grand Manor

When the Spaniards came to the New World, they brought a wonderful tradition of housing style. This two-story home exemplifies the special look with a tile roof, large entry columns, arched windows and stucco siding.

Made for an indoor/outdoor lifestyle, the floor plan of this home concentrates on living easy. The gigantic family room, with covered porch access and a sunken conversation area, shares a through-fireplace with the study. An L-shaped kitchen has an attached, glass-surrounded breakfast room and is conveniently located next to the dining room/living room combination.

Besides the luxury-appointed master suite, there are two family bedrooms and a full bath upstairs. Notice that the master bath enjoys a through-fireplace from the bedroom.

Additional products and services available. See page 4.

141

DESIGN HH3449

First Floor:	1,336 sq. ft.
Second Floor:	1,186 sq. ft.
Total:	2,522 sq. ft.

Grand Opening Statement

Make a dramatic opening statement when you entertain. This home's regal covered entry opens to a lofty foyer with a curved stairway, open living and dining rooms and a balcony over-look from the second floor. A well-placed powder room serves the needs of guests enjoying these beautifully formal areas.

The rear of the home is devoted to more casual pursuits. A family room, with a through-fireplace to the breakfast nook, also accesses a terrace outside. The U-shaped kitchen is both convenient and attractive.

The bedrooms are found on the second floor. The master suite has a sitting area, a private covered deck and a corner-placed whirlpool spa. Secondary bedrooms include one with a walk-in closet.

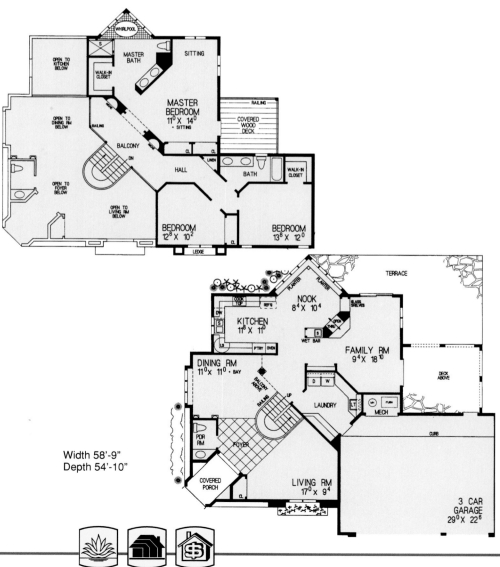

Width 58'-9"
Depth 54'-10"

Additional products and services available. See page 4.

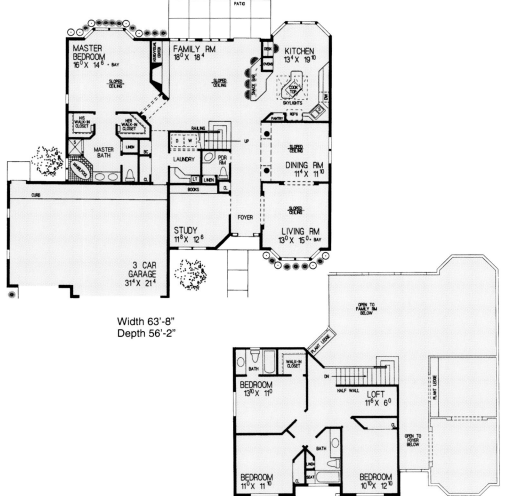

Width 63'-8"
Depth 56'-2"

DESIGN HH3441

First Floor:	2,022 sq. ft.
Second Floor:	845 sq. ft.
Total:	2,867 sq. ft.

Somewhere To Call Home

You don't just want a house—you're looking for a home. Somewhere you can forget the worries of the day. Somewhere your kids can feel safe and comfortable. A place to keep for years to come. This handsome stucco design has many of the special features you're looking for: a snack bar, an audio-visual center and a fireplace in the family room; a desk, an island cook top, a bay and skylights in the kitchen area; two columns and a plant ledge in the formal dining room.

The first-floor master suite includes His and Hers walk-in closets, a spacious bath and a bay window. On the second floor, one bedroom features a walk-in closet and private bath, while two additional bedrooms share a full bath. Don't miss the three-car garage and private study with built-in bookshelves.

Additional products and services available. See page 4.

143

DESIGN HH3436

Square Footage:	2,573

Sunny Stucco Home

Here's a test to see if this is the home for you: 1) You live to be outside; 2) When you're inside, you're looking outside; 3) If you can't be near a window, you go stir crazy. Answering yes to any one or all of the above means you should immediately build this home. You'll get patio access from every major living area, plus private patios at the master suite and one of the two family bedrooms.

You'll also be impressed with the many interior features: an expansive gathering room/dining area with a sloped ceiling; the kitchen which includes a large pantry and an adjoining break-fast area with a fireplace; and a three-car garage!

Each of the bedrooms includes a walk-in closet and convenient access to a full bath. A laundry and workshop are special additions.

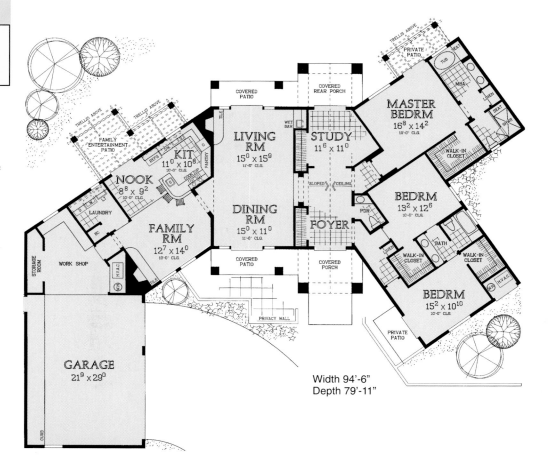

Width 94'-6"
Depth 79'-11"

 Additional products and services available. See page 4.

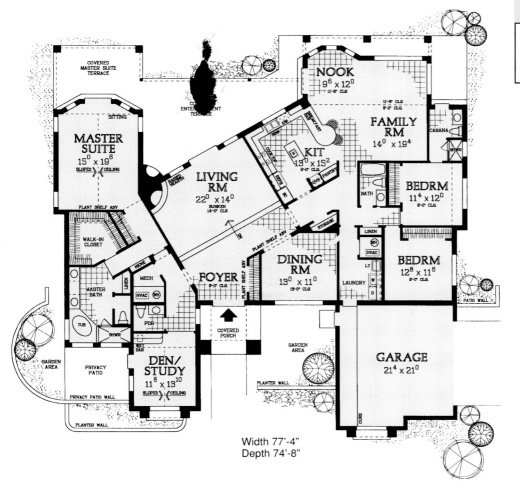

Width 77'-4"
Depth 74'-8"

DESIGN HH3475

Square Footage: 3,286

Unique Spanish Styling

There's something uniquely captivating about Spanish design. A colorful, tiled hipped roof contrasts with varying roof planes and wide overhangs. The sheltered front entrance is both dramatic and inviting with double doors opening to the central foyer.

In the sunken living room, a curved, raised-hearth fireplace acts as a focal point. Double glass doors lead to a covered terrace. The U-shaped kitchen is efficient with its island work surface, breakfast bar, pantry and broom closet. An informal nook features a projecting bay and high ceiling. This generous, open area extends to include the family room. Opposite the more formal living room is the separate dining room, which looks out on the garden court. Notice the complete separation of the parents' and children's bedrooms.

DESIGN HH3430

Square Footage:	2,394

Entertaining In Open Style

This is the home for entertaining. And it won't matter if your style is casual weekend parties with friends or very formal dinner parties with the boss. This plan can handle both. Its open floor plan holds a sunken conversation area as the centerpiece. The formal living and dining rooms encompass a large space to the right and are graced by a sloping ceiling. The family room shares a through-fireplace with the conversation area and also has a sloped ceiling. The kitchen features a snack bar and attaches to a bayed breakfast room.

Split zoning places the master bedroom to the left of the plan and family bedrooms to the right. The master contains a walk-in closet, whirlpool tub and rear-porch access.

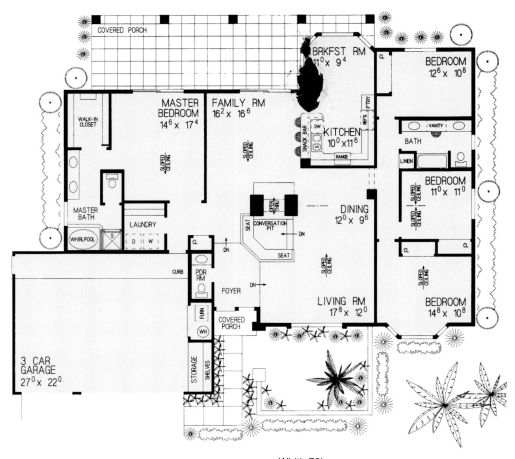

Width 72'
Depth 60'-6"

Additional products and services available. See page 4.

Photos by Allen Maertz

This home, as shown in the photograph, may differ from the actual blueprints.
For more detailed information, please check the floor plans carefully.

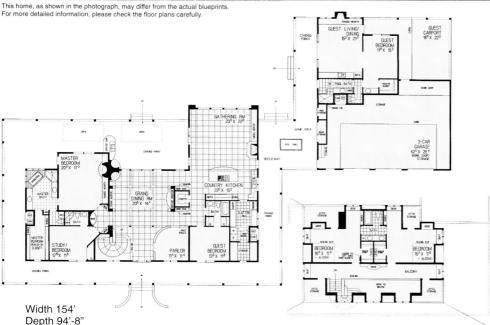

Width 154'
Depth 94'-8"

DESIGN HH3471

First Floor:	3,166 sq. ft.
Second Floor:	950 sq. ft.
Guest Living Area:	680 sq. ft.
Total:	4,796 sq. ft.

Home On The Range

Conjuring up dreams of round-ups, prairie moons and wide-open spaces, this contemporary farmhouse is the essence of Western living. The central entrance leads into a cozy parlor—half walls provide a view of the grand dining room, with built-in china alcove, service counter and fireplace. The country kitchen, with a large island cooktop, overlooks the gathering room with its full wall of glass.

The master bedroom will satisfy even the most discerning tastes. It boasts a raised hearth, porch access and a bath with a walk-in closet, separate vanities and a whirlpool. You may want to use one of the additional first-floor bedrooms as a study, the other as a guest room.

Two family bedrooms and attic storage make up the second floor. Note, too, the separate garage and guest house which make this such a winning design.

DESIGN HH3440

Square Footage: 2,290

Volume-Look Western

Don't let this plan fool you. It looks like it might harbor bedrooms on a second floor. But it really is a convenient, easy-to-build one-story design. The trick is in the volume-look ceilings that make the living areas seem open and airy. Take the gathering room, for example. Its charm is centered in a through-fireplace to the dining room, an audio/visual center and handy outdoor access. The nearby kitchen includes a wide pantry, a snack bar and a separate eating area.

There are even three bedrooms in the plan! (Or reconfigure the den/study as a fourth bedroom.) The master suite features two walk-in closets, a separate shower and whirlpool tub, dual vanities and linen storage. The huge three-car garage means never getting soaked on your way to work again.

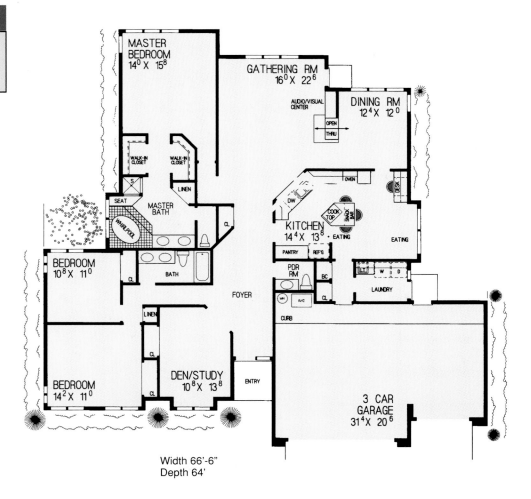

Width 66'-6"
Depth 64'

Additional products and services available. See page 4.

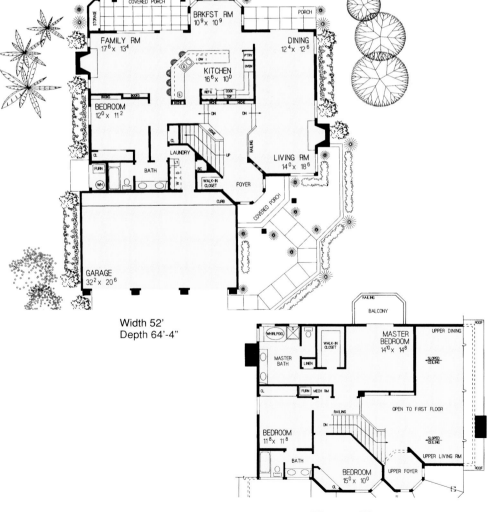

Width 52'
Depth 64'-4"

DESIGN HH3425

First Floor:	1,776 sq. ft.
Second Floor:	1,035 sq. ft.
Total:	2,811 sq. ft.

Southwest With A Slant

Here's a new angle on Southwest design: the entry is angled to the basic layout of the home. Above it is a quaint tower structure that actually contains the upper foyer and admits light to this area. Inside is an interesting floor plan containing rooms with a variety of shapes. Formal areas are to the right of the entry tower: a living room with a fireplace and a large dining room. The kitchen has loads of counter space and is complemented by a bumped-out breakfast room. Note the second fireplace in the family room and the first-floor bedroom.

Three second-floor bedrooms radiate around the upper foyer. The master suite has a private balcony, a large walk-in closet and a separate tub and shower. The two family bedrooms share a full, compartmented bath.

DESIGN HH3435

First Floor:	1,946 sq. ft.
Second Floor:	986 sq. ft.
Total:	2,932 sq. ft.

Manor With A Mission

Mission styling is not for everyone. But for those who appreciate its historic grace and grand presence, nothing else will do. In the Mission manner, this home exudes an elegance that is hard to find in simpler homes. Enter at the angled foyer which contains a curved staircase to the second floor. Family bedrooms are here along with a spacious guest suite. All have private balconies.

The master bedroom is found on the first floor and has a private patio and whirlpool overlooking an enclosed garden area. Besides a living room and dining room connected by a through-fireplace, there is a family room with casual eating space. There is also a library with a large closet. Built-ins and interesting shapes abound throughout the house.

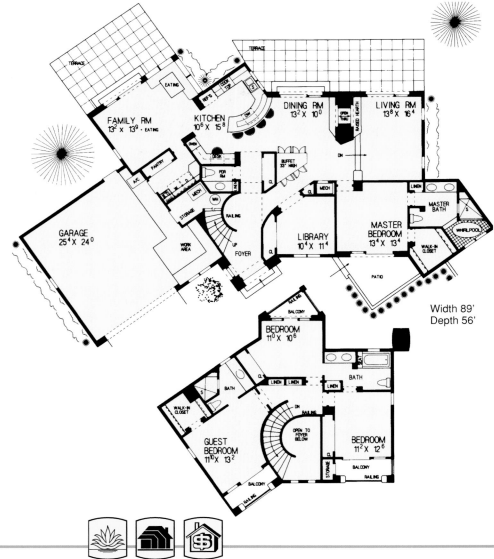

Width 89'
Depth 56'

Additional products and services available. See page 4.

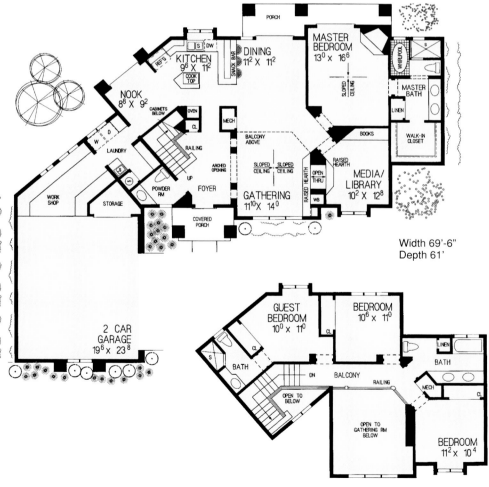

Width 69'-6"
Depth 61'

DESIGN HH3437

First Floor:	1,522 sq. ft.
Second Floor:	800 sq. ft.
Total:	2,322 sq. ft.

Fully Customizable

You'll be amazed at the amount of room available in this two-story Mission-style home, and all in just over 2,300 square feet! And if you're not quite happy with the way the floor plan lays out, it can be customized to your specifications.

The first-floor master suite features a fireplace and a gracious bath with a walk-in closet, a whirlpool, a shower, dual vanities and linen storage. The kitchen, with an island cooktop, includes a snack bar and an adjoining breakfast nook. The gathering room has a lovely sloped ceiling and through-fireplace to the media room or library. A larger space for more formal dining connects the gathering room to the rear porch.

Second-floor bedrooms include a private guest suite with a separate bath. A balcony overlooks the gathering room below.

DESIGN HH3407

First Floor:	2,401 sq. ft.
Second Floor:	927 sq. ft.
Total:	3,328 sq. ft.

Song Of Santa Fe

When early explorers talked of searching for the Seven Cities of Gold, what they found were communities of homes that created the basis for this distinctive Santa Fe design. Stucco, rounded corners, balconies, vigas and an in-line plan are characteristics.

On the first floor: a large two-story gathering room with a bee-hive fireplace; a gallery leading to the kitchen and breakfast area; a media room with a full entertainment center and a master suite with special appointments and nearby study.

The second floor contains three bedrooms, each with a huge closet. A full, compartmented bath is shared by the three. A quiet reading loft, with built-in bookshelves, finishes this floor. Outdoor areas abound: a full covered patio with a built-in barbecue to the rear; two covered porches at the front; and a private patio just off the study.

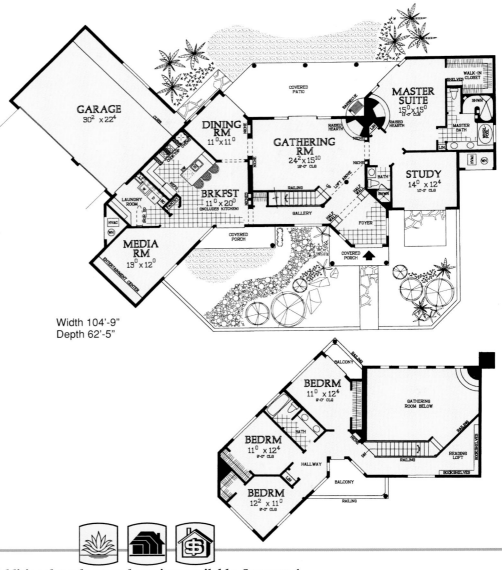

Width 104'-9"
Depth 62'-5"

Additional products and services available. See page 4.

Width 90'
Depth 51'-8"

DESIGN HH3432

First Floor:	1,966 sq. ft.
Second Floor:	831 sq. ft.
Total:	2,797 sq. ft.

Large Entry Court

Southwestern homes are famous for their significant contribution to outdoor spaces. Patios, decks, balconies and courtyards are found in abundance in the typical example. This Santa Fe-styled two-story is no exception. It begins with a large entry courtyard with covered areas at the dining room and a bedroom. Additional patios are in the back off the living room and another bedroom, and the family room and kitchen. Balconies grace the master bedroom as well as the guest room on the second floor.

But don't ignore the indoor livability. The entry foyer leads to living areas at the back of the plan: a living room with a corner fireplace and a family room connected to the kitchen via a built-in eating nook. Upstairs, the master suite features a grand bath and a large walk-in closet. The guest bedroom also has a private bath.

DESIGN HH3433

Square Footage:	2,350

Santa Fe Signature

Certain styles have a signature all their own. They are so distinctive, they are easily recognizable by almost everyone. This exquisite one-story exudes a Santa Fe style that creates interesting angles. A grand entrance leads through a courtyard into the foyer with a circular skylight, closet space, niches and a convenient powder room.

Turn right to the master suite with a deluxe bath and a bedroom closet at hand, perfect for a nursery, home office or an exercise room. Two more family bedrooms are placed quietly in the far wing of the house.

Fireplaces in the living room, dining room and on the covered porch create various shapes. Make note of the island range in the kitchen, the extra storage in the garage and the covered porches on three sides.

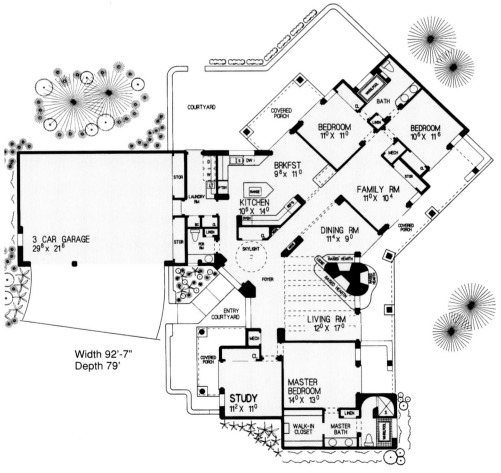

Width 92'-7"
Depth 79'

Additional products and services available. See page 4.

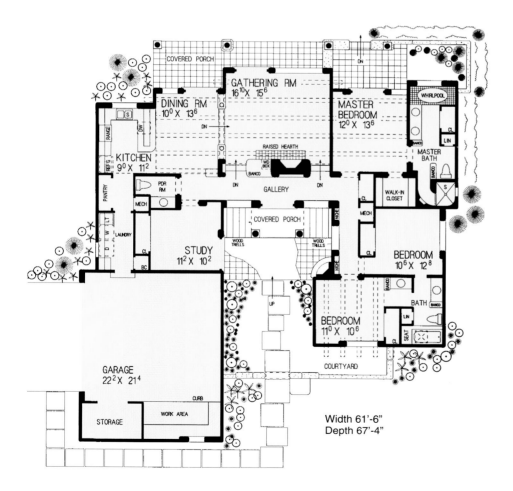

Width 61'-6"
Depth 67'-4"

DESIGN HH3431

Square Footage: 1,907

Old-Style Courtyard

The original Santa Fe homes often featured a courtyard area just past the front gate. It allowed a quiet, cool place for relaxing and protected the home from outside noise and weather. Our smaller one-story design shown here mimics this winsome feature. Graceful curves welcome you into the courtyard and then, inside, a gallery directs traffic to the work zone on the left or the sleeping zone on the right.

Straight ahead lies a sunken gathering room with a beam ceiling and a raised-hearth fireplace. The covered rear porch is accessible from the dining room, gathering room and secluded master bedroom.

The master bath has a whirlpool tub, a separate shower, a double vanity and lots of closet space. Two family bedrooms share a compartmented bath.

DESIGN HH2949

Square Footage: 2,922

Home For Upscale Living

The amenities and floor plan of this home make it seem like an estate of over 4,000 square feet! It matches traditional South-western design elements such as stucco, tile, and exposed rafters (called vigas) with an up-to-date floor plan. The 43-foot gathering room provides a dramatic multi-purpose living area that opens to a formal dining area and has a snack bar through to the kitchen. Other features include a morning room with a sunny bay and a media room which could serve as a third bedroom.

The master bedroom contains a walk-in closet and an amenity-filled bath with a whirlpool tub. A secondary or guest bedroom has its own bath and a huge walk-in closet.

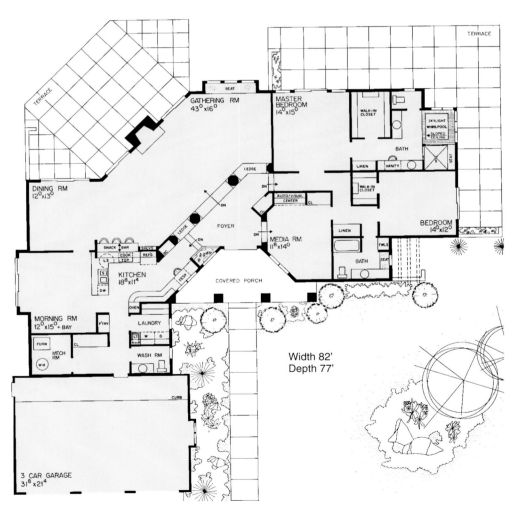

Width 82'
Depth 77'

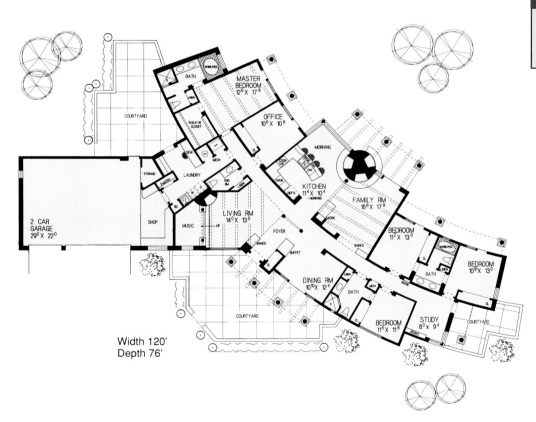

Width 120'
Depth 76'

DESIGN HH3329

Square Footage:　2,968

Drama On The Curve

We'll throw you a curve with this dramatic plan—so be ready for exciting Santa Fe style. Projecting wood beams, called vigas, add a decorative touch to the exterior. A courtyard leads to the entryway. To the left of the foyer rests a living room with a beam ceiling, a corner fireplace and a music alcove. Past the formal dining room on the right is the family room with a fireplace and outdoor access. The kitchen offers yet another fireplace, along with a snack bar and an adjacent morning room.

The master bedroom, with a beam ceiling, is placed quietly to the left of the home. The master bath includes a whirlpool tub, a separate shower, dual vanities and a linen closet. At the opposite end of the home are three family bedrooms, two baths and a study with a built-in bookcase.

DESIGN HH3434

Square Footage: 3,428

Plan For A Large Family

Need a place for three or four children to have a room of their own? Need extra space for guests or in-laws? Love Santa Fe style? This plan's for you! Striking a beautiful combination of historic exterior detailing and open floor planning, it lives as good as it looks.

Formal living and dining rooms are complemented by a large casual area containing a family room, morning room and kitchen. All are warmed by a circular hearth that extends outside.

Three family bedrooms are found on the right side of the plan, as is a bonus room—perfect for hobbies, games or an additional bedroom. The master suite is on the left side of the plan, adjacent to a handy home office. Note the extra-large laundry area.

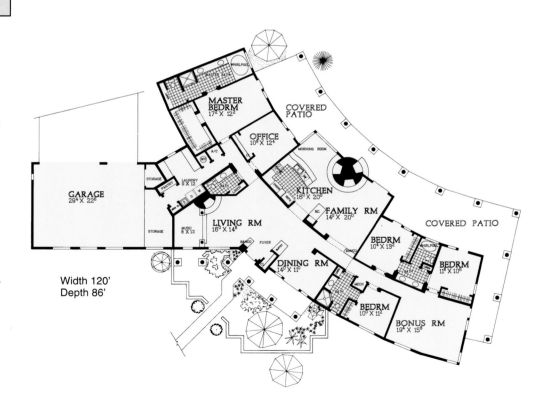

Width 120'
Depth 86'

Additional products and services available. See page 4.

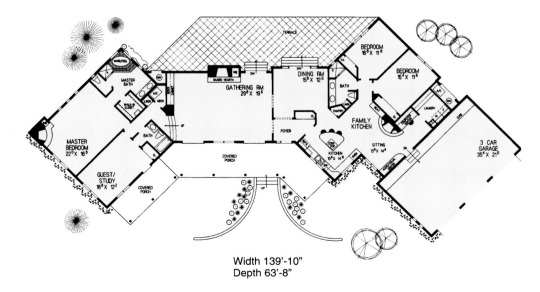

Width 139'-10"
Depth 63'-8"

DESIGN HH3405

Square Footage:	3,144

Split-Bedroom Planning For Extra Privacy

Pioneer living was never like this! Most of the original Santa Fe homes contained one or, at best, two bedrooms. This replica features four bedrooms (or three plus a study) that are split—master and guest room on one side and family bedrooms on the other.

A covered porch running the width of the facade leads to an entry foyer that connects to a huge gathering room with a fireplace and a formal dining room. The family kitchen allows special space for casual gatherings.

Built-ins abound throughout the house: bookshelves and cabinets, benches, audio-visual center, and computer center. A three-car garage is near the laundry and opens to the family room/family kitchen.

DESIGN HH2922

Square Footage:	3,505

Spanish Magnifico!

Drawn directly from classic Spanish styling that was so popular in the early West, this home hums to the strum of a softly played guitar. Designed for wide-open spaces, it is loaded with custom features. There's an enormous sunken gathering room which connects to a cozy study with a warming fireplace. The dining room is connected as well and opens onto a private eating terrace. The country-style kitchen contains an efficient work area, as well as space for relaxing in the morning room and sitting room. Two nice-sized bedrooms and a luxurious master suite round out the plan.

The master suite is of real interest. It features a fireplace with an alcove and a built-in sitting area; an enormous dressing room with walk-in closets for him and for her; a skylit whirlpool tub; and a private terrace.

Width 110'-7"
Depth 66'-11"

Additional products and services available. See page 4.

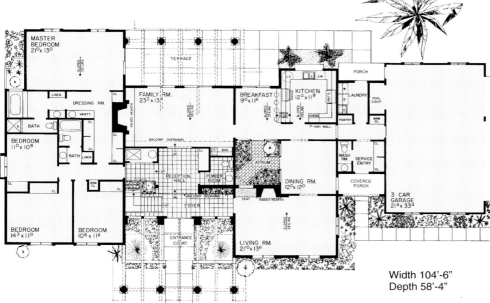

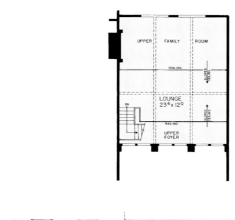

DESIGN HH2670

Square Footage:	3,058 sq. ft.
Lounge:	279 sq. ft.

Reception Hall And Atrium

Sunny climates demand lots of light-gathering areas and outdoor spaces. This home delivers with a covered entry foyer, enclosed atrium, long rear terrace and plenty of windows. The atrium has a built-in seat and will bring light to its adjacent rooms: living room, dining room and breakfast room. Beyond the foyer, sunken one step, is the tiled reception hall that includes a powder room. This area leads to the sleeping wing and up one step to the family room with a raised-hearth fireplace and sliding glass doors to the rear terrace. Overlooking the family room is a railed lounge which can be used for various activities.

Sleeping areas include a master suite and three family bedrooms. The master features a sloped ceiling, a dressing room with a vanity sink, a separate tub and shower and terrace access. Family bedrooms share a full bath.

Width 104'-6"
Depth 58'-4"

Additional products and services available. See page 4.

161

DESIGN HH2850

Main Level:	1,530 sq. ft.
Upper Level:	984 sq. ft.
Lower Level:	951 sq. ft.
Total:	3,465 sq. ft.

Multi-Level Spanish Design

You'd be hard pressed to find a better looking and better planned Spanish-style design. The main level has plenty going for it (it's got a nifty little pool): family room with raised-hearth fireplace and sloped ceiling, rear terrace, and a small porch leading into a mudroom.

Down below is just the right spot for kids and teens: a 300-square-foot activity room with a fireplace and access to a covered terrace out back. Here, too, are a discreetly placed study and extra bedroom.

The upper level features three bedrooms, including a master suite with a dressing room, a mammoth walk-in closet and a private balcony. The upper-level family bedrooms share a full bath with twin vanities. Both of these bedrooms have charming box windows.

Width 90'
Depth 56'

Additional products and services available. See page 4.

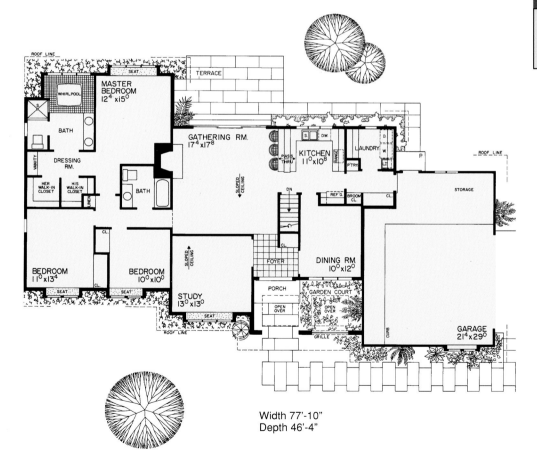

Width 77'-10"
Depth 46'-4"

DESIGN HH2875

Square Footage: 1,913

Cozy Plan With Special Features

Special details make a big difference in the livability of this one-story Spanish plan. An open garden court introduces the plan; each of the bedrooms has a unique window seat; and the garage has a huge storage area.

The kitchen contains a pass-through to a large gathering room with a fireplace and a sloped ceiling. Other features include a dining room, a laundry room and a study off the foyer. Barbecues and lazy Sundays with the paper happen on the rear terrace.

Three bedrooms, including a master bedroom with its own whirlpool, dominate the left side of the plan. Pampering elements in the master suite include a dressing room—with double walk-in closets—and a vanity area.

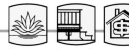

DESIGN HH2912

Square Footage: 1,864

Spanish-Styled Ranch

Beauty is not just skin deep. If a home is not livable, it is only just another pretty face. This low-slung design with smart Spanish styling incorporates careful zoning by room functions. All three bedrooms, including a master bedroom suite, are isolated at one end of the home. The master has features we'll bet you haven't even thought of: dressing room with vanity, huge walk-in closet, separate tub and shower, and access to the terrace.

Entry to a breakfast room and kitchen is possible through a mud room off the garage. That's good news when you're carrying groceries from car to kitchen or slipping off muddy shoes. The kitchen includes a snack bar and a convenient cooktop. There's also a nearby formal dining room.

A large rear gathering room features a sloped ceiling and a fireplace. A covered porch furthers living potential.

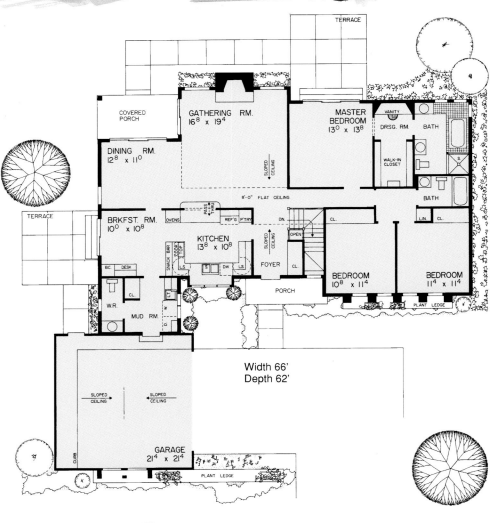

Width 66'
Depth 62'

Additional products and services available. See page 4.

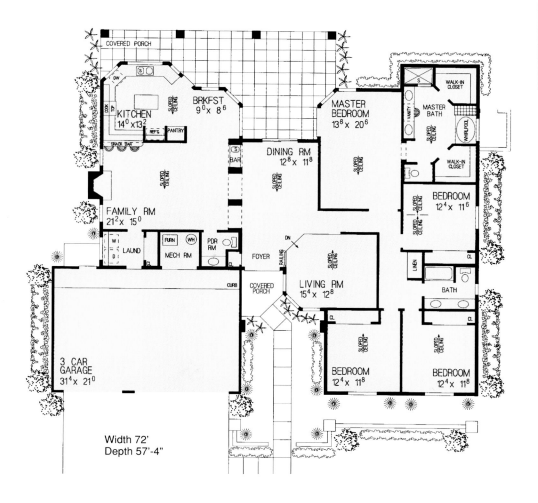

Width 72'
Depth 57'-4"

DESIGN HH3423

Square Footage: 2,577

Take A Walk In Western Boots

The Southwest holds special appeal—far-ranging landscapes, casual lifestyles, room to roam. This spacious design mimics all the elements of the Southwest that draws its ardent admirers. The exterior is classic stucco styling with a grand entry and lots of windows. Beyond the open entry foyer are the dining room and step-down living room with bay window. The informal family room has a sloped ceiling and cozy fireplace for cool desert evenings. Nearby is an efficient kitchen and breakfast room. A myriad of windows here creates a light-filled space for informal eating.

Four bedrooms are found to the right of the plan. The family bedrooms share a fine bath. The master suite is as large as you've dreamed and has double walk-in closets and a whirlpool tub. It also features access to the rear covered porch.

DESIGN HH2948

Square Footage:	1,830

Perfect For The Southwest. . . Or Anywhere!

Styled for Southwest living, this home is a good choice in just about any area. Among its many highlights are a gathering room/dining room combination that includes a fireplace, a snack-bar pass-through, and sliding glass doors to the rear terrace. The kitchen is uniquely shaped and sports a huge walk-in pantry plus a breakfast room with windows on the front covered porch.

Bedrooms include a master suite with a sloped ceiling, access to the rear terrace, a whirlpool spa and a double vanity. Two additional bedrooms share a full bath. One of these bedrooms makes a fine study and features built-in shelves for books as well as a built-in cabinet.

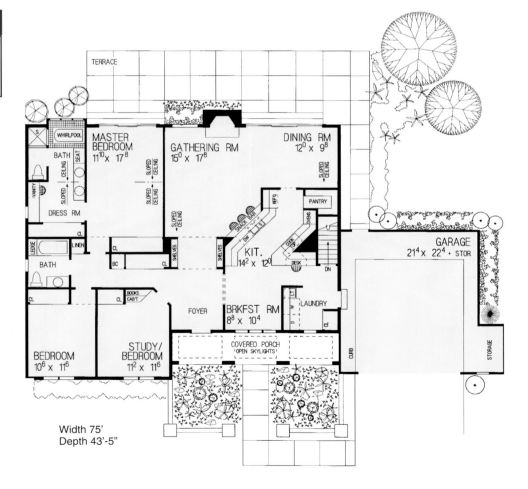

Width 75'
Depth 43'-5"

BALCONY

MASTER
BEDROOM
16⁰ X 9¹⁰

BEDRM.
12⁰ X 11⁰

BALCONY

BATH

WHIRL
POOL

MASTER
BATH

LIN.

LIN.

BEDRM.
11⁰ X 12⁸

SHOWER

WALK-IN CL.

DN

RAILING

UPPER
FOYER

WALK-IN
CLOSET

UPPER
LIVING RM.

COVERED PORCH

TERRACE

COVERED PORCH

FAMILY
ROOM
14⁰ X 15⁶

KITCHEN
BRKFST.
19⁰ X 12⁴

ISLAND

HEARTH

FIRE
PLACE

SHLVS

SHLVS

OVN.

REFS.

PTRY.

DINING
RM.
11⁰ X 12⁴

PWDR.
RM.

WORKSHOP

CL.

LNDRY

W.

D.

DN

FOYER

UP

CL.

LIVING ROOM
18⁴ X 13⁴

PORCH

GARAGE
20⁰ X 23⁸

BALCONY

Width 48'
Depth 58'

DESIGN HH3457

First Floor:	1,252 sq. ft.
Second Floor:	972 sq. ft.
Total:	2,224 sq. ft.

Grand Gables

Gables, gables everywhere—
and a cool stucco facade with
multi-paned windows add up to a
great exterior style. But be sure
to take a close look at the floor
plan. For family living, this
delightful three-bedroom plan
scores big. The family room
focuses on a fireplace and enjoys
direct access to a covered porch.
The breakfast room allows plenty of space for friendly meals—
the island kitchen remains open
to this room thus providing ease
in serving meals and, of course,
conversations with the cook.
From the two-car garage, a utility
area opens to the main-floor living areas.

Upstairs, the master suite
affords a quiet retreat with its
private bath. Here you'll find a
whirlpool tub set in a sunny
nook. A balcony further
enhances this bedroom. The two
secondary bedrooms share a full
hall bath with a double vanity.

DESIGN HH2905

First Floor:	1,342 sq. ft.
Second Floor:	619 sq. ft.
Total:	1,961 sq. ft.

The Beauty Of The Mix

Mixed materials—stone and vertical wood siding—go a long way to enhance the rustic transitional look of this two-story home. Great floor planning makes it very comfortable. Because the livability is in the rear, the home is shielded from street noise and each first-floor room (except the kitchen) has access to the rear terrace via sliding glass doors. This plan is also great for a narrow lot; its width is just under 50 feet.

The sleeping accommodations are also comfortable. There's a large master bedroom on the first floor with a walk-in closet and terrace access. Two family bedrooms are found on the second floor along with a full bath and balcony lounge.

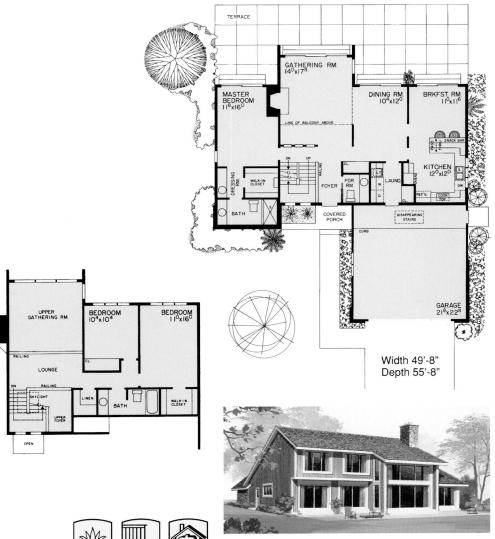

Width 49'-8"
Depth 55'-8"

Additional products and services available. See page 4.

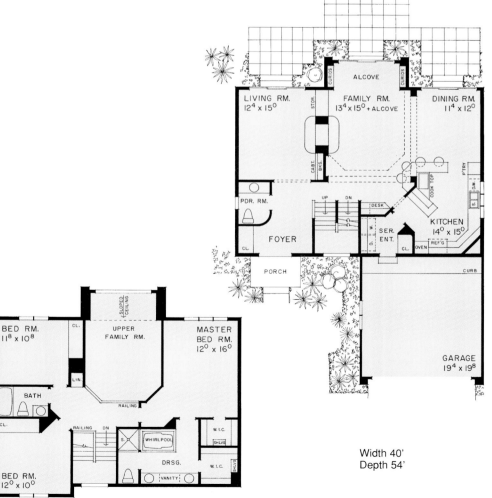

Width 40'
Depth 54'

DESIGN HH3562

First Floor:	1,182 sq. ft.
Second Floor:	927 sq. ft.
Total:	2,109 sq. ft.

Contemporary With A Touch Of Classic Tudor

Though transitional by design, the exterior of this home maintains a touch of Old World with a suggestion of Tudor details and jack arches. While its interesting detailing marks it as a beauty, its interior makes it a livable option for any family. Entry occurs through double doors to the left side of the plan. A powder room with a curved wall is handy to the entry. The formal living room shares a through-fireplace with the large family room. The dining room is adjoining and has a pass-through counter to the L-shaped kitchen. Special details on this floor include a wealth of sliding glass doors to the rear terrace and built-ins throughout.

Upstairs are three bedrooms with two full baths. The master contains two walk-in closets and a royal bath.

Additional products and services available. See page 4.

169

DESIGN HH3341

First Floor:	1,055 sq. ft.
Second Floor:	981 sq. ft.
Total:	2,036 sq. ft.

Tudor Transitional

Designed for the empty-nester, small family, or as a second home, this appealing Tudor adaptation holds a most livable floor plan. A lovely enclosed courtyard at the entry entices your green thumb. It leads to an entry that opens to first-floor living areas. Besides the 31' gathering room/dining room area and U-shaped kitchen with a nearby washroom, there is a front study with a large storage closet on the first floor.

Three bedrooms on the second floor meet sleeping needs without a hitch. Notice the walk-in closets and the master-bedroom balcony. The master suite also sports a handsome whirlpool tub, a separate shower with seat and a double-bowl vanity. Don't miss the built-in cabinets in the second-floor hall.

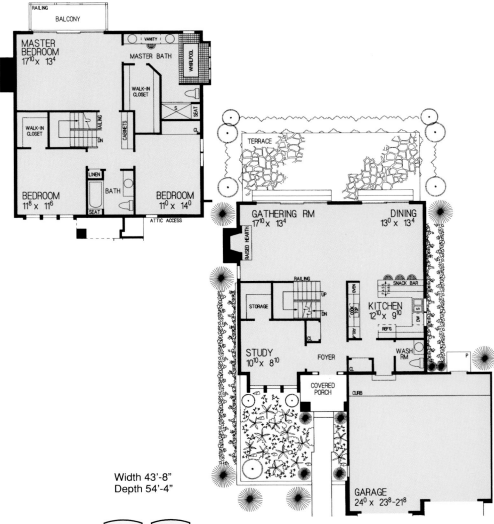

Width 43'-8"
Depth 54'-4"

This home, as shown in the photograph, may differ from the actual blueprints. For more detailed information, please check the floor plans carefully.

Photos by Andrew D, Lautman

Width 49'
Depth 54'-4"

Alternate kitchen/
dining room/ breakfast room plan

DESIGN HH2826

First Floor:	1,112 sq. ft.
Second Floor:	881 sq. ft.
Total:	1,993 sq. ft.

Best Transitional Design

Transitional design at its best! Easy-going and informal, this home meets all lifestyle demands. Notice the spacious gathering room which shares a through-fireplace with the quiet study; the formal and informal dining areas; and the roomy U-shaped kitchen. If you choose, you can build the alternate kitchen/dining room/breakfast room plan which puts the dining room to the front of the home. A captivating rear terrace and deck provide outdoor space that extends the gathering room, the dining room and the study.

Upstairs, the master bedroom suite is set off by a railed balcony lounge from family bedrooms. It contains a walk-in closet, a bath with double vanities and built-in cabinets and shelves.

Additional products and services available. See page 4.

171

DESIGN HH3563

First Floor:	1,023 sq. ft.
Second Floor:	866 sq. ft.
Total:	1,889 sq. ft.

Juliet's Balcony

Romantics take heart—you may see yourself reciting Shakespeare from the second-floor balcony of this wonderful home. The plan combines the best of contemporary and traditional styling. Its stucco exterior is enhanced by arched windows and a recessed arched entry plus a lovely balcony off the second-floor master bedroom. A walled entry court extends the living room on the outside. The double front doors open to a foyer with a hall closet and powder room. The service entrance is just to the right and accesses the two-car garage. The large living room adjoins directly to the dining room. The family room is set off behind the garage and features a sloped ceiling and fireplace.

Sleeping quarters consist of two secondary bedrooms with a shared bath and a generous master suite with a well-appointed bath.

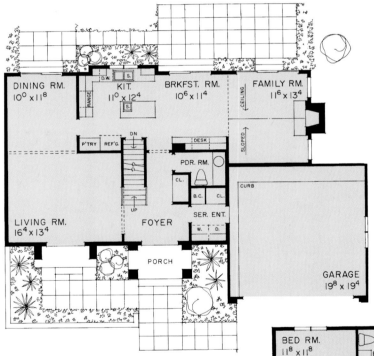

Width 52'-4"
Depth 34'-8"

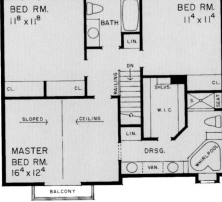

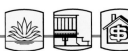

Width 63'-6"
Depth 51'-6"

DESIGN HH3326

First Floor:	1,595 sq. ft.
Second Floor:	1,112 sq. ft.
Total:	2,707 sq. ft.

A Small Slice Of The Southwest

A touch of Spanish flavor tickles your design appetite in this transitional two-story. The wraparound front porch, the varying roof planes highlighted by colorful tiles and the paneled front door flanked by twin glass panels all blend to create a grand first impression. Inside, there are two living areas: the formal front living room and the informal rear family room. The latter will serve effectively as the hub for family activities as it sports a raised-hearth fireplace, twin shelves and access to the entertainment patio.

Four bedrooms and two baths highlight the second floor. In the master suite you'll find a walk-in closet in addition to a long wardrobe closet. The master bath is outstanding with its twin lavatories, whirlpool, stall shower and compartmented toilet.

DESIGN HH3338

First Floor:	1,314 sq. ft.
Second Floor:	970 sq. ft.
Total:	2,284 sq. ft.

Brick Is Back

Brick is back by popular demand. It's not only a beautiful exterior choice, but works well on contemporary as well as traditional facades. You'll love what it does for this transitional design. For new parents or empty-nesters, this plan's master suite has an attached nursery or sitting room. A separate bath and dressing room are additional enhancements. Two family bedrooms and a full bath with a whirlpool round out the second floor.

Downstairs there are a formal living room and dining room and the more casual family room with a snack-bar eating area. A covered porch is accessible from the family room. The front study is near a handy powder room. Laundry facilities are found near the two-car garage.

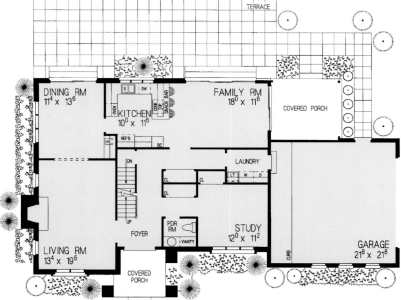

Width 65'-6"
Depth 35'

Additional products and services available. See page 4.

This home, as shown in the photograph, may differ from the actual blueprints. For more detailed information, please check the floor plans carefully.

Photo by Bob Greenspan

Width 53'
Depth 51'-8"

DESIGN HH2490

First Floor:	1,414 sq. ft.
Second Floor:	620 sq. ft.
Total:	2,034 sq. ft.

Picture Perfect

Be prepared for the flash of cameras and the oohs and ahs throughout the neighborhood when this home is built. It's model quality is worth bragging about. Split-bedroom planning makes the most of the floor plan. The master suite pampers with a fireplace and lavish bath that includes a whirlpool tub, separate shower, double-bowl vanity and walk-in closet. Additional bedrooms are upstairs. They share a full bath; one bedroom has a private balcony.

The living areas are open and have easy access to the rear terrace. A huge gathering room has a fireplace and is open to the formal dining room. A snack bar separates this area from the efficient kitchen. A laundry room and a washroom connect the main house to the two-car garage.

DESIGN HH3346

Square Footage:	2,032

Something Old Is New Again

Some styles are just too good to go away. The Tudor is one of those whose popularity remains—even when adapted as we've done in this rendition. By adding a thoroughly updated floor plan, the home takes on even more appeal. Though compact, there's plenty of living space: a large study with a fireplace, a huge gathering room with a wet bar and sloped ceiling, a fine formal dining room with an attached covered porch, and a handy breakfast room with an eating terrace.

The master bedroom has an attached bath with a whirlpool tub, twin walk-in closets and a compartmented toilet. The bedroom also features a private covered porch. One additional bedroom has its own bath. Note the two-car garage with storage space.

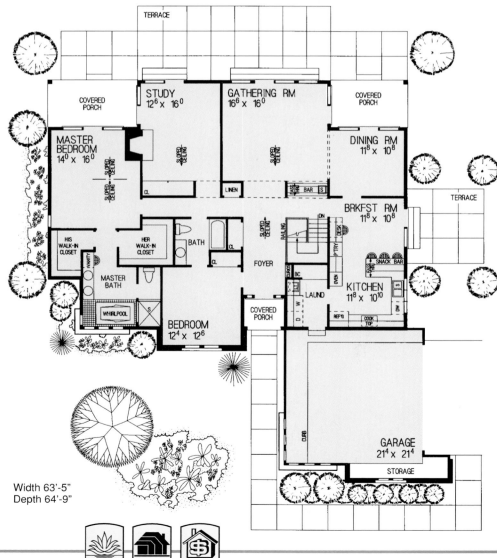

Width 63'-5"
Depth 64'-9"

Additional products and services available. See page 4.

This home, as shown in the photograph, may differ from the actual blueprints. For more detailed information, please check the floor plans carefully.

Photo by Andrew D. Lautman

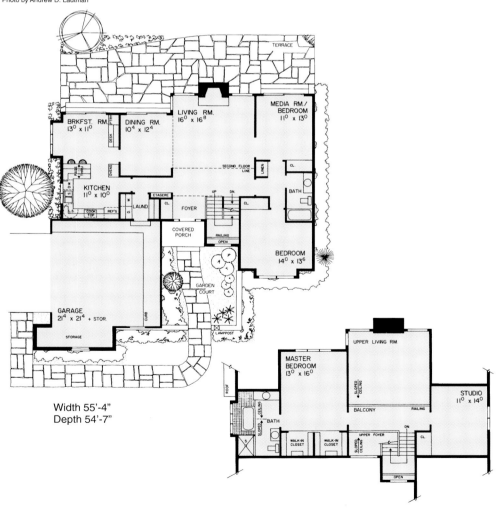

Width 55'-4"
Depth 54'-7"

DESIGN HH2927

First Floor:	1,425 sq. ft.
Second Floor:	704 sq. ft.
Total:	2,129 sq. ft.

Warm And Inviting, Inside And Out

This charming Early American adaptation with brick-and-board exterior almost resounds with the refrains of a fife and drumcorps. And it's just as warm on the inside! Features include a complete second-floor master bedroom suite, a balcony overlooking the living room and a studio. The master bathroom features a sloped ceiling and a luxury tub.

Look to the first floor for a convenient kitchen with a pass-through to a breakfast room. There's also a formal dining room just steps away in the rear of the house. An adjacent rear living room enjoys its own fireplace.

Other features include a rear media room or optional third bedroom. A downstairs bedroom enjoys an excellent front view.

DESIGN HH3454

Square Footage:	1,699

High Style For Modest Budgets

The cherished volume look in this design is achieved through the use of a high-pitched, hipped roof. The front gable with lower-projecting brick pillars acts a pleasing architectural feature. Another delightful architectural feature is the radial window above the front door; it brings an extra measure of natural light to the foyer. Through a pair of columns, an open living and dining room area creates a warm space for all sorts of living pursuits. The L-shaped kitchen has an island work surface, a practical planning desk and an informal eating space. The breakfast area has access to an outdoor living area—perfect for enjoying a morning cup of coffee.

Sleeping arrangements are emphasized by the master suite with its tray ceiling and sliding glass doors to the yard.

Width 52'-8"
Depth 49'

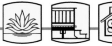

Additional products and services available. See page 4.

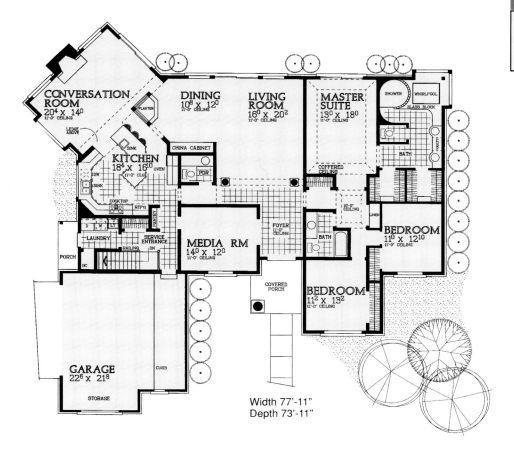

Width 77'-11"
Depth 73'-11"

DESIGN HH3327

Square Footage:	2,881

Traditional Home With Modern Moxie

The high, massive hipped roof of this home creates an imposing facade while varying roof planes and projecting gables enhance appeal. A central, high-ceilinged foyer routes traffic efficiently to the sleeping, formal and informal zones of the house. Note the sliding glass doors that provide access to outdoor living facilities. A built-in china cabinet and planter unit are fine decor features in the dining room. In the angular kitchen, a high ceiling and efficient work patterning set the pace. The conversation room may act as a multi-purpose room. For TV time, a media room caters to audio-visual buffs.

Sleeping quarters include a spacious master bedroom. An abundance of wall space for effective and flexible furniture arrangement further characterizes the room. Two sizable bedrooms serve the children or guests.

DESIGN HH3468

First Floor:	1,618 sq. ft.
Second Floor:	510 sq. ft.
Total:	2,128 sq. ft.

Farmhouse Of The Future

Old MacDonald never had it so good: a wraparound porch, dormer windows, attached garage, and a high, volume roof. And that's just on the outside. Inside, the great room sports a fireplace and lots of natural light. Grab a snack at the kitchen island/snack bar or the breakfast room. The vaulted foyer grandly introduces the dining room and parlor.

The master bedroom is much more than Old Mac could have dreamed. Do a careful study and you'll see a tray ceiling, a fireplace, a luxury bath and a walk-in closet. Stairs lead up to a quaint loft/bedroom, a full bath and an additional bedroom with a full bath. Designated storage space makes this one a winner.

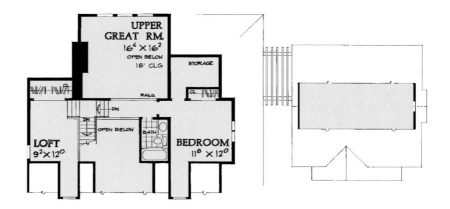

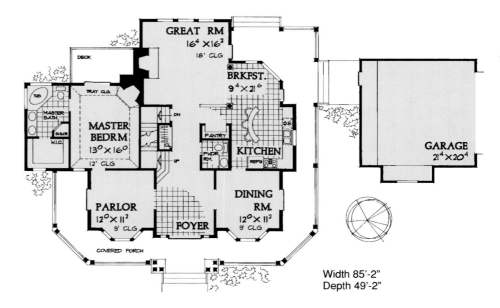

Width 85'-2"
Depth 49'-2"

Additional products and services available. See page 4.

DESIGN HH3438

First Floor:	1,489 sq. ft.
Second Floor:	741 sq. ft.
Total:	2,230 sq. ft.

Town Or Country Home

A unique farmhouse plan which provides a grand floor plan, this home is comfortable in country or suburban settings. Formal entertaining areas share first-floor space with family gathering rooms and work and service areas. The master suite is also on this floor for convenience and privacy.

Upstairs is a guest bedroom, private bath and loft area that makes a perfect studio. Special features make this a great place to come home to: built-in dressers, a private deck and porches, a three-way fireplace, a built-in table, and loads of storage.

Width 59'
Depth 30'

Additional products and services available. See page 4.

DESIGN HH3446

First Floor:	1,532 sq. ft.
Second Floor:	1,200 sq. ft.
Total:	2,732 sq. ft.

Large-Family Livability

The massive twin chimneys of this house impress with their decorative caps and sculptured patterns. The recessed front entrance has appealing twin columns that form a covered porch. The spacious, well-lighted foyer with a high ceiling looks up to a dramatic balcony. This foyer also efficiently routes traffic to all areas of the house.

To the left is the formal living room with a fireplace and, to the rear is the dining room—both function well together through the employment of an open, columned room divider. A quiet study sits off to the right. You may decide to use it as a media room, sewing room or guest room. The kitchen remains spacious and delights with its irregular shape and well-appointed work areas.

Upstairs, three bedrooms serve the children while the master suite is more secluded and features an outstanding bath.

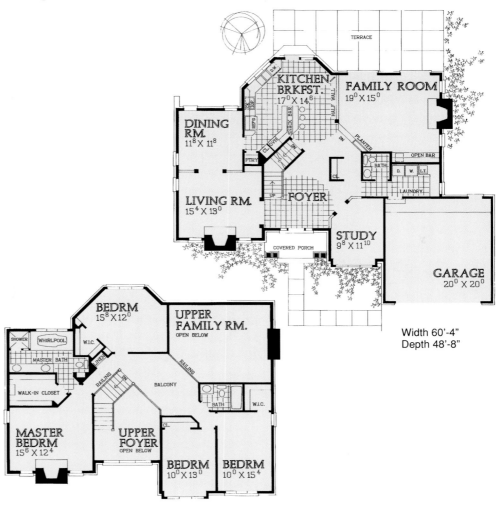

Width 60'-4"
Depth 48'-8"

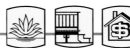

    Additional products and services available. See page 4.

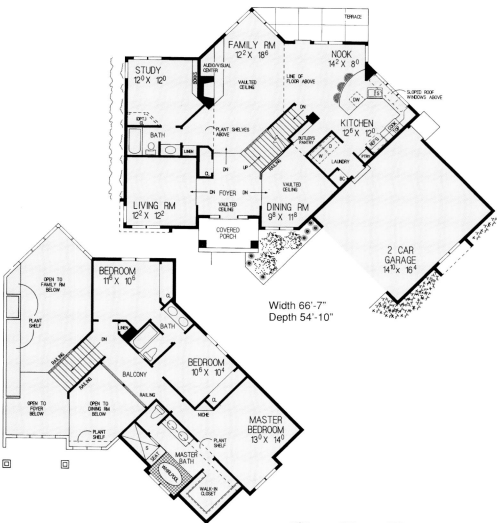

Width 66'-7"
Depth 54'-10"

DESIGN HH3439

First Floor:	1,424 sq. ft.
Second Floor:	995 sq. ft.
Total:	2,419 sq. ft.

Great From All Angles

Featuring a facade of wood and window glass, this home makes a striking first impression. Its floor plan is equally as splendid. Formal living and dining areas flank the entry foyer—both are sunken two steps down. Also sunken from the foyer is the family room with an attached breakfast nook. A fireplace in this area sits adjacent to a built-in audio-visual center. A nearby study with an adjacent full bath doubles as a guest room.

Upstairs are three bedrooms including a master suite with a whirlpool spa and a walk-in closet. Plant shelves adorn the entire floor plan.

DESIGN HH3572

First Floor:	2,778 sq. ft.
Second Floor:	841 sq. ft.
Total:	3,619 sq. ft.

Talk Of The Town

For a change of pace, this California transitional design offers the finest in modern livability. The tiled foyer presents an open floor plan that affords elegance and practicality. The large living room and library will make impressive entertaining spaces while the family room, with its oversized fireplace, provides a comfortable atmosphere for casual living. The three-car garage opens to a utility area off the kitchen and breakfast room.

Located on the first floor for privacy, the master bedroom boasts a curved wall of glass and a pampering bath with a whirlpool tub, separate vanities and a walk-in closet. Upstairs, three bedrooms include one with a balcony and one with a private bath.

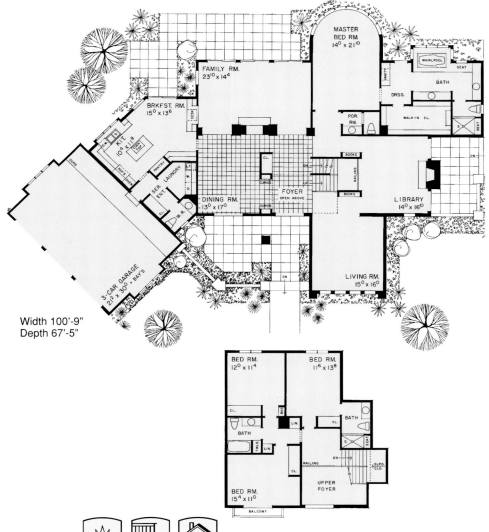

Width 100'-9"
Depth 67'-5"

Additional products and services available. See page 4.

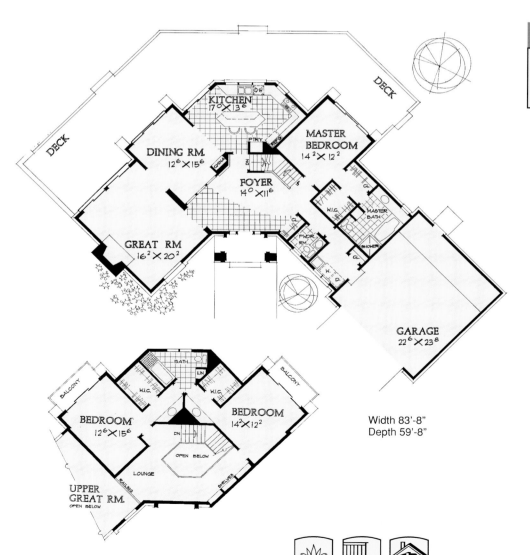

DECK

KITCHEN
17⁰×13⁶

MASTER
BEDROOM
14²×12²

DINING RM.
12⁶×15⁶

DECK

FOYER
14⁰×11⁶

W.I.C.

MASTER
BATH

SHOWER

GREAT RM
16²×20²

PWDR.
RM.

W.D.

GARAGE
22⁶×23⁸

BALCONY

BATH

LIN.

W.I.C.

W.I.C.

BALCONY

BEDROOM
12⁶×15⁶

BEDROOM
14²×12²

DN

OPEN BELOW

LOUNGE

UPPER
GREAT RM.
OPEN BELOW

RAILING

SHELVES

Width 83'-8"
Depth 59'-8"

DESIGN HH3310

First Floor:	1,668 sq. ft.
Second Floor:	905 sq. ft.
Total:	2,573 sq. ft.

Elegance On A Small Scale

In Japan, building sites are small. Yet the Japanese love to build estate-sized homes. The solution—keep all the style of estate, but scale it down. That's exactly what we've done with this plan.

The open foyer creates a rich atmosphere. To the left you'll find a great room with raised brick hearth and sliding glass doors that lead out onto a wrap-around deck. The kitchen heads up the first floor and includes a snack bar and deck access. The master bedroom, with its own deck access and bath with whirlpool, is located on the first floor for privacy.

Upstairs, two family bedrooms, both with balconies and walk-in closets, share a full bath. Don't overlook the lounge and elliptical window that give the second floor added charisma.

DESIGN HH3366

Main Level:	1,638 sq. ft.
Upper Level:	650 sq. ft.
Lower Level:	934 sq. ft.
Total:	3,222 sq. ft.

Walk-Out Basement

There is much more to this design than meets the eye. While it may look like a 1½-story plan, bonus recreation and hobby space in the walk-out basement adds almost 1,000 square feet. The first floor holds living and dining areas as well as the master bedroom suite.

Two family bedrooms on the second floor are connected by a balcony that overlooks the gathering room below. Notice the covered porch beyond the breakfast and dining rooms.

Width 57'
Depth 51'-8"

Additional products and services available. See page 4.

This home, as shown in the photograph, may differ from the actual blueprints. For more detailed information, please check the floor plans carefully.

Photo by Laszlo Regos

Width 44'
Depth 32'

DESIGN HH2488

First Floor:	1,113 sq. ft.
Second Floor:	543 sq. ft.
Total:	1,656 sq. ft.

Large Corner Hearth

For a lakeside retreat or as a retirement haven, this charming design offers the best in livability. Its rustic exterior is highlighted by vertical wood siding and a deep roof overhang, plus lots of large windows to take in the sights. The gathering room with a corner fireplace, the U-shaped kitchen with an attached dining room, the lovely deck and the first-floor master suite make a complete and comfortable living space. A deck just off the dining room allows space for outdoor dining and relaxing.

Two bedrooms with a full bath and a balcony lounge upstairs complement the design and provide sleeping accommodations for family and guests. Note the ample attic storage area and additional storage in the master bath.

DESIGN HH2871

| Square Footage: | 1,824 |

Country Contemporary

For a contemporary with a rustic touch, this high-roofed one-story is hard to beat. Stone, wood and glass combine for a textured look on the outside. A rear greenhouse, the kitchen bay window and the front terrace with exposed beams are added elements. Living areas are directly connected to the entry foyer. Working areas include a gourmet kitchen with a break-fast room and a handy mud room with a wash area. The living room connects directly to the dining room and has a sloped ceiling and fireplace.

The bedrooms dominate the left side of the plan. The master features a walk-in closet and terrace access. Two family bedrooms share a full bath.

Width 80'-4"'
Depth 43'

Additional products and services available. See page 4.

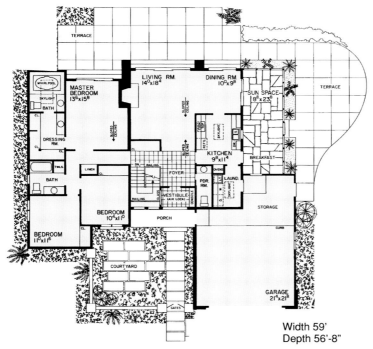

Width 59'
Depth 56'-8"

DESIGN HH2902

Square Footage:	1,632

Super Solar Design

A sun space highlights this passive solar design. It features access from the kitchen, the dining room and the garage. Three skylights highlight the interior—one in the kitchen, laundry and master bath. An air-locked vestibule helps this design's energy efficiency.

Interior livability is excellent. The living/dining room rises with a sloped ceiling and enjoys a fireplace and two sets of sliding glass doors to the terrace.

Three bedrooms are in the sleeping wing. The master bedroom has a private bath with a luxurious whirlpool tub.

DESIGN HH2864

Square Footage: 1,387

Narrow-Lot Plan

Projecting the garage to the front of a house is very economical in two ways. One, it reduces the required lot size, and two, it will protect the interior from street noise. Many other characteristics of this design deserve mention, too. The entry leads to various areas of the house. The interior kitchen has a breakfast room and a snack bar on the gathering-room side. The adjacent study contains a wet bar and can serve as a guest bedroom if needed. Sliding glass doors in three rooms—the dining room, the study and the master bedroom—open to the terrace.

The two main bedrooms include a family bedroom with a full bath and skylight, and the master bedroom. The master is all you might ever want in a private retreat. It contains a dressing room and a full bath with a skylight. It also features sloped ceilings.

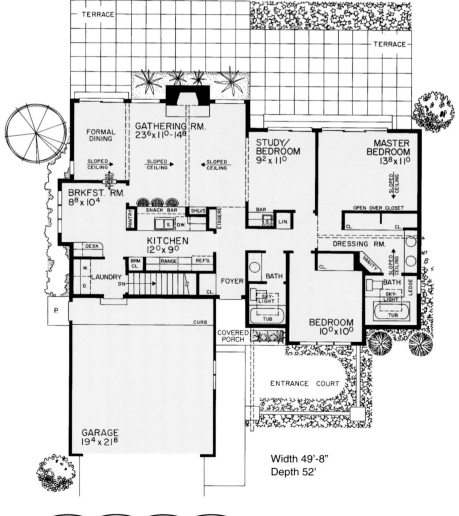

Width 49'-8"
Depth 52'

Additional products and services available. See page 4.

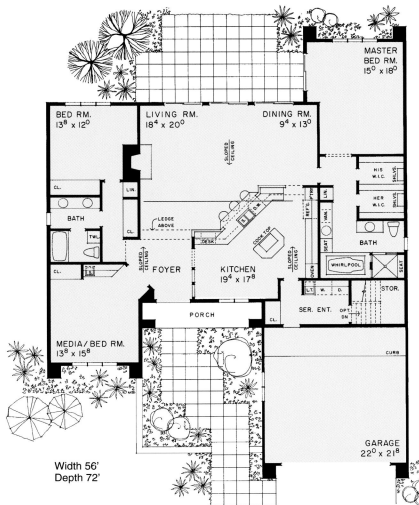

Width 56'
Depth 72'

DESIGN HH3560

Square Footage: 2,189

Simply Good Looking

Simplicity is the key to the stylish good looks of this home's facade. A walled garden entry and large window areas appeal to outdoor enthusiasts. Inside, the kitchen forms the hub of the plan. It opens directly off the foyer and contains an island counter and a work counter with eating space on the living area side. A sloped ceiling, a fireplace and sliding glass doors to a rear terrace are highlights in the living area.

The master bedroom also sports sliding glass doors to the terrace. Its dressing area is enhanced with double walk-in closets and lavatories. A whirlpool tub and seated shower are additional amenities. Two family bedrooms are found on the opposite side of the house. They share a full bath with twin lavatories.

Photos by Bob Greenspan

DESIGN HH2920

First Floor:	3,067 sq. ft.
Second Floor:	648 sq. ft.
Total:	3,715 sq. ft.

Best-Selling Contemporary

It must be something about its clean, bold lines. Or perhaps it's the way the floor plan lays out. Or maybe it's some indecipherable quality that just can't be defined. Whatever it is, it makes this plan one of our most popular contemporaries ever.

A fireplace opens up to both the living room and country kitchen. The first-floor master bedroom is away from the traffic of the house and features a dressing/exercise room, a whirlpool tub and shower and a spacious walk-in closet. Two more bedrooms and a full bath are on the second floor. The cheerful sun room adds 296 square feet to the total.

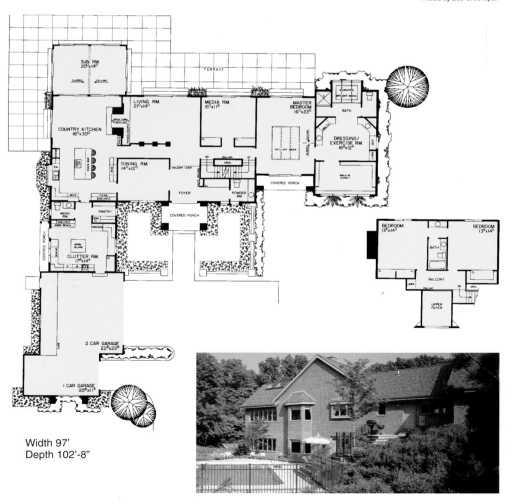

Width 97'
Depth 102'-8"

Additional products and services available. See page 4.

Width 81'-4"
Depth 78'

DESIGN HH2915

Square Footage: 2,758

The Smaller Version

If you really like the look of one-story contemporary homes but find that many are just too big, take a close look at this one. It has nearly everything going for it. Start with the 340-square-foot-country kitchen, which sports a fireplace, snack bar and greenhouse next door. Move to the media room, where there's a wall of built-ins, and then on to the combination living room/dining area (note the sloped ceiling, raised-hearth fireplace and doors leading to the terrace in back).

Also check out both the king-sized master suite with His and Hers walk-ins and whirlpool made for two, and all the extra storage space.

DESIGN HH2608

Main Level:	728 sq. ft.
Upper Level:	874 sq. ft.
Lower Level:	310 sq. ft.
Total:	1,912 sq. ft.

Two Terraces

Tri-level living works to great advantage in this rustic design. Not only can you enjoy the three levels but there is also a fourth basement level for bulk storage and, perhaps, a shop area. The interior livability is outstanding. The main level has an L-shaped formal living/dining area with a fireplace in the living room, sliding glass doors in the dining room leading to the upper terrace, a U-shaped kitchen and an informal eating area. Down a few steps to the lower level is the family room with another fireplace and sliding doors to the lower terrace, a washroom and a laundry.

The upper level houses all of the bedrooms including three family bedrooms, a bath and the master suite. The master sports a walk-in closet and a private balcony.

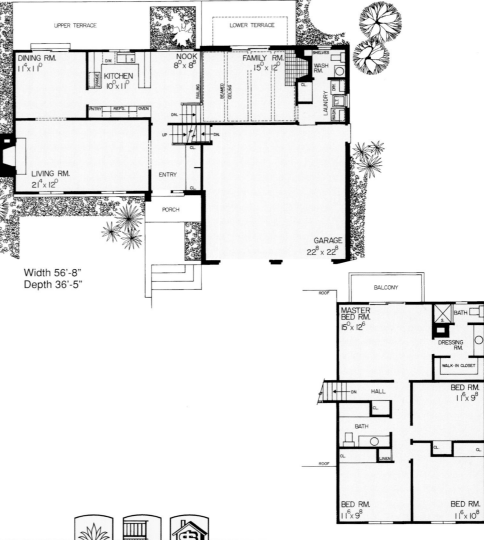

Additional products and services available. See page 4.

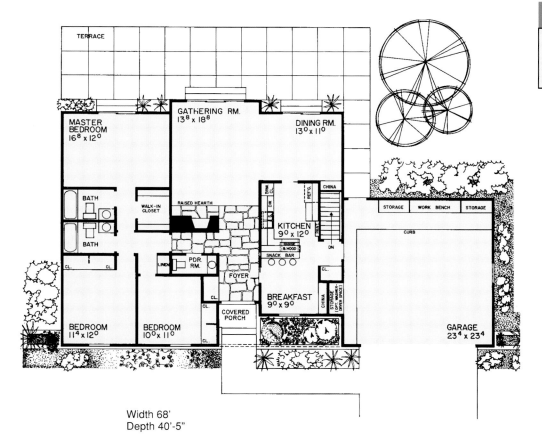

TERRACE

MASTER
BEDROOM
16⁸ x 12⁰

GATHERING RM.
13⁸ x 18⁸

DINING RM.
13⁰ x 11⁰

BATH

WALK-IN
CLOSET

RAISED HEARTH

CHINA

STORAGE WORK BENCH STORAGE

CURB

BATH

KITCHEN
9⁰ x 12⁰

CL.   CL.

PDR.
RM.

LINEN

SNACK BAR

FOYER

DN

BEDROOM
11⁴ x 12⁰

BEDROOM
10⁰ x 11⁰

COVERED
PORCH

BREAKFAST
9⁰ x 9⁰

CHINA

STORAGE

GARAGE
23⁴ x 23⁴

Width 68'
Depth 40'-5"

DESIGN HH2671

Square Footage: 1,589

Rustic Ranch

Built for big-sky country, this rustic ranch design is THE choice for Western style. Its exterior features vertical wood siding, a deep roof overhang and a long, low profile. The entry foyer is floored with flagstone and leads to other areas of the home. The living area, consisting of a gathering room and a dining room, also enjoys access to the terrace. The work center is efficiently planned and includes a kitchen with a snack bar, the breakfast room with a built-in china cabinet and stairs to the basement.

The sleeping area features three bedrooms. The master bedroom utilizes sliding glass doors to the rear terrace.

The plan is enhanced by such special amenities as a raised-hearth fireplace and a walk-in closet in the master bedroom.

DESIGN HH2818

Square Footage:	1,566

Optional Basement

One outstanding feature of contemporary homes is their simple, clean lines. This flawless contemporary design has that feature plus a recessed front entry with a covered porch. The rear gathering room has a sloped ceiling, a raised-hearth fireplace, sliding glass doors to the terrace and a snack bar with a pass-through to the kitchen. The formal dining room is also convenient to the kitchen. A laundry with a pantry and a broom closet connects the main house to the garage.

Three bedrooms are found on the left side of the plan. Family bedrooms share a full bath. The master bedroom has a private bath and terrace access. This plan includes details for the construction of an optional basement.

Optional Basement Plan

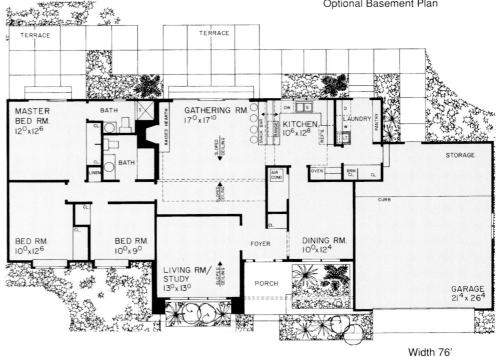

Width 76'
Depth 34'-4"

Additional products and services available. See page 4.

DESIGN HH3368

Square Footage:	2,720

Rooflines Add To Style

Rooflines are the key to the interesting exterior of this design. Their configuration allows for sloped ceilings in the gathering room and large foyer. But there's much more to appreciate in the living areas: a wet bar between the gathering room and media room (use the media room as an extra bedroom if needed), a fireplace in the gathering room, a laundry room and a huge walk-in closet at the service entrance. The kitchen is L-shaped and includes a large conversation bay and island cooktop. A large terrace to the rear is accessed from the gathering room, dining room and conversation bay.

The master bedroom suite has a huge walk-in closet, a garden whirlpool and a separate shower. Two family bedrooms share a full bath.

Width 78'
Depth 54'-4"

DESIGN HH2781

First Floor:	2,132 sq. ft.
Second Floor:	1,156 sq. ft.
Total:	3,288 sq. ft.

Window Wonderland

On a clear day, you can see forever from almost any room in this eye-catching contemporary design. Vertical siding and a long shed roof (containing a skylight into the upper-story lounge) hold a special appeal. The floor plan is a perfect complement. Of particular interest is the huge sunken gathering room that features a fireplace and balcony overlook from the upper lounge. The front kitchen features an island range, an adjacent breakfast nook and a pass-through to a formal dining room. The master suite offers a spacious walk-in closet and dressing room. The side terrace can be reached from the master suite, the gathering room and the study.

The second floor contains three bedrooms and storage space galore. The center lounge offers a sloped ceiling and skylight.

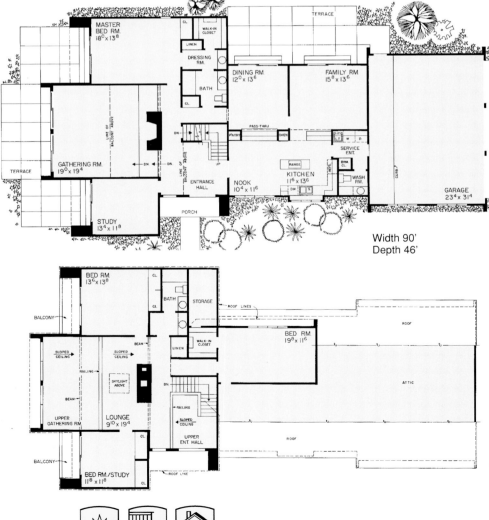

Width 90'
Depth 46'

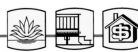

Additional products and services available. See page 4.

This home, as shown in the photograph, may differ from the actual blueprints. For more detailed information, please check the floor plans carefully.

Photos by Andrew D. Lautman

UPPER GREAT RM.

RAILING

LOUNGE / HOBBIES
16⁰ x 9²

CL.

CL.

DN   RAILING

UPPER FOYER

STOR. / BATH

RAILING

BALCONY

LOUNGE / GUEST RM. / GRANDCHILDREN'S RM.
16⁰ x 19²

CL.

CL.

DN   RAILING

UPPER FOYER

BATH

RAILING

Alternate Second Floor

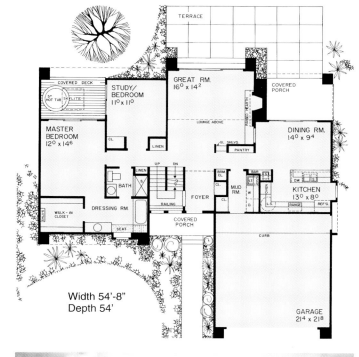

TERRACE

COVERED DECK

5" HOT TUB   SKYLITE

STUDY / BEDROOM
11⁰ x 11⁰

GREAT RM.
16⁰ x 14²

COVERED PORCH

MASTER BEDROOM
12⁰ x 14⁶

CL.

LINEN

LOUNGE ABOVE

DINING RM.
14⁰ x 9⁴

GL. SHLVS.

PANTRY

BATH

LINEN   UP DN

BRM CL.

BAR

KITCHEN
13⁰ x 8⁰

DW

WALK-IN CLOSET

DRESSING RM.

SEAT

RAILING

FOYER

MUD RM.

OVEN

RANGE   REF'G

COVERED PORCH

CURB

GARAGE
21⁴ x 21⁸

Width 54'-8"
Depth 54'

DESIGN HH2822

First Floor:	1,363 sq. ft.
Second Floor:	351 sq. ft.
Total:	1,714 sq. ft.

Excellent Empty-Nester

Flexibility and livability are the hallmarks of this affordable plan, which is tailor-made for small families and empty-nesters. Basically a one-level design with second-floor possibilities, the room upstairs (see alternate layouts) can be nearly anything you want it to be: lounge, guest room, play room for the kids or grand-children, partitioned or open.

Downstairs, a little space goes a long way. In less than 1,400 square feet is the great room with a fireplace, the separate dining room with an adjacent porch, the study/bedroom and the sizable master suite. Look for distinctive features such as the covered porch off the dining room, the covered deck with hot-tub space off the master suite, the mud room with a closet, and the seat in the dressing room. A two-car garage can open to the front or to the side.

DESIGN HH2711

First Floor:	975 sq. ft.
Second Floor:	1,024 sq. ft.
Total:	1,999 sq. ft.

Rustic Contemporary

A woodsy plan, yet it has clean contemporary lines. The vertical siding is purely modern, but keeping it natural and adding a brick fireplace adds a provincial touch. But there's nothing rustic about the floor plan. It keeps pace with today's lifestyles. There's a bedroom for everyone with a complete master suite with a private balcony plus two more bedrooms upstairs.

The first floor has a study with a storage closet. A convenient snack bar is located between the kitchen and the dining room. The kitchen offers many built-in appliances. The gathering room—with a raised-hearth fireplace—and dining room combination measures 31 feet wide. Be sure to check out the rear terrace which runs the full width of the house.

Width 40'-4"
Depth 52'

Additional products and services available. See page 4.

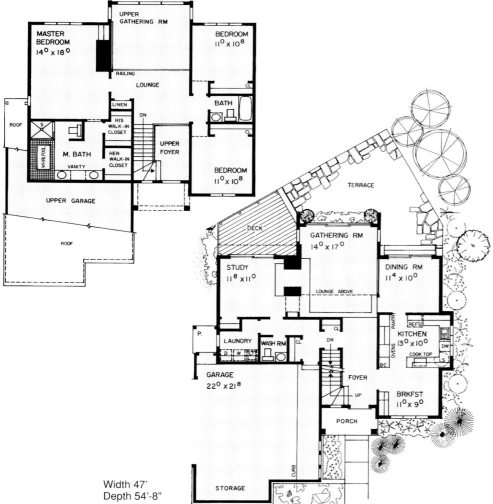

MASTER BEDROOM 14⁰ x 18⁰

UPPER GATHERING RM

BEDROOM 11⁰ x 10⁸

RAILING

LOUNGE

ROOF

LINEN

HIS WALK-IN CLOSET

DN

BATH

CL

M. BATH

HER WALK-IN CLOSET

UPPER FOYER

VANITY

BEDROOM 11⁰ x 10⁸

UPPER GARAGE

ROOF

TERRACE

DECK

GATHERING RM 14⁰ x 17⁰

STUDY 11⁸ x 11⁰

DINING RM 11⁴ x 10⁰

LOUNGE ABOVE

PANTRY

REF

KITCHEN 13⁰ x 10⁰

OVENS

COOK TOP

DW

S

LAUNDRY

WASH RM

CL

DN

BC

GARAGE 22⁰ x 21⁸

FOYER

UP

BRKFST 11⁰ x 9⁰

PORCH

Width 47'
Depth 54'-8"

STORAGE

CURB

DESIGN HH3352

First Floor:	1,148 sq. ft.
Second Floor:	1,010 sq. ft.
Total:	2,158 sq. ft.

Contemporary Mix

In most instances, a mix of exterior materials heralds a purely traditional design. However, in this rustic two-story, we've managed to use both stone and vertical wood siding to create a truly unique contemporary. Open spaces characterize its interior plan. The first floor is dedicated to casual living—sunken gathering room with pass-through fireplace to a study, nearby dining room, kitchen with attached breakfast area. All rear living areas have access through sliding glass doors to an outdoor deck or terrace.

Upstairs rooms include a magnificent master suite with a garden whirlpool tub, a balcony lounge area and two family bedrooms with a full bath between.

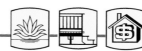

Additional products and services available. See page 4.

201

DESIGN HH3565

First Floor:	1,248 sq. ft.
Second Floor:	1,012 sq. ft.
Total:	2,260 sq. ft.

Simple Yet Elegant

Though tending toward European details, this plan evolved into a modern design. The exterior is simple yet elegant, while interior floor planning is thorough yet efficient. The formal living and dining rooms are to the left of the home, separated by columns. The living room features a wall of windows and a fireplace. The kitchen with an island cooktop is adjacent to the large family room with terrace access. A study with additional terrace access completes the first floor.

The master bedroom features a balcony and a spectacular bath with a whirlpool tub, a shower with seat, separate vanities and a walk-in closet. Two family bedrooms share access to a full bath. Also notice the three-car garage.

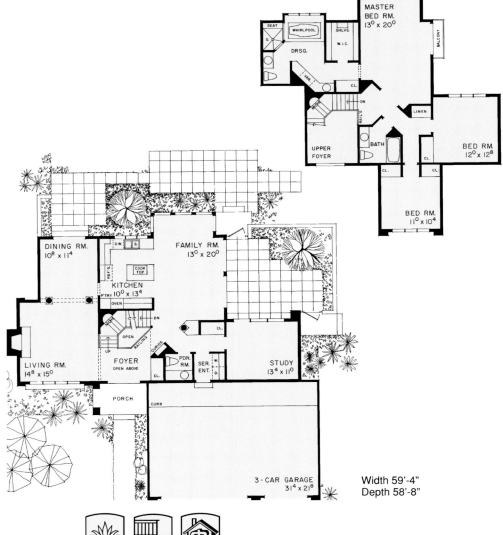

Width 59'-4"
Depth 58'-8"

Additional products and services available. See page 4.

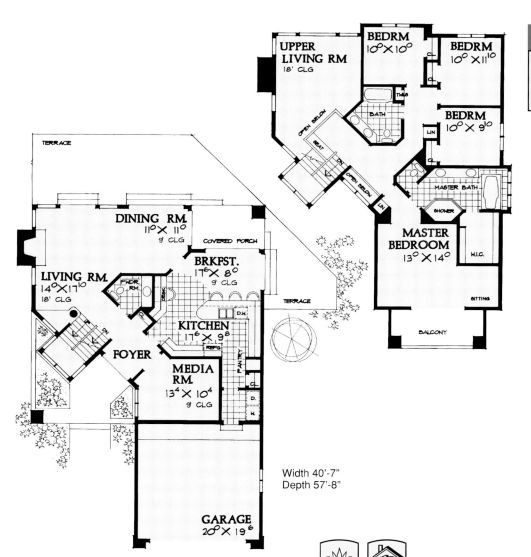

UPPER LIVING RM
18' CLG

BEDRM
10⁰ X 10⁰

BEDRM
10⁰ X 11¹⁰

BEDRM
10⁰ X 9¹⁰

BATH

MASTER BATH

SHOWER

MASTER BEDROOM
13⁰ X 14⁰

W.I.C.

SITTING

BALCONY

TERRACE

DINING RM
11⁰ X 11⁰
9' CLG

COVERED PORCH

BRKFST.
17⁶ X 8⁰
9' CLG

LIVING RM
14⁰ X 17¹⁰
18' CLG

KITCHEN
17⁶ X 9⁸

FOYER

MEDIA RM
13⁴ X 10⁴
9' CLG

TERRACE

GARAGE
20⁰ X 19⁶

Width 40'-7"
Depth 57'-8"

DESIGN HH3456

First Floor:	1,130 sq. ft.
Second Floor:	1,189 sq. ft.
Total:	2,319 sq. ft.

The Angle On Volume

Hipped roofs are not common on contemporary homes. But this one works well with the high volume look created by large, two-story windows. The angled entry opens to a media room on the right and formal living and dining rooms on the left. Remaining exposed to the dining room, the living room contains a marbled hearth and sliding glass doors to the back terrace. A covered porch, accessed from both the dining and breakfast rooms, adds outdoor dining possibilities. The kitchen utilizes a built-in desk and a snack-bar pass-through to the breakfast area. A large pantry and closet lead to the laundry near the garage.

Upstairs, four bedrooms accommodate the large family well. In the master suite, amenities such as a sitting area and a balcony add definition. The master bath sports a whirlpool and a walk-in closet.

DESIGN HH3409

First Floor:	1,481 sq. ft.
Second Floor:	1,287 sq. ft.
Total:	2,768 sq. ft.

Southwestern Style With A Twist Of Contemporary

Stucco and a tiled roof are clear signals that this two-story home is Southwestern by nature. But its other elements shout contemporary all the way. Glass block walls and a foyer with a barrel-vaulted ceiling create an interesting exterior. Covered porches to the front and rear provide for excellent indoor/outdoor living relationships.

Inside, a large planter and through-fireplace enhance the living room and family room. A desk, eating area and a snack bar are special features in the kitchen. The master suite is highlighted by a large walk-in closet, a bath with a separate shower and tub and a private deck. Three additional bedrooms upstairs share a full bath.

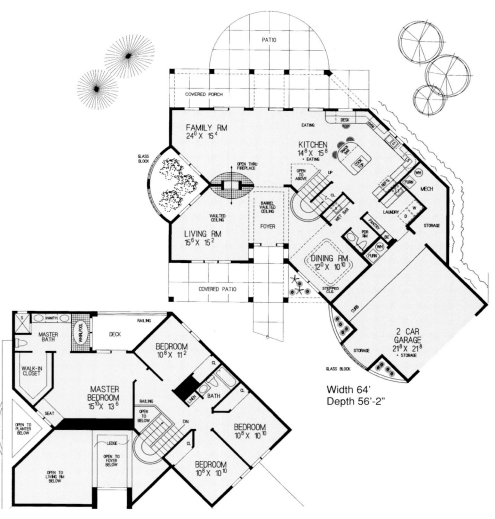

Width 64'
Depth 56'-2"

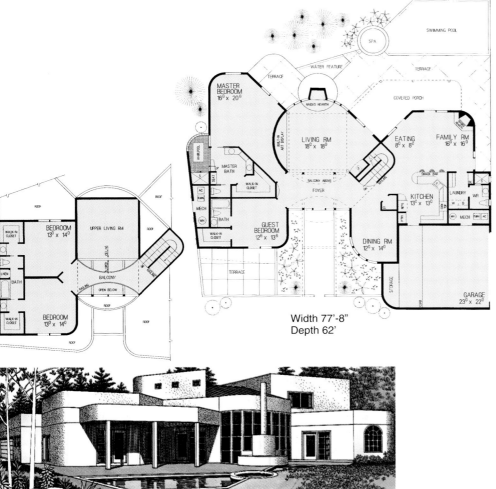

Width 77'-8"
Depth 62'

DESIGN HH3403

First Floor:	2,240 sq. ft.
Second Floor:	660 sq. ft.
Total:	2,900 sq. ft.

California Contemporary

Fast cars, wind-swept beaches, sunny summer days and lazy, languid nights. There's something alluring about the California lifestyle—captured perfectly in this ultra-modern contemporary. There is no end to the distinctive features in its floor plan. Formal living areas are concentrated in the center of the plan—the kitchen and family room function well together as an informal living area. The optional guest bedroom or den and the master bedroom are located to the left of the plan. The master is as sumptuous as you might imagine: private terrace, walk-in closet, whirlpool tub and dual vanities.

The second floor holds two bedrooms and a full bath. Each has a walk-in closet and a private vanity. The curved balcony on the second floor overlooks the entry and the living room.

DESIGN HH3362

First Floor:	1,305 sq. ft.
Second Floor:	862 sq. ft.
Lower Level:	1,140 sq. ft.
Total:	3,307 sq. ft.

Walk-Out Basement Level

You'd never guess by looking at just the front of this home that a walk-out basement adds over 1,000 square feet to its total livability. It actually provides space for a huge activities room with a fireplace, a wet bar and a third bedroom with a bath.

The main level holds the gathering room and dining room—a space over 37' in width. A pass-through snack bar to the island kitchen is handy for more casual meals. A tucked-away media room has built-ins to hold a TV, VCR and stereo equipment.

On the second floor are two bedrooms with two full baths. The master bedroom has a private balcony, His and Hers walk-in closets and twin vanities. The balcony area overlooks the gathering room below and also the entry foyer.

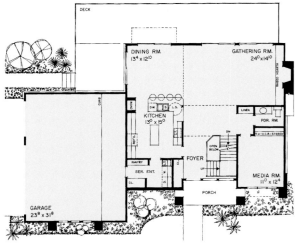

Width 62'-8"
Depth 44'

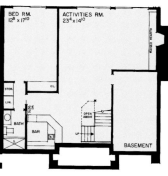

Additional products and services available. See page 4.

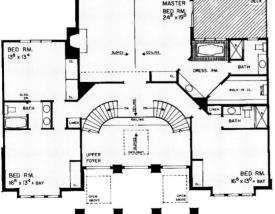

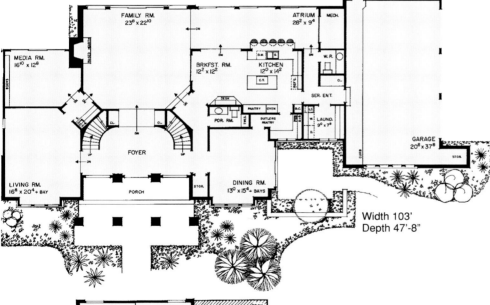

Width 103'
Depth 47'-8"

DESIGN HH3364

First Floor:	2,861 sq. ft.
Second Floor:	1,859 sq. ft.
Total:	4,720 sq. ft.

Contemporary Estate

No English lord would ever live here. Maybe a Texas cattle baron. Or even a Hollywood-movie type. It's too easy-living to appeal to stuffy royalty. But you'll enjoy its many estate-like features. Notice the varying levels—a family room, living room, media room and atrium are down a few steps from the elegant entry foyer. The large L-shaped kitchen is highlighted by an island work center and a pass-through snack bar to the atrium.

A double curved staircase leads to a second floor where four bedrooms and three baths are found. One family bedroom has its own bath with a linen closet. The other two family bedrooms share a full bath with a double vanity. The master suite is fit for royalty with a private deck, a fireplace, a walk-in closet and an unbelievable bath.

DESIGN HH2879

First Floor:	3,173 sq. ft.
Upper Lounge:	267 sq. ft.
Total:	3,440 sq. ft.

One-Story Living With A Bonus

Volume design is not necessarily "just for looks" as this lavish contemporary design proves. It includes an upper lounge that overlooks the family room below, has views out the large windows at the entry and can be used for living space or additional sleeping space if needed. A centrally located atrium with a skylight provides focal interest downstairs. A large, efficient kitchen with snack-bar service to the breakfast room enjoys its own greenhouse window. The spacious family room shares a warming fireplace and a view of the rear covered terrace. To the front, a living room with a fireplace delights in a view of the garden court and the atrium.

The deluxe master suite features a relaxing whirlpool, a dressing area and an abundance of walk-in closets.

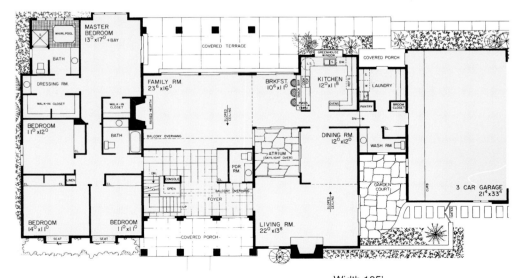

Width 105'
Depth 52'-8"

Additional products and services available. See page 4.

DESIGN HH2534

Square Footage:	3,262

Unique, Angular Style

Using the best of Western design with in-line floor planning, this grand ranch house is made for open spaces. The wings effectively balance a truly dramatic front entrance. Massive masonry walls support the wide overhanging roof with its exposed beams. The patterned double front doors are surrounded by delightful expanses of glass. The raised planter and the masses of quarried stone (or brick if you prefer) enhance the exterior appeal.

Inside, a distinctive and practical floor plan emerges. The entry is impressive and leads through gates to the grand gathering room. The right wing holds the three bedrooms, each of which has terrace access. The master has three closets (two are walk-in!) and a dressing area in the bath. The left wing holds the kitchen, dining room and service areas. Be sure to notice the many terraces and porches.

Width 144'-8"
Depth 71'-7"

Additional products and services available. See page 4.

209

DESIGN HH2511

Main Level:	1,043 sq. ft.
Upper Level:	703 sq. ft.
Lower Level:	794 sq. ft.
Total:	2,540 sq. ft.

One Of Our Best Multi-Levels

This outstanding multi-level home comes complete with outdoor deck and balconies. The entry level provides full living space: gathering room with fireplace, study (or optional bedroom) with bath, dining room, and U-shaped kitchen. A bedroom and bunkroom on the upper level are joined by a wide balcony area and full bath. Lower-level space includes a large activities room with fireplace, an additional bunk room and a full bath.

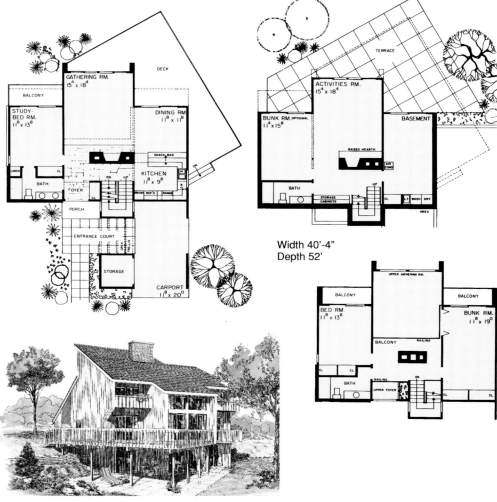

Width 40'-4"
Depth 52'

Additional products and services available. See page 4.

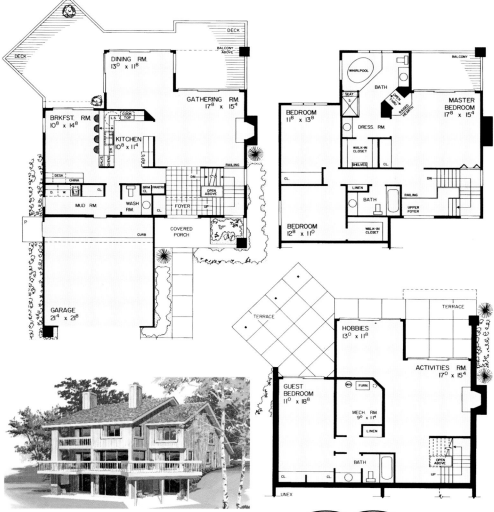

DESIGN HH2937

Main Level:	1,096 sq. ft.
Upper Level:	1,115 sq. ft.
Lower Level:	1,104 sq. ft.
Total:	3,315 sq. ft.

Hillside Tamer

A great place for those who love the outdoors! The gathering room (with fireplace), dining room and breakfast room all lead out to a deck off the main level. Similarly, the lower-level activity room (another fireplace!) hobby room and guest bedroom contain separate sliding glass doors to the back-yard terrace.

Upstairs are three bedrooms, including a suite with a through-fireplace, a private balcony, a walk-in closet, a dressing room and a whirlpool.

Width 40'
Depth 58'

DESIGN HH3361

Main Level:	3,548 sq. ft.
Lower Level:	1,036 sq. ft.
Total:	4,584 sq. ft.

Bi-Level Beauty

Got more family members than room to keep them? What appears initially as a one-story design is really a bi-level home that allows space for the whole gang. On the main level are a gathering room/dining room combination, a U-shaped kitchen, a breakfast room, two family bedrooms and the master suite.

The lower level holds a huge activities room with a summer kitchen and another bedroom with a walk-in closet and full bath.

Width 74'
Depth 68'-8"

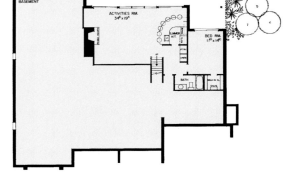

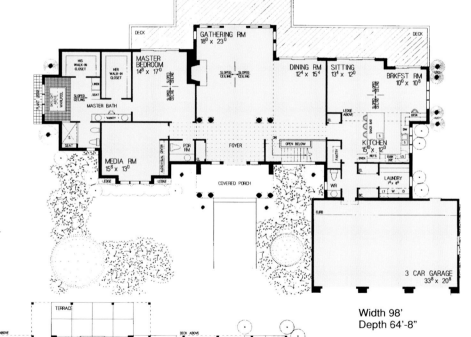

DECK

DECK

GATHERING RM
18⁰ x 23⁰

DECK

HIS WALK-IN CLOSET

MASTER BEDROOM
14⁸ x 17⁰

HER WALK-IN CLOSET

LINEN

SEAT

SLOPED CEILING

SLOPED CEILING

DINING RM
12⁴ x 15⁴

SITTING
13⁴ x 12⁰

BRKFST RM
10⁰ x 10⁸

LEDGE ABOVE

MASTER BATH

SLOPED CEILING

VANITY

KITCHEN
15¹⁰ x 12⁰

SNACK BAR

DESK

FOYER

OPEN BELOW

DW

OVEN

REF

COOK TOP

MEDIA RM
15⁸ x 13⁰

POR RM

SEAT

LEDGE

LEDGE

COVERED PORCH

LAUNDRY

LT W D

WR

CURB

3 CAR GARAGE
33⁸ x 20⁸

PLANT LEDGE

Width 98'
Depth 64'-8"

TERRACE

DECK ABOVE

ACTIVITIES RM
18⁰ x 22⁰

TERRACE

DECK ABOVE

TERRACE

FURN

WH

BEDROOM
13⁰ x 15⁰

WALK-IN CLOSET

DECK

BEDROOM
16⁰ x 12⁴

BASEMENT

WALK-IN CLOSET

SNACK BAR

RANGE

SUMMER KIT.
13⁸ x 10⁰

OPEN ABOVE

STORAGE

LINEN

BATH

VANITY

REFG

PANTRY

UNEX

UNEX

DESIGN HH3311

Main Level:	2,662 sq. ft.
Lower Level:	1,548 sq. ft.
Total:	4,210 sq. ft.

Suited For Sloping Lots

Here's a hillside haven for family living with plenty of room to entertain in style. The gathering room is straight back and adjoins a formal dining area. A true gourmet kitchen with plenty of room for casual eating is nearby. The abundantly appointed master suite is complemented by a luxurious bath. Note the media room to the front of the house.

On the lower level are two more bedrooms, a full bath, a large activity area with a fireplace and a convenient summer kitchen.

When You're Ready To Order . . .

Let Us Show You Our Home Blueprint Package.

Building a home? Planning a home? Our Blueprint Package has nearly everything you need to get the job done right, whether you're working on your own or with help from an architect, designer, builder or subcontractors. Each Blueprint Package is the result of many hours of work by licensed architects or professional designers.

QUALITY

Hundreds of hours of painstaking effort have gone into the development of your blueprint set. Each home has been quality-checked by professionals to insure accuracy and buildability.

VALUE

Because we sell in volume, you can buy professional-quality blueprints at a fraction of their development cost. With our plans, your dream home design costs only a few hundred dollars, not the thousands of dollars that custom architects charge.

SERVICE

Once you've chosen your favorite home plan, you'll receive fast, efficient service whether you choose to mail or fax your order to us or call us toll free at 1-800-521-6797. For customer service, call toll free 1-888-690-1116.

SATISFACTION

Over 50 years of service to satisfied home plan buyers provide us unparalleled experience and knowledge in producing quality blueprints. What this means to you is satisfaction with our product and performance.

ORDER TOLL FREE 1-800-521-6797

After you've looked over our Blueprint Package and Important Extras on the following pages, simply mail the order form on page 189 or call toll free on our Blueprint Hotline: 1-800-521-6797. We're ready and eager to serve you. For customer service, call toll free 1-888-690-1116.

. . . .

Each set of blueprints is an interrelated collection of detail sheets which includes components such as floor plans, interior and exterior elevations, dimensions, cross-sections, diagrams and notations. These sheets show exactly how your house is to be built.

Among the sheets included may be:

Frontal Sheet
This artist's sketch of the exterior of the house gives you an idea of how the house will look when built and landscaped. Large ink-line floor plans show all levels of the house and provide an overview of your new home's livability, as well as a handy reference for deciding on furniture placement.

Foundation Plan
This sheet shows the foundation layout includ-

SAMPLE PACKAGE

ing support walls, excavated and unexcavated areas, if any, and foundation notes. If slab construction rather than basement, the plan shows footings and details for a monolithic slab. This page, or another in the set, may include a sample plot plan for locating your house on a building site.

Detailed Floor Plans
These plans show the layout of each floor of the house. Rooms and interior spaces are carefully dimensioned and keys are given for cross-section details provided later in the plans. The positions of electrical outlets and switches are shown.

House Cross-Sections
Large-scale views show sections or cut-aways of the foundation, interior walls, exterior walls, floors, stairways and roof details. Additional cross-sections may show important changes in floor, ceiling or roof heights or the relationship of one level to another. Extremely valuable for construction, these sections show exactly how the various parts of the house fit together.

Interior Elevations
Many of our drawings show the design and placement of kitchen and bathroom cabinets, laundry areas, fireplaces, bookcases and other built-ins. Little "extras," such as mantelpiece and wainscoting drawings, plus moulding sections, provide details that give your home that custom touch.

Exterior Elevations
These drawings show the front, rear and sides of your house and give necessary notes on exterior materials and finishes. Particular attention is given to cornice detail, brick and stone accents or other finish items that make your home unique.

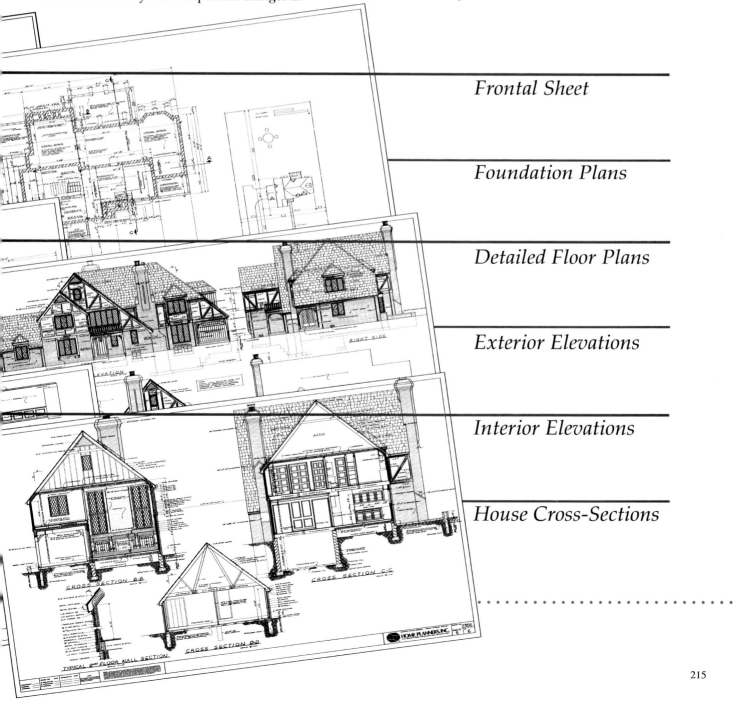

Frontal Sheet

Foundation Plans

Detailed Floor Plans

Exterior Elevations

Interior Elevations

House Cross-Sections

Important Extras To Do The Job Right!

Introducing eight important planning and construction aids developed by our professionals to help you succeed in your home-building project.

MATERIALS LIST

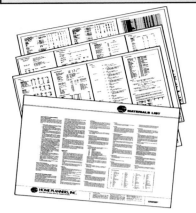

(Note: Because of the diversity of local building codes, our Materials List does not include mechanical materials.)

For many of the designs in our portfolio, we offer a customized materials take-off that is invaluable in planning and estimating the cost of your new home. This Materials List outlines the quantity, type and size of materials needed to build your house (with the exception of mechanical system items). Included are framing lumber, windows and doors, kitchen and bath cabinetry, rough and finish hardware, and much more. This handy list helps you or your builder cost out materials and serves as a reference sheet when you're compiling bids.

SPECIFICATION OUTLINE

This valuable 16-page document is critical to building your house correctly. Designed to be filled in by you or your builder, this book lists 166 stages or items crucial to the building process. It provides a comprehensive review of the construction process and helps in making choices of materials. When combined with the blueprints, a signed contract, and a schedule, it becomes a legal document and record for the building of your home.

QUOTE ONE®

Summary Cost Report / Materials Cost Report

A new service for estimating the cost of building select designs, the Quote One® system is available in two separate stages: The Summary Cost Report and the Materials Cost Report.

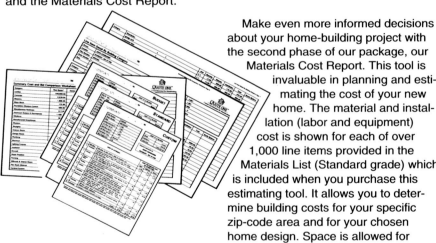

The Summary Cost Report is the first stage in the package and shows the total cost per square foot for your chosen home in your zip-code area and then breaks that cost down into ten categories showing the costs for building materials, labor and installation. The total cost for the report (which includes three grades: Budget, Standard and Custom) is just $19.95 for one home, and additionals are only $14.95. These reports allow you to evaluate your building budget and compare the costs of building a variety of homes in your area.

Make even more informed decisions about your home-building project with the second phase of our package, our Materials Cost Report. This tool is invaluable in planning and estimating the cost of your new home. The material and installation (labor and equipment) cost is shown for each of over 1,000 line items provided in the Materials List (Standard grade) which is included when you purchase this estimating tool. It allows you to determine building costs for your specific zip-code area and for your chosen home design. Space is allowed for additional estimates from contractors and subcontractors, such as for mechanical materials, which are not included in our packages. This invaluable tool is available for a price of $110 ($120 for a Schedule E plan) which includes a Materials List.

The Quote One® program is continually updated with new plans. If you are interested in a plan that is not indicated as Quote One®, please call and ask our sales reps, they will be happy to verify the status for you. To order these invaluable reports, use the order form on page 221 or call 1-800-521-6797.

CONSTRUCTION INFORMATION

If you want to know more about techniques—and deal more confidently with subcontractors we offer these useful sheets. Each set is an excellent tool that will add to your understanding of these technical subjects.

Plan-A-Home®

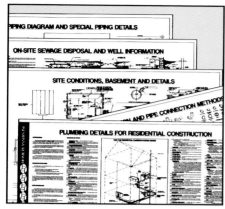

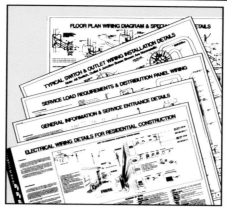

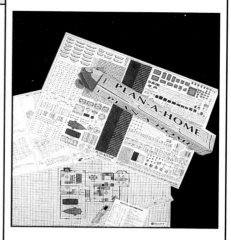

PLUMBING

The Blueprint Package includes locations for all the plumbing fixtures in your new house, including sinks, lavatories, tubs, showers, toilets, laundry trays and water heaters. However, if you want to know more about the complete plumbing system, these 24x36-inch detail sheets will prove very useful. Prepared to meet requirements of the National Plumbing Code, these six fact-filled sheets give general information on pipe schedules, fittings, sump-pump details, water-softener hookups, septic system details and much more. Color-coded sheets include a glossary of terms.

ELECTRICAL

The locations for every electrical switch, plug and outlet are shown in your Blueprint Package. However, these Electrical Details go further to take the mystery out of household electrical systems. Prepared to meet requirements of the National Electrical Code, these comprehensive 24x36-inch drawings come packed with helpful information, including wire sizing, switch-installation schematics, cable-routing details, appliance wattage, door-bell hookups, typical service panel circuitry and much more. Six sheets are bound together and color-coded for easy reference. A glossary of terms is also included.

Plan-A-Home® is an easy-to-use tool that helps you design a new home, arrange furniture in a new or existing home, or plan a remodeling project. Each package contains:

- **More than 700 reusable peel-off planning symbols** on a self-stick vinyl sheet, including walls, windows, doors, all types of furniture, kitchen components, bath fixtures and many more.

- **A reusable, transparent, 1/4-inch scale planning grid** that matches the scale of actual working drawings (1/4-inch equals 1 foot). This grid provides the basis for house layouts of up to 140x92 feet.

- **Tracing paper** and a protective sheet for copying or transferring your completed plan.

- **A felt-tip pen,** with water-soluble ink that wipes away quickly.

Plan-A-Home® lets you lay out areas as large as a 7,500 square foot, six-bedroom, seven-bath house.

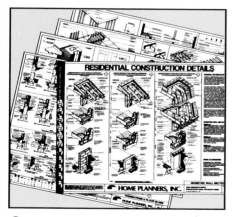

CONSTRUCTION

The Blueprint Package contains everything an experienced builder needs to construct a particular house. However, it doesn't show all the ways that houses can be built, nor does it explain alternate construction methods. To help you understand how your house will be built—and offer additional techniques—this set of drawings depicts the materials and methods used to build foundations, fireplaces, walls, floors and roofs. Where appropriate, the drawings show acceptable alternatives. These six sheets will answer questions for the advanced do-it-yourselfer or home planner.

MECHANICAL

This package contains fundamental principles and useful data that will help you make informed decisions and communicate with subcontractors about heating and cooling systems. The 24x36-inch drawings contain instructions and samples that allow you to make simple load calculations and preliminary sizing and costing analysis. Covered are today's most commonly used systems from heat pumps to solar fuel systems. The package is packed full of illustrations and diagrams to help you visualize components and how they relate to one another.

To Order, Call Toll Free
1-800-521-6797

To add these important extras to your Blueprint Package, simply indicate your choices on the order form on page 221 or call us Toll Free 1-800-521-6797 and we'll tell you more about these exciting products. For customer service, call toll free 1-888-690-1116.

Price Schedule & Plans Index

These pages contain all the information you need to price your blueprints. In general, the larger and more complicated the house, the more it costs to design and thus the higher the price we must charge for the blueprints. Remember, however, that these prices are far less than you would normally pay for the services of a licensed architect or professional designer.

Custom home designs and related architectural services often cost thousands of dollars, ranging from 5% to 15% of the cost of construction. By ordering our blueprints you are potentially saving enough money to afford a larger house, or to add those "extra" amenities such as a patio, deck, swimming pool or even an upgraded kitchen or luxurious master suite.

House Blueprint Price Schedule
(Prices guaranteed through December 31, 1999)

Tier	1-set Study Package	4-set Building Package	8-set Building Package	1-set Reproducible Sepias	Home Customizer® Package
A	$390	$435	$495	$595	$645
B	$430	$475	$535	$655	$705
C	$470	$515	$575	$715	$765
D	$510	$555	$615	$775	$825
E	$630	$675	$735	$835	$885
F	$730	$775	$835	$935	$985
G	$830	$875	$935	$1035	$1085

Prices for 4- or 8-set Building Packages honored only at time of original order.

Additional Identical Blueprints in same order..............$50 per set
Reverse Blueprints (mirror image)................................$50 per set
Specification Outlines...$10 each
Materials Lists ....$50 each

Materials Lists for "E" price plans are an additional $10.

Deck Plans Price Schedule

CUSTOM DECK PLANS

Price Group	Q	R	S
1 Set Custom Plans	$25	$30	$35

Additional identical sets ....$10 each
Reverse sets (mirror image)...........................$10 each

STANDARD DECK DETAILS
1 Set Generic Construction Details...........................$14.95 each

COMPLETE DECK BUILDING PACKAGE

Price Group	Q	R	S
1 Set Custom Plans, plus 1 Set Standard Deck Details	$35	$40	$45

Landscape Plans Price Schedule

Price Group	X	Y	Z
1 set	$35	$45	$55
3 sets	$50	$60	$70
6 sets	$65	$75	$85

Additional Identical Sets ....$10 each
Reverse Sets (mirror image)...........................$10 each

Index

To use the Index below, refer to the design number listed in numerical order (a helpful page reference is also given). Note the price index letter and refer to the House Blueprint Price Schedule above for the cost of one, four or eight sets of blueprints or the cost of a reproducible sepia. Additional prices are shown for identical and reverse blueprint sets, as well as a very useful Materials List for some of the plans. Also note in the Index below those plans that have matching or complementary Deck Plans or Landscape Plans. Refer to the schedules

above for prices of these plans. Some of our plans can be customized with Home Planners' Home Customizer® Package. These plans are indicated below with this symbol: ☎. See page 221 for information. Some plans are also part of our Quote One® estimating service and are indicated by this symbol: 🏠. See page 216 for more information.

To Order: Fill in and send the order form on page 221—or call toll free 1-800-521-6797 or 520-297-8200.

DESIGN	PRICE	PAGE	CUSTOMIZABLE	QUOTE ONE®	DECK	DECK PRICE	LANDSCAPE	LANDSCAPE PRICE	REGIONS
HH1113	A	28		🏠	D113	R	L202	X	1-3,5,6,8
HH1323	A	29			D117	S	L225	X	1-3,5,6,8
HH1791	B	21			D114	R	L205	Y	1-3,5,6,8
HH1850	B	34		🏠					
HH1920	B	98		🏠			L225	X	1-3,5,6,8
HH1956	A	32	☎	🏠	D117	S			
HH1957	A	33		🏠	D100	Q	L228	Y	1-8
HH2145	A	20		🏠			L209	Y	1-6,8
HH2206	B	73		🏠			L220	Y	1-3,5,6,8
HH2488	A	187	☎	🏠	D102	Q			
HH2490	A	175	☎	🏠					
HH2491	A	79	☎	🏠					
HH2505	A	100	☎	🏠	D113	R	L226	X	1-8
HH2511	B	210		🏠	D108	R	L229	Y	1-8
HH2534	D	209					L227	Z	1-8
HH2563	B	15	☎	🏠	D114	R	L201	Y	1-3,5,6,8
HH2565	B	126		🏠	D101	R	L225	X	1-3,5,6,8
HH2597	B	101		🏠	D114	R	L226	X	1-8
HH2603	B	113			D106	S	L220	Y	1-3,5,6,8
HH2606	A	75	☎	🏠			L221	Y	1-3,5,6,8
HH2608	A	194		🏠	D112	R	L228	Y	1-8
HH2610	C	31		🏠	D114	R	L204	Y	1-3,5,6,8
HH2615	D	22			D106	S	L211	Y	1-8
HH2622	A	30	☎	🏠	D103	R	L200	X	1-3,5,6,8
HH2657	B	18					L200	X	1-8
HH2659	A	35		🏠	D113	R	L205	Y	1-3,5,6,8
HH2661	A	16	☎	🏠	D113	R	L202	X	1-3,5,6,8
HH2662	C	37					L216	Y	1-3,5,6,8
HH2665	D	42		🏠					
HH2668	B	43					L214	Z	1-3,5,6,8
HH2670	D	161		🏠			L236	Z	3,4,7
HH2671	D	195			D114	R	L234	Y	1-8
HH2672	B	99		🏠	D112	R	L226	X	1-8
HH2682	A	17	☎	🏠	D115	Q	L200	X	1-3,5,6,8
HH2683	D	39			D101	R	L214	Z	1-3,5,6,8
HH2694	C	56					L209	Y	1-6,8
HH2699	C	26					L211	Y	1-8
HH2707	A	108	☎	🏠	D117	S	L226	X	1-8
HH2711	B	200			D105	R	L229	Y	1-8
HH2774	B	61		🏠	D100	Q	L207	Z	1-6,8
HH2776	B	52	☎	🏠	D113	Q	L207	Z	1-6,8
HH2779	D	88		🏠	D100	Q	L217	Y	1-8

218

DESIGN	PRICE	PAGE	CUSTOMIZABLE	QUOTE ONE®	DECK	DECK PRICE	LANDSCAPE	LANDSCAPE PRICE	REGIONS
HH2781	C	198		✓	D121	S	L230	Z	1-8
HH2800	B	81		✓	D113	R	L220	Y	1-3,5,6,8
HH2802	B	74	✓	✓	D118	R	L220	Y	1-3,5,6,8
HH2805	B	109		✓	D113	R	L220	Y	1-3,5,6,8
HH2810	B	105		✓	D112	R	L204	Y	1-3,5,6,8
HH2818	B	196	✓	✓	D101	R	L234	Y	1-8
HH2822	A	199		✓			L229	Y	1-8
HH2826	B	171	✓	✓	D116	R			
HH2850	C	162		✓	D122	S	L236	Z	3,4,7
HH2851	C	89		✓			L217	Y	1-8
HH2854	B	77	✓	✓	D112	R	L220	Y	1-3,5,6,8
HH2855	B	80	✓	✓	D103	R	L219	Z	1-3,5,6,8
HH2864	A	190		✓	D100	Q	L225	X	1-3,5,6,8
HH2871	B	188		✓	D117	S			
HH2875	B	163		✓	D113	R	L236	Z	3,4,7
HH2878	B	106	✓	✓	D112	R	L200	X	1-3,5,6,8
HH2879	D	208		✓					
HH2880	C	24	✓	✓	D114	R	L212	Z	1-8
HH2889	D	38		✓	D107	S	L215	Z	1-6,8
HH2902	B	189		✓			L234	Y	1-8
HH2905	B	168		✓	D121	S	L229	Y	1-8
HH2908	B	57	✓	✓	D117	S	L205	Y	1-3,5,6,8
HH2912	B	164		✓					
HH2915	C	193		✓	D114	R	L212	Z	1-8
HH2916	C	23		✓			L221	X	1-3,5,6,8
HH2920	D	192	✓	✓	D104	S	L212	Z	1-8
HH2921	D	25		✓	D104	S	L212	Z	1-8
HH2922	D	160		✓					
HH2927	B	177	✓	✓	D100	Q			
HH2937	C	211		✓			L229	Y	1-8
HH2940	E	92		✓	D114	R	L230	Z	1-8
HH2946	C	58	✓	✓	D114	R	L207	Z	1-6,8
HH2947	B	95	✓	✓	D112	R	L200	X	1-3,5,6,8
HH2948	B	166	✓	✓					
HH2949	C	156		✓					
HH2950	C	135		✓					
HH2953	E	68		✓	D111	S	L223	Z	1-3,5,6,8
HH2962	B	71	✓	✓					
HH2964	B	76		✓					
HH2968	E	93		✓			L227	Z	1-8
HH2970	D	67		✓			L223	Z	1-3,5,6,8
HH2973	B	66	✓	✓			L223	Z	1-3,5,6,8
HH2974	B	63		✓			L223	Z	1-3,5,6,8
HH2995	D	27		✓	D106	S	L217	Y	1-8
HH3303	D	41		✓			L215	Z	1-6,8
HH3304	E	69		✓			L209	Y	1-6,8
HH3307	C	51		✓	D111	S	L207	Z	1-6,8
HH3309	B	62		✓			L209	Y	1-6,8
HH3310	C	185		✓	D111	S	L227	Z	1-8
HH3311	D	213		✓	D109	S	L220	Y	1-3,5,6,8
HH3313	B	121		✓			L200	X	1-3,5,6,8
HH3314	B	72		✓			L200	X	1-3,5,6,8
HH3315	D	120		✓			L200	X	1-3,5,6,8
HH3316	A	118		✓			L202	X	1-3,5,6,8
HH3318	B	117	✓	✓	D111	S	L202	X	1-3,5,6,8
HH3319	C	122	✓	✓	D112	R	L217	Y	1-8
HH3321	C	123	✓	✓	D116	R	L209	Y	1-6,8
HH3323	C	140	✓	✓			L223	Z	1-3,5,6,8
HH3325	C	59	✓	✓	D100	Q	L238	Y	3,4,7,8
HH3326	C	173	✓	✓			L220	Y	1-3,5,6,8
HH3327	C	179	✓	✓	D110	R	L217	Y	1-8
HH3329	C	157	✓	✓			L233	Y	3,4,7
HH3331	A	78		✓			L203	Y	1-3,5,6,8
HH3332	B	97		✓			L200	X	1-3,5,6,8
HH3333	C	44		✓			L204	Y	1-3,5,6,8
HH3334	C	103		✓			L207	Z	1-6,8
HH3337	D	40		✓			L214	Z	1-3,5,6,8
HH3338	B	174		✓			L204	Y	1-3,5,6,8
HH3340	B	102		✓			L224	Y	1-3,5,6,8
HH3341	B	170		✓			L234	Y	1-8
HH3342	B	82		✓			L217	Y	1-8
HH3345	B	107	✓	✓			L220	Y	1-3,5,6,8
HH3346	B	176	✓	✓			L204	Y	1-3,5,6,8
HH3348	C	96		✓			L200	X	1-3,5,6,8
HH3350	B	111		✓	D115	Q	L205	Y	1-3,5,6,8
HH3351	C	104		✓	D115	Q	L209	Y	1-6,8
HH3352	B	201		✓	D108	R	L229	Y	1-8
HH3355	A	116	✓	✓	D117	S	L220	Y	1-3,5,6,8
HH3357	D	112		✓	D115	Q	L211	Y	1-8
HH3360	D	125		✓			L207	Z	1-6,8
HH3361	D	212		✓			L230	Z	1-8
HH3362	D	206		✓					
HH3364	D	207		✓			L204	Y	1-3,5,6,8
HH3366	D	186		✓			L220	Y	1-3,5,6,8
HH3368	C	197		✓	D104	S	L220	Y	1-3,5,6,8
HH3376	B	110		✓	D114	R	L205	Y	1-3,5,6,8
HH3380	E	94		✓					
HH3382	C	64		✓	D110	R	L202	X	1-3,5,6,8
HH3385	C	65		✓	D100	Q	L207	Z	1-6,8
HH3396	C	53		✓	D111	S	L207	Z	1-6,8
HH3398	C	54		✓	D111	S	L224	Y	1-3,5,6,8
HH3399	D	55		✓	D110	R	L224	Y	1-3,5,6,8
HH3403	C	205		✓			L237	Y	7
HH3405	D	159	✓	✓			L236	Z	3,4,7
HH3407	C	152		✓			L237	Y	7
HH3409	C	204		✓			L230	Z	1-8
HH3411	C	133	✓	✓			L233	Y	3,4,7
HH3413	C	136	✓	✓			L238	Y	3,4,7,8
HH3414	C	139	✓	✓			L233	Y	3,4,7
HH3415	C	132	✓	✓			L233	Y	3,4,7
HH3416	A	128	✓	✓			L239	Z	1-8
HH3419	B	129		✓			L239	Z	1-8
HH3421	B	137	✓	✓			L238	Y	3,4,7,8
HH3422	B	127	✓	✓			L239	Z	1-8
HH3423	C	165	✓	✓					
HH3424	B	141	✓	✓			L233	Y	3,4,7
HH3425	C	149		✓					
HH3429	C	138	✓	✓			L233	Y	3,4,7
HH3430	C	146	✓	✓			L233	Y	3,4,7
HH3431	B	155		✓					
HH3432	C	153	✓	✓			L233	Y	3,4,7
HH3433	C	154	✓	✓			L213	Z	1-8
HH3434	D	158	✓	✓			L233	Y	3,4,7
HH3435	C	150	✓	✓			L227	Z	1-8
HH3436	C	144	✓	✓			L227	Z	1-8
HH3437	C	151	✓	✓			L212	Z	1-8
HH3438	C	181	✓	✓			L209	Y	1-6,8
HH3439	C	183		✓			L205	Y	1-3,5,6,8
HH3440	C	148	✓	✓			L233	Y	3,4,7
HH3441	C	143	✓	✓			L239	Z	1-8
HH3442	A	47	✓	✓	D115	Q	L200	X	1-3,5,6,8
HH3446	C	182		✓	D115	Q	L220	Y	1-3,5,6,8
HH3449	C	142	✓	✓			L236	Z	3,4,7
HH3454	B	178		✓	D110	R	L220	Y	1-3,5,6,8
HH3456	C	203		✓			L238	Y	3,4,7,8
HH3457	B	167		✓			L217	Y	1-8
HH3458	C	114		✓	D105	R	L222	Y	1-3,5,6,8
HH3459	C	90		✓			L220	Y	1-3,5,6,8
HH3460	A	46	✓	✓			L200	X	1-3,5,6,8
HH3461	B	50		✓			L204	Y	1-3,5,6,8
HH3462	B	60		✓			L207	Z	1-6,8
HH3463	C	91		✓			L238	Y	3,4,7,8
HH3465	A	49		✓			L205	Y	1-3,5,6,8
HH3466	B	48	✓	✓	D110	R	L207	Z	1-6,8
HH3468	B	180	✓	✓			L209	Y	1-6,8
HH3471	E	147		✓			L236	Z	3,4,7
HH3475	D	145	✓	✓			L236	Z	3,4,7
HH3478	B	130	✓	✓			L238	Y	3,4,7,8
HH3480	B	131	✓	✓	D112	R	L238	Y	3,4,7,8
HH3497	B	119		✓					
HH3502	E	70		✓	D111	S	L224	Y	1-3,5,6,8
HH3503	E	36		✓	D108	R	L210	Y	1-3,5,6,8
HH3558	C	83		✓	D105	R	L203	Y	1-3,5,6,8
HH3559	C	86	✓	✓	D111	S	L217	Y	1-8
HH3560	B	191		✓			L234	Y	1-8
HH3562	B	169		✓	D110	R	L238	Y	3,4,7,8
HH3563	B	172		✓	D115	Q	L233	Y	3,4,7
HH3565	C	202		✓	D110	R	L233	Y	3,4,7
HH3568	D	124		✓	D115	Q	L205	Y	1-3,5,6,8
HH3569	B	84		✓	D105	R	L238	Y	3,4,7,8
HH3571	B	19		✓	D115	Q	L202	X	1-3,5,6,8
HH3572	D	184		✓	D110	R	L227	Z	1-8
HH3600	C	115	✓	✓			L200	X	1-3,5,6,8
HH3601	C	115	✓	✓			L200	X	1-3,5,6,8
HH3602	C	87	✓	✓			L220	Y	1-3,5,6,8
HH3603	C	85		✓			L220	Y	1-3,5,6,8
HH3639	C	134	✓	✓			L217	Y	1-8
HH4061	A	45		✓	D115	Q			

Before You Order . . .

Before filling out the coupon at right or calling us on our Toll-Free Blueprint Hotline, you may want to learn more about our services and products. Here's some information you will find helpful.

Quick Turnaround

We process and ship every blueprint order from our office within 48 hours. Because of this quick turnaround, we won't send a formal notice acknowledging receipt of your order.

Our Exchange Policy

Since blueprints are printed in response to your order, we cannot honor requests for refunds. However, we will exchange your entire first order for an equal number of blueprints at a price of $50 for the first set and $10 for each additional set; $70 total exchange fee for 4 sets; $100 total exchange fee for 8 sets . . . *plus* the difference in cost if exchanging for a design in a higher price bracket or *less* the difference in cost if exchanging for a design in lower price bracket. One exchange is allowed within a year of purchase date. **(Sepias are not exchangeable.)** All sets from the first order must be returned before the exchange can take place. Please add $18 for postage and handling via ground service; $30 via Second Day Air; $40 via Next Day Air.

About Reverse Blueprints

If you want to build in reverse of the plan as shown, we will include an extra set of reverse blueprints (mirror image) for an additional fee of $50. Although lettering and dimensions will appear backward, reverses will be a useful aid if you decide to flop the plan.

Revising, Modifying and Customizing Plans

The wide variety of designs available in this publication allows you to select ideas and concepts for a home to fit your building site and match your family's needs, wants and budget. Like many homeowners who buy these plans, you and your builder, architect or engineer may want to make changes to them. Some minor changes may be made by your builder, but we recommend that most changes be made by a licensed architect or engineer. If you need to make alterations to a design that is customizable, you need only order our Home Customizer® Package to get you started. As set forth below, we cannot assume any responsibility for blueprints which have been changed, whether by you, your builder or by professionals selected by you or referred to you by us, because such individuals are outside our supervision and control.

Architectural and Engineering Seals

Some cities and states are now requiring that a licensed architect or engineer review and "seal" a blueprint, or officially approve it, prior to construction due to concerns over energy costs, safety and other factors. Prior to application for a building permit or the start of actual construction, we strongly advise that you consult your local building official who can tell you if such a review is required.

About the Designers

The architects and designers whose work appears in this publication are among America's leading residential designers. Each plan was designed to meet the requirements of a nationally recognized model building code in effect at the time and place the plan was drawn. Because national building codes change from time to time, plans may not comply with any such code at the time they are sold to a customer. In addition, building officials may not accept these plans as final construction documents of record as the plans may need to be modified and additional drawings and details added to suit local conditions and requirements. We strongly advise that purchasers consult a licensed architect or engineer, and their local building official, before starting any construction related to these plans.

Local Building Codes and Zoning Requirements

At the time of creation, our plans are drawn to specifications published by the Building Officials and Code Administrators (BOCA) International, Inc.; the Southern Building Code Congress (SBCCI) International, Inc.; the International Conference of Building Officials; or the Council of American Building Officials (CABO). Our plans are designed to meet or exceed national building standards. Because of the great differences in geography and climate throughout the United States and Canada, each state, county and municipality has its own building codes, zone requirements, ordinances and building regulations. Your plan may need to be modified to comply with local requirements regarding snow loads, energy codes, soil and seismic conditions and a wide range of other matters. In addition, you may need to obtain permits or inspections from local governments before and in the course of construction. Prior to using blueprints ordered from us, we strongly advise that you consult a licensed architect or engineer—and speak with your local building official—before applying for any permit or beginning construction. We authorize the use of our blueprints on the express condition that you strictly comply with all local building codes, zoning requirements and other applicable laws, regulations, ordinances and requirements. **Notice:** Plans for homes to be built in Nevada must be re-drawn by a Nevada-registered professional. Consult your building official for more information on this subject.

Foundation and Exterior Wall Changes

Most of our plans are drawn with either a full or partial basement foundation. Depending on your specific climate or regional building practices, you may wish to change this basement to a slab or crawlspace. Most professional contractors and builders can easily adapt your plans to alternate foundation types. Likewise, most can easily change 2x4 wall construction to 2x6, or vice versa.

Disclaimer

We and the designers we work with have put substantial care and effort into the creation of our blueprints. However, because we cannot provide on-site consultation, supervision and control over actual construction, and because of the great variance in local building requirements, building practices and soil, seismic, weather and other conditions, WE CANNOT MAKE ANY WARRANTY, EXPRESS OR IMPLIED, WITH RESPECT TO THE CONTENT OR USE OF OUR BLUEPRINTS, INCLUDING BUT NOT LIMITED TO ANY WARRANTY OF MERCHANTABILITY OR OF FITNESS FOR A PARTICULAR PURPOSE.

Terms and Conditions

These designs are protected under the terms of United States copyright Law and may not be copied or reproduced in any way, by any means, unless you have purchased Sepias or Reproducibles which clearly indicate your right to copy or reproduce. We authorize the use of your chosen design as an aid in the construction of one single-family home only. You may not use this design to build a second or multiple dwellings without purchasing another blueprint or blueprints or paying additional design fees.

How Many Blueprints Do You Need?

A single set of blueprints is sufficient to study a home in greater detail. However, if you are planning to obtain cost estimates from a contractor or subcontractors—or if you are planning to build immediately—you will need more sets. Because additional sets are cheaper when ordered in quantity with the original order, make sure you order enough blueprints to satisfy all requirements. The following checklist will help you determine how many you need:

____ Owner

____ Builder (generally requires at least three sets; one as a legal document, one to use during inspections, and at least one to give to subcontractors)

____ Local Building Department (often requires two sets)

____ Mortgage Lender (usually one set for a conventional loan; three sets for FHA or VA loans)

____ TOTAL NUMBER OF SETS

Toll Free 1-800-521-6797

Regular Office Hours:
8:00 a.m. to 8:00 p.m. Eastern Time, Monday through Friday
Our staff will gladly answer any questions during regular office hours. Our answering service can place orders after hours or on weekends.

If we receive your order by 4:00 p.m. Eastern Time, Monday through Friday, we'll process it and ship within 48 hours. When ordering by phone, please have your charge card ready. We'll also ask you for the Order Form Key Number at the bottom of the coupon.

By FAX: Copy the Order Form on the next page and send it on our FAX line: 1-800-224-6699 or 1-520-544-3086.

Canadian Customers
Order Toll-Free 1-800-561-4169

For faster service and plans that are modified for building in Canada, customers may now call in orders directly to our Canadian supplier of plans and charge the purchase to a charge card. Or, you may complete the order form at right, adding 40% to all prices and mail in Canadian funds to:

The Plan Centre 60 Baffin Place
Unit 5
Waterloo, Ontario N2V 1Z7

OR: Copy the Order Form and send it via our Canadian FAX line: 1-800-719-3291.

The Home Customizer®

"This house is perfect...if only the family room were two feet wider." Sound familiar? In response to the numerous requests for this type of modification, Home Planners has developed **The Home Customizer® Package**. This exclusive package offers our top-of-the-line materials to make it easy for anyone, anywhere to customize any Home Planners design to fit their needs. Check the index on page 186 for those plans which are customizable.

Some of the changes you can make to any of our plans include:
- exterior elevation changes
- kitchen and bath modifications
- roof, wall and foundation changes
- room additions and more!

The Home Customizer® Package includes everything you'll need to make the necessary changes to your favorite Home Planners design. The package includes:
- instruction book with examples
- architectural scale and clear work film
- erasable red marker and removable correction tape
- ¼"-scale furniture cutouts
- 1 set reproducible, erasable Sepias
- 1 set study blueprints for communicating changes to your design professional
- a copyright release letter so you can make copies as you need them
- referral letter with the name, address and telephone number of the professional in your region who is trained in modifying Home Planners designs efficiently and inexpensively.

The price of the **Home Customizer® Package** ranges from $605 to $845, depending on the price schedule of the design you have chosen. **The Home Customizer® Package** will not only save you 25% to 75% of the cost of drawing the plans from scratch with a custom architect or engineer, it will also give you the flexibility to have your changes and modifications made by our referral network or by the professional of your choice. Now it's even easier and more affordable to have the custom home you've always wanted.

For Customer Service, call toll free 1-888-690-1116.

 For information about any of our services or to order call 1-800-521-6797.

BLUEPRINTS ARE NOT RETURNABLE

Helpful Books & Software

Home Planners wants your building experience to be as pleasant and trouble-free as possible. That's why we've expanded our library of Do-It-Yourself titles to help you along. In addition to our beautiful plans books, we've added books to guide you through specific projects as well as the construction process. In fact, these are titles that will be as useful after your dream home is built as they are right now.

ONE-STORY

1 448 designs for all lifestyles. 860 to 5,400 square feet. 384 pages $9.95

TWO-STORY

2 460 designs for one-and-a-half and two stories. 1,245 to 7,275 square feet. 384 pages $9.95

VACATION

3 345 designs for recreation, retirement and leisure. 312 pages $8.95

MULTI-LEVEL
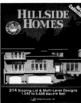
4 312 designs for split-levels, bi-levels, multi-levels and walkouts. 224 pages $8.95

COUNTRY

5 200 country designs from classic to contemporary by 7 winning designers. 224 pages $8.95

MOVE-UP

6 200 stylish designs for today's growing families from 9 hot designers. 224 pages $8.95

NARROW-LOT

7 200 unique homes less than 60' wide from 7 designers. Up to 3,000 square feet. 224 pages $8.95

SMALL HOUSE

8 200 beautiful designs chosen for versatility and affordability. 224 pages $8.95

BUDGET-SMART

9 200 efficient plans from 7 top designers, that you can really afford to build! 224 pages $8.95

EXPANDABLES

10 200 flexible plans that expand with your needs from 7 top designers. 240 pages $8.95

ENCYCLOPEDIA

11 500 exceptional plans for all styles and budgets—the best book of its kind! 352 pages $9.95

AFFORDABLE

12 Completely revised and updated, featuring 300 designs for modest budgets. 256 pages $9.95

ENCYCLOPEDIA 2

13 500 Completely new plans. Spacious and stylish designs for every budget and taste. 352 pages $9.95

VICTORIAN

14 160 striking Victorian and Farmhouse designs from three leading designers. 192 pages $12.95

EASY-LIVING

15 216 Efficient and sophisticated plans that are small in size, but big on livability. 224 pages $8.95

LUXURY
16 154 fine luxury plans-loaded with luscious amenities! 192 pages $14.95

LIGHT-FILLED

17 223 great designs that make the most of natural sunlight. 240 pages $8.95

BEST SELLERS

18 Our 50th Anniversary book with 200 of our very best designs in full color! 224 pages $12.95

SPECIAL COLLECTION

19 70 Romantic house plans that capture the classic tradition of home design. 160 pages $17.95

COUNTRY HOUSES

20 208 Unique home plans that combine traditional style and modern livability. 224 pages $9.95

TRADITIONAL

21 403 designs of classic beauty and elegance. 304 pages $9.95

MODERN & CLASSIC

22 341 impressive homes featuring the latest in contemporary design. 304 pages $9.95

NEW ENGLAND

23 260 of the best in Colonial home design. Special interior design sections, too. 384 pages $14.95

SOUTHERN

24 207 homes rich in Southern styling and comfort. 240 pages $8.95

SUNBELT

25 215 Designs that capture the spirit of the Southwest. 208 pages $10.95

WESTERN

26 215 designs that capture the spirit and diversity of the Western lifestyle. 208 pages $9.95

Landscape Designs

EASY CARE

27 41 special landscapes designed for beauty and low maintenance. 160 pages $14.95

FRONT & BACK

28 The first book of do-it-yourself landscapes. 40 front, 15 backyards. 208 pages $14.95

BACKYARDS

29 40 designs focused solely on creating your own specially themed backyard oasis. 160 pages $14.95

Outdoor Projects

OUTDOOR

30 42 unique outdoor projects. Gazebos, strombellas, bridges, sheds, playsets and more! 96 pages $7.95

GARAGES & MORE

31 101 Multi-use garages and outdoor structures to enhance any home. 96 pages $7.95

DECKS

32 25 outstanding single-, double- and multi-level decks you can build. 112 pages $7.95

Design Software

BOOK & CD ROM	3D DESIGN SUITE	ENERGY GUIDE	BATHROOMS	KITCHENS	HOUSE CONTRACTING	WINDOWS & DOORS	CONTRACTING GUIDE

33 Both the Home Planners Gold book and matching Windows™ CD ROM with 3D floorplans. $24.95

34 Home design made easy! View designs in 3D, take a virtual reality tour, add decorating details and more. $59.95

35 The most comprehensive energy efficiency and conservation guide available. 280 pages $35.00

36 An innovative guide to organizing, remodeling and decorating your bathroom. 96 pages $8.95

37 An imaginative guide to designing the perfect kitchen. Chock full of bright ideas to make your job easier. 176 pages $14.95

38 Everything you need to know to act as your own general contractor...and save up to 25% off building costs. 134 pages $12.95

39 Installation techniques and tips that make your project easier and more professional looking. 80 pages $7.95

40 Loaded with information to make you more confident in dealing with contractors and subcontractors. 287 pages $18.95

ROOFING	FRAMING	VISUAL HANDBOOK	BASIC WIRING	PATIOS & WALKS	TILE	PLUMBING	TRIM & MOLDING

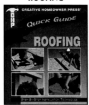      

41 Information on the latest tools, materials and techniques for roof installation or repair. 80 pages $7.95

42 For those who want to take a more-hands on approach to their dream. 319 pages $19.95

43 A plain-talk guide to the construction process; financing to final walk-through, this book covers it all. 498 pages $19.95

44 A straight forward guide to one of the most misunderstood systems in the home. 160 pages $12.95

45 Clear step-by-step instructions take you from the basic design stages to the finished project. 80 pages $7.95

46 Every kind of tile for every kind of application. Includes tips on use installation and repair. 176 pages $12.95

47 Tackle any plumbing installation or repair as quickly and efficiently as a professional. 160 pages $12.95

48 Step-by-step instructions for installing baseboards, window and door casings and more. 80 pages $7.95

Additional Books Order Form

To order your books, just check the box of the book numbered below and complete the coupon. We will process your order and ship it from our office within 48 hours. Send coupon and check (in U.S. funds).

YES! Please send me the books I've indicated:

☐ 1:VO $9.95	☐ 25:SW $10.95
☐ 2:VT $9.95	☐ 26:WH $9.95
☐ 3:VH $8.95	☐ 27:ECL $14.95
☐ 4:VS $8.95	☐ 28:HL $14.95
☐ 5:FH $8.95	☐ 29:BYL $14.95
☐ 6:MU $8.95	☐ 30:YG $7.95
☐ 7:NL $8.95	☐ 31:GG $7.95
☐ 8:SM $8.95	☐ 32:DP $7.95
☐ 9:BS $8.95	☐ 33:HPGC . . . $24.95
☐ 10:EX $8.95	☐ 34:PLANSUITE . $59.95
☐ 11:EN $9.95	☐ 35:RES $35.00
☐ 12:AF $9.95	☐ 36:CDB $8.95
☐ 13:E2 . . . . . $9.95	☐ 37:CKI $14.95
☐ 14:VDH . . . $12.95	☐ 38:SBC $12.95
☐ 15:EL $8.95	☐ 39:CGD $7.95
☐ 16:LD2 . . . $14.95	☐ 40:BCC $18.95
☐ 17:NA $8.95	☐ 41:CGR $7.95
☐ 18:HPG . . . $12.95	☐ 42:SRF $19.95
☐ 19:WEP . . . $17.95	☐ 43:RVH $19.95
☐ 20:CN $9.95	☐ 44:CBW $12.95
☐ 21:ET $9.95	☐ 45:CGW $7.95
☐ 22:EC $9.95	☐ 46:CWT $12.95
☐ 23:NES . . . $14.95	☐ 47:CMP $12.95
☐ 24:SH $8.95	☐ 48:CGT $7.95

Canadian Customers
Order Toll-Free 1-800-561-4169

Additional Books Sub-Total $_____
ADD Postage and Handling $ 3.00
Sales Tax: (AZ, CA, DC, IL, MI, MN, NY & WA residents, please add appropriate state and local sales tax.) $_____
YOUR TOTAL (Sub-Total, Postage/Handling, Tax) $_____

YOUR ADDRESS (Please print)

Name _____

Street _____

City _____ State_____ Zip _____

Phone (_____) _____—_____

YOUR PAYMENT
Check one: ☐ Check ☐ Visa ☐ MasterCard ☐ Discover Card
Required credit card information:

Credit Card Number_____

Expiration Date (Month/Year) _____/ _____

Signature Required _____

 Home Planners, LLC
Wholly owned by Hanley-Wood, Inc.
3275 W Ina Road, Suite 110, Dept. BK, Tucson, AZ 85741

TB50B

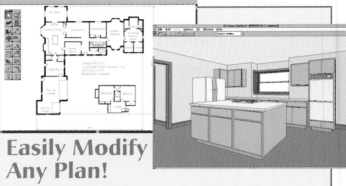

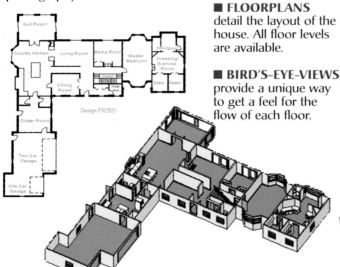